Project
Fatherhood

A STORY OF COURAGE AND HEALING IN
ONE OF AMERICA'S TOUGHEST COMMUNITIES

Jorja Leap

BEACON PRESS
BOSTON

Beacon Press
Boston, Massachusetts
www.beacon.org

Beacon Press books
are published under the auspices of
the Unitarian Universalist Association of Congregations.

18 17 16 15   8 7 6 5 4 3 2 1

This book is printed on acid-free paper that meets the uncoated paper
ANSI/NISO specifications for permanence as revised in 1992.

Text design and composition by Wilsted & Taylor Publishing Services

Some names and identifying characteristics of people mentioned
in this work have been changed to protect their identities.

Library of Congress Cataloging-in-Publication Data

Leap, Jorja.
    Project Fatherhood : a story of courage and healing in one of America's toughest
communities / Jorja Leap.
        pages cm
    ISBN 978-0-8070-1452-3 (hardback) — ISBN 978-0-8070-1453-0 (ebook)
    1. Fatherhood—California—Los Angeles. 2. Father and child—California—Los
Angeles. 3. Parenting—California—Los Angeles. I. Title.
        HQ756.L43 2015
        306.874'2—dc23   2014043792

This book is for my brothers,
Tony and Chris,

and for our father,
Daniel Manos

*But God bless the child
that's got his own.*

BILLIE HOLIDAY

CONTENTS

ONE

Watts

*Watts is home. Born and raised in Watts . . . I since moved
but Watts will always be home for me, I love everything about
it, it's where I come from. Even though Watts is known for its
low income, gang infested, drug infested streets, it made me
the person I am today . . . coming from Watts motivates me
to do better and have a better life. But Watts will always be
home. . . . WATTS UP!!!!*

—Vince, February 21, 2011, 4:13 p.m.,
"Mapping L.A., Neighborhoods:
Tell us what Watts means to you,"
Los Angeles Times online

Watts is worth it.
—Watts United

My relationship with Watts began with a riot.

In 1965, I was nine years old and thrilled to be spending the night
with my aunt and uncle—"Thea" Adrienne and "Theo" Pete—at their
home in South Los Angeles. In my extended, Greek family, Theo Pete
was clearly my favorite relative. I loved listening to him talk: he was a
high school history teacher and I was a willing pupil.

He had put himself in charge of my philosophical education for as
far back as I could remember, giving me books, assuring me that Com-
munists were not evil human beings, and encouraging me to become an
astronaut or a UN ambassador. He also was on the lookout for any signs
of perfectionism in my already compulsive personality, informing me
that there were only three perfect people on earth: "Pope Paul, Theo
Pete, and Mary Poppins."

Because of this, I listened raptly as he explained what we were watching unfold on the black-and-white television in the kitchen. But the sense of distance the TV coverage created was an illusion. Rampant violence was occurring less than five miles away. It was a hot August night, and the normally active streets of South Los Angeles were empty. Panic and dread mingled as my aunt repeatedly answered the ringing phone. Despite Thea Adrienne's calm, there was no mistaking the look on her face. I knew something terrible was happening in my nine-year-old world. All night long, the calls charted rumors about the course of the rioters. They were six blocks away—no ten blocks away. They would be in Inglewood by morning. The police couldn't get them under control. The National Guard was coming and it would all be better in a matter of hours.

I didn't understand who "they" were.

In the midst of all the false reports, Theo Pete explained that "they" were the people who lived in Watts, a small community nestled in the easternmost corner of South Los Angeles. He said they were rebelling against injustice, then added that the rioting had to be viewed in a historical context. The problems in Watts were economic and revolved around the issue of race. The term African American had not yet slipped into popular usage as Theo Pete explained how the people of the "Negro" race had been subjected to discrimination at every level, how they experienced the worst forms of social exclusion based solely on the color of their skin and fantasies about their differences from "whites." What Theo Pete told me burned into my brain: the rioters were justified, the police were out of control, and after all, what could you expect when the gap between whites and blacks was so large in all facets of life—jobs, housing, schools, resources, the future?

That night is a memory of multiple images: the TV depiction of the police in their riot gear, the black faces filled with despair and rage as they tried to protect themselves from the swinging billy clubs, the smell of smoke and burning rubber. People packed up their wedding photographs and good silver and left town for a few days. But throughout the six days of television coverage and mainstream hysteria, Theo Pete refused to divert from the narrative he offered.

"The riots were inevitable. Watts has always been the poorest part of Los Angeles. People pretend it doesn't exist. And we're not watching a riot—it's actually a social protest. The problem is what the violence is doing. Everyone is afraid instead of understanding the problem. And the worst thing is, these poor people—they're burning their own neighborhood and their own stores. We're all so scared they're going to do something to us. They're only hurting themselves." Theo Pete stopped talking long enough to shake his head. "But all of this will drive home the truth. Things are gonna change."

At times, during the decades that followed, his predictions appeared overly optimistic. The retail businesses that burned down during the six days of the Watts riots closed and never returned to South Los Angeles, limiting residents to a forced choice between liquor stores run by southern European immigrants or "mom and pop" grocery stores operated by Korean families. In the years that followed, many parts of Watts looked like a wasteland of boarded-up buildings and abandoned houses.

However, there was also room for hope. In the aftermath of the riots, Martin Luther King, Jr. General Hospital was built in the heart of Watts, the civil rights movement flourished, and affirmative action measures were implemented. Eventually, decades later, an African American man was elected president of the United States. I sometimes allowed myself to think that things might actually be changing.

But on a February night, forty-seven years later, I wasn't so sure.

It has been two days since a black teenager, Trayvon Martin, was shot and killed by George Zimmerman, a neighborhood watch volunteer in central Florida. Nothing has happened to Zimmerman even though there has been a national outcry that *something must be done*. Just what that is depends on who is talking. Right-wing advocates have established a "George Zimmerman legal defense fund" with a website that has already collected $100,000. President Obama has announced that if he had a son, that young man could have been Trayvon Martin. There have been demonstrations outside of the Florida police department that arrested and then released Zimmerman. Both the twenty-four-hour television news cycle and the blogosphere are pulsating with commentators anticipating the potentially violent reaction of the black community. All of this rhetoric conceals a multitude of misunderstandings, because a high school student wearing a hoodie—who might or might not have been at the wrong place at the wrong time, who might or might not have been a gang member—was shot and is now dead. And there were other problems.

Trayvon Martin was black. George Zimmerman—despite his vaguely Jewish-sounding last name—was brown. In Los Angeles, many felt additional uneasiness because of the conflict between the African American and Latino communities. Over the past decade, as the demography of Southern California shifted, South Los Angeles in particular has evolved into a divided region, with a virtual Mason-Dixon Line running between the two groups. Resentment between African Americans and Latinos was part of life, and it wasn't just gang versus gang. The frisson of anxiety in the air was palpable and the LAPD was on tactical alert. Everyone was trying to work around the sense of imminent danger, the feeling that something was going to happen. So many believed that somewhere, sometime, the African American community would explode. As I drove into South Los Angeles that afternoon, a National Public Radio commentator posed the question "How does the black community feel?"

I was about to find out.

Two hours later, a group of black and brown men—active and former gang members, post-prison felons, and adolescents—sits in a small room at a community recreation center in the middle of the Jordan Downs housing development. This group has been meeting every Wednesday night for over a year, but tonight is different. The room is silent. A wave of tension rises, like heat from the sidewalk. Slowly, one of the men begins to speak.

"Y'know, if Trayvon was white, they would have already killed George Zimmerman. He'd be dead."

The men all nod. Another speaks.

"He just wanted Skittles. They saw a black kid with a hoodie and they think—boom—'gang member.' He was just a little kid who wanted Skittles."

"He was talkin' to his girlfriend on the cell phone."

"It's the cops. You know, Zimmerman wasn't a cop, but he wanted to be a cop. They let him get away with it."

"That could be any of our kids."

"It's happenin' again."

"What do you mean again? It never *stopped* happenin' in this community."

"It shows you it doesn't matter if Obama—if a black man—*is* president of the United States. Young black men still have a big target on their backs."

"Our graveyards are too full."

"And the white man is still sitting on top of it all, still in control. Still tryin' to destroy our young men."

"And the white man—all he wants is to keep us down."

Sorrow and anger merge as the men speak. But there is something else in their voices, in their faces. Some of the men hang their heads, in confusion and impotence. They look hurt, betrayed. Slowly, Big Mike, the group's leader, begins to speak.

"We need to talk about what we are feelin'. It's time to speak the truth."

"It makes me so angry. I want to do somethin'—anything!" one man blurts out. His shaved head glistens in the fluorescent overhead light.

I am watching all of this, silent. I keep thinking how we are sitting together right in the heart of Watts, where people have suffered inequality and felt rage and wound up expressing it in dramatic—and destructive—activity. I am thinking of Theo Pete and the Watts riots. But I am also remembering that twenty years earlier and three miles north of this room, at the intersection of Florence and Normandie, a white man, Reginald Denny, was pulled from the truck he was driving and beaten nearly to death in the aftermath of the Rodney King verdict. And yet, I don't feel scared. Other feelings are at war inside of me. Trust. Recklessness. Faith. Defiance. And there is something else. Shame.

"YOU KNOW THEY DO THIS TO US HERE ALLA THE TIME. IT'S THE COPS. AND THAT GUY ZIMMERMAN THOUGHT HE WAS A COP. HE WAS WORSE THAN A COP. HE WAS A WANNABE."

One man—Donald "Twin" James—is screaming. He rarely talks, and when he does, he explodes. The other men laugh warily.

"Come on, Twin, he wasn't a cop. He was just a muthafucka with a gun."

"He was a Mexican—a Latino, whatcha call it, I don't care."

"Stop talkin' like that."

"Yeah, quit it."

"You know we didn't mean you—Luis and Aaron. We didn't mean you guys."

Not everyone in the room is African American. While the majority of the men here are black, there are others participating in the conversation who have been in prison alongside them, who are poor alongside them—but they are brown.

Because of this, the group finds one thing about which they can agree.

The killing all comes down to white racism.

"It's not the brown man; it's not the black man."

"You just know what they're like in Florida."

"It's the white man. They want money and power and control."

"This is alla conspiracy. They don't want us to have anything—if we make it, if we get ahead, the white man is gonna take it away. Trayvon wasn't in the ghetto. He wasn't in a housing development—his daddy owned the house he lived in."

"We gotta do something—they wanna kill all of us."

The men's voices grow louder and angrier. One man stands up and says, "I'm just feelin' frustrated," and slams the wall with his fist. But just as the discussion appears ready to erupt into violence, someone declares, "It doesn't matter what's gone on. It's not the white man killing us."

There is silence. All eyes turn to Sy, and he continues speaking.

"Listen to alla us. We're lyin'. And we're fools. It's not white men coming here to Watts to kill us. We're so stupid, we're doin' the job for them. We got our black young men shootin' our brown young men, and our brown young men shootin' our black young men. But even worse than that, we got our black young men shootin'—*and killin'*—each other." Sy pauses and looks at each man in the group. "We gotta stop this now. We gotta save our children."

The conversation—and the rage—freezes.

Somewhere in the distance, a child can be heard shouting, then laughing.

"We gotta save our children," the men begin to repeat—as if it is a mantra.

"We gotta stop killing each other."

"We gotta make sure no more children grow up to go into the pen."

The men glance quickly at one another and nod. Big Mike stands and hits the table in front of him with both hands.

"Now what do we want to do?"

The group is silent. Big Mike and I are the official co-leaders of this group, but it's clear that certain men are in control. One of them, Debois, softly asks, "Do you ever wonder why this keeps happening to our young black men?" The other men in the group shake their heads and sit quietly for a moment. Then Leelee intones, "It's the same story over and over again. And we gotta watch out for our young men—the ones that are here and the ones that ain't here." He looks at Matt, the teenager sitting next to him.

Throughout the discussion, Matt has been sitting to the side, silent and thoughtful. He is the exact same age as Trayvon Martin. But on this night he is not worried about national politics. He is thinking instead of his girlfriend who may be pregnant.

The men in the room are smart. The men in the room are angry. Many of these men are victims of the ill-fated "war on drugs" and disproportionate sentencing of the 1990s. They have been released from prison sometime in the last five years and are still trying to "come home," without knowing just exactly how to do that. They have physically returned to their communities but have no idea how to move forward with their lives. They are silent as Big Mike repeats the question.

"I'm askin' you—as fathers, as men. We see what the problem is. What are we gonna do?"

This book is the story of how one group of men, born and raised in Watts, in South Los Angeles, set out to answer that question, both within their families and in their community. Through a program called Project Fatherhood, the men met on a weekly basis to examine issues surrounding their roles as parents. However, the group slowly grew to mean much more to these men; it was a place where they could share both jokes and traumatic experiences, where they could discuss the joys and sorrows of attempting to connect with their children after being separated from them because of incarceration or estrangement. Finally, it provided a place for the men to plan and carry out activities in the Watts community, to heal the neighborhood they had once sought to destroy.

I was recruited as a co-leader, but I soon realized the group had a story that called out to be told. I drew upon my background as an anthropologist and trained ethnographer. The task of collecting the fathers' stories was intense and emotional. As I began to get to know many of the men individually outside of the group setting, I realized it was critical to understand exactly how each life had unfolded over the past decades, before the meetings started. Their experiences offered stark evidence of the abuses perpetrated by the police, the havoc caused by the so-called "war on drugs," and the true human cost of poverty. But their lives were also a testimony to the inherent strength and resilience that composed the content of their character. The men were strong, funny, angry, outrageous, and—more than anything—able to relate and be intimate. As I lived within the Watts community and spent time with these fathers, I recorded repeated instances when they confronted tremendous obstacles. However, an unexpected outcome emerged as I documented their lives amid the ongoing inequities of life in South Los Angeles. In listening to their stories, I was ultimately able to bear witness to the process of healing they had undertaken. For the past four years, I have chronicled what has happened to these men—and to me— as our lives have been shared and transformed. This book is the story of that transformation.

TWO

The Father Wound

"How does it feel to be hugged by your father?"
"It feels great."
"I wonder what that would feel like."
—transcript from The California Endowment
Boys and Men of Color Youth Camp, 2013

When my cell phone buzzed, I was watching Jon Stewart. My anxiety immediately kicked into overdrive. It was summer; it was night; and the caller ID read "Big Mike." These were all signs of the perfect storm. Big Mike—or Elder Michael Cummings—had once been a gang member and drug dealer; he still played multiple roles in Watts but now worked as a combination tow-truck driver, activist, and street interventionist. More than anything, he was a man devoted to keeping the peace in Watts. He responded to any street violence with a bagful of strategies for de-escalating tension and preventing retaliation. I dreaded answering his call, knowing something major—perhaps tragic—had probably occurred.

"Doctorjorjaleap," he began, running my official title and first and last name all into one word. "You're a master social worker." This was clearly a question disguised as a statement. While I knew a great deal about his life and work, when it came to describing my job, Big Mike was on shaky ground. He was aware that I taught at the University of California at Los Angeles and that my writing had something to do with gangs and public policy, but beyond that he didn't quite know what I did. Most days, neither did I. Officially, I was a combination researcher-writer-activist. As impressive as this looked on paper, I was less a Renaissance woman than an anthropologist with a perpetual identity crisis. Nevertheless, I possessed the necessary MSW and had been on the

9

faculty of the UCLA Department of Social Welfare for over twenty years, so I could in good faith answer yes.

"Okay, good. We're starting a fathers' group at Jordan Downs and we need a master social worker. Can you be our social worker?"

I exhaled. Nothing tragic had occurred. Despite the sense of relief, my heart kept pounding. What I was experiencing was pretty much the professional equivalent of bumping into an old boyfriend. Watts—the most crime-ridden community in South Los Angeles—and I had broken up long before, and I had moved on to work with gangs in other settings throughout California. But, deep in my heart, I still carried a torch for three violence-torn public housing projects in a corner of South Los Angeles: Jordan Downs, Nickerson Gardens, and Imperial Courts. In my rush to get back to the streets of Watts, I answered yes with such force and enthusiasm that Big Mike was taken aback.

"I would *love* to!"

"Okay, okay, slow down. We're gonna see if this even happens. Can you be at Jordan Downs next Wednesday night? You, Andre, and me— we've gotta have a planning meeting."

"Okay. I *am* excited. And I'm gonna slow down. But you need to tell me what this is about."

"We're gonna get a group of men together to meet and talk about fatherhood. We're gonna try to help them to be good fathers to their children. You know, a lotta these guys have been locked up, so we are gonna help them after they get out of prison or support them if they're tryin' to stay out of prison."

Despite my enthusiasm, I felt wary. Somehow this need for a social worker smacked of institutional accountability—someone, somewhere was trying to cover his ass.

"Who's organizing this, Mike?"

"It's all part of something called Project Fatherhood. Do you know Dr. Hershel Swinger?"

"Yeah, I know Dr. Swinger. I worked with him."

"See, I knew you were the right one to ask. Dr. Swinger is helpin' us to set up Project Fatherhood because he wants us to teach men how to be good fathers."

Whatever Big Mike might be talking about, if Hershel Swinger was involved, it had something to do with strengthening families—an approach Swinger and many others believed in passionately. This was not a Trojan horse trotted through the community gates by social conservatives, promoting "family values" while sneaking in hopelessly discriminatory legislation. Instead, it was a school of thought that advocated turning traditional ideas about families—particularly poor families—upside down. Rather than searching for dysfunction, mainly among marginalized and impoverished families, this approach identified and built upon the families' strengths. Instead of wishful thinking, it offered a nuanced view of families bound and gagged by a system that failed to understand the complexities of their lives. Early in my career, I had quickly learned that every family I encountered—even the most troubled—invariably had positive characteristics somewhere, operating in some ways. None of this knowledge came from published research. I knew this from my Rolodex of shot-callers, people who would have made great attorneys or finance experts; they were the ones who "provided" for brothers and sisters and aging grandparents. I had "case-managed" too many drug dealers who multitasked and orchestrated the exchange of cash for product, even as they responded to phone calls from multiple baby mamas. They picked their kids up from school and took them on camping trips, all while they were dealing meth or heroin or marijuana. The picture was complicated. Their lives and their families were complicated.

This whole notion of "family strengths" went against the helping professions' past conventional wisdom, which had been all about pathology. Traditionally, social workers and therapists were trained to identify problems and develop plans to solve them. I practically had been breast-fed this worldview in graduate school, from Daniel Moynihan's observations on "black matriarchy" to Oscar Lewis's analysis of the "culture of poverty." The focus on deficits reinforced the idea that poor families were dysfunctional, and it mainly implicated families that were African American or Latino. These discussions, both inside and outside of the classroom, contrasted with explorations of other ethnic groups—Japanese, Chinese, or other Asians—whose families were often portrayed as integrated and strong. Of course, the era gave rise to the smug aphorism "family is just a synonym for dysfunction," with its implied message that professionals knew what families needed, and that they were in the best position to correct things. Even as an inexperienced and naïve social worker in the 1970s and 1980s, I was uncomfortable with this approach. The chain of cause and effect didn't make a lot of sense to me; pathology involved multiple factors, including biology, history, and economics, much more than it did problematic families. Despite its shortcomings, the perspective guided most social work interventions and approaches, until the idea of family strengths emerged in the mid-1980s.

Changing the dominant mindset was not easy. Resistance was everywhere, including among thought leaders who emphasized a combination of marriage, chastity, and religion as the best and only answer to the struggles parents and children faced. And then there was the challenge of just how to use hidden talents and strengths to solidify families. All this percolated as I was making changes in my own work, turning from practice and training to research and evaluation. Strangely enough, my new work brought me into direct contact with Dr. Hershel Swinger.

I got to know Swinger when I worked as part of a research team led by Dr. Todd Franke evaluating the effectiveness of the Partnership for Families (PFF), a child-abuse prevention initiative dedicated to strengthening families. Swinger, an African American professor with a PhD in clinical psychology, emerged as a voice for family strengths. He was one of the key designers of the PFF program, sponsored by First Five LA as part of its comprehensive state effort offering programs for children during their first five years of life. Everyone in the Los Angeles social work and human services community knew Dr. Swinger; his work commanded respect. It went beyond examining family strengths to shed light on how children dealt with the trauma they suffered as a result of community and family violence. In particular, Swinger's work illuminated how children with absentee fathers suffered more anxiety and depression, and experienced higher rates of drug abuse, school dropout, and—the most common item on the urban curriculum vita— involvement with the criminal justice system. What I didn't know until the call came from Big Mike was that Swinger had been talking about fatherhood long before it became a rallying cry of politicians and policymakers.

In 1996, Swinger began organizing and implementing Project Fatherhood. The program was structured to reduce child abuse, neglect, and involvement with children's protective services by supporting and strengthening high-risk, urban fathers. Swinger's emphasis on the critical role of fathers eventually attracted national attention from both Republicans and Democrats. After the program received a $7.5 million federal grant in 2006 under the Bush administration, Swinger oversaw its replication at fifty agencies throughout Los Angeles County. In 2010, the Obama administration recognized Project Fatherhood as a "model program."

But I knew very little about this. When I told Big Mike I would show up for the planning meeting at Jordan Downs, I had only a rough sense that I was joining an effort that included work in child abuse prevention but encompassed a great deal more. It was an undertaking that went beyond issues of gangs or violence—right to questions of fatherhood, male identity, and families' experiences of both pain and loss. I wasn't thinking too deeply about any of this. All that played in my head was the mantra *I want to get back to Jordan Downs. I want to go home to Watts.*

This was a pretty peculiar desire. Most people—whatever their color—looked at me skeptically when I brought up the subject of Watts. "You gotta remember, Watts is different," Kenny Green said while we ate lunch, when I mentioned that I was returning there to potentially co-lead some sort of fatherhood group. Kenny had been a gang interventionist for seventeen years, guiding and at times protecting me while I worked in the streets.

"I know, but I think this program sounds like a great idea."

He shook his head and warned me, "You keep forgetting—it gets crazy there in a totally different way than anywhere in Los Angeles, even South Los Angeles." I understood his cautionary tone. For most people, Watts was synonymous with riots, poverty, and danger. But for me it was where I had come of age as a social worker and fallen in love with the man who would be my first husband, and where I had felt adopted by black families living in the projects, people who told me, "You just a skinny little white thing who don't know much. Hush up and listen." Watts always felt like home to me. I wanted to help with whatever was going on with family strengths and Project Fatherhood.

In truth, I was ill-equipped for the task. I had come to the game of parenthood late with the adoption of my daughter, Shannon, and I possessed a boatload of insecurities about my relationship to her. Fatherhood? I had enough trouble being a mother. The entire arena of fatherhood was pretty much alien to me. The relationship I was building with my own father had been cut short when he died of cancer while I was in college. For me, fatherhood was invariably associated with masculinity, wordless bonds, and—more than anything—loss.

These associations were all reinforced in 2008 when I started observing the work of Father Greg Boyle at Homeboy Industries, a Los Angeles–based gang intervention agency. There I quickly realized that, for the former gang members enrolled in Homeboy's reentry program, fatherhood was intertwined with a deep wound and profound yearning.

Greg was very clear about all of this. He told me over and over again, "There is a hole in the soul of every homie here—in the shape of their father. Most of these youngsters have never had a father in their life. And they want it. Look at some of the kids you see who come in here—their mothers are doing all they can—but they miss that father, they miss that presence in their lives. Then there's the homies whose fathers have had long-term drug problems. So even if they're around, they're not present, they're not part of their lives. All these kids want is a father—someone to care about them. They know that's how life should be. And they want that for their own children. We have to help with that."

Despite all the attention that Homeboy received for its social enterprise efforts and its work to obtain jobs for program graduates, Father Greg, or "G," was adamant that former gang members who received only job training, job placement services, or actual employment would not truly heal or resolve their identity issues.

"Any kind of job program *has* to be accompanied by a therapeutic community, so these individuals can work on themselves, on their trauma and their losses. This is where the hope comes from. Because we know: a hopeful kid never joins a gang or goes back to his neighborhood." It was clear to me that Greg—and by association, Homeboy Industries—was trying to provide a parenting experience within its walls. This was integral to the needs of former gang members I came to know.

After five years of being embedded at Homeboy, I came to find their stories achingly familiar. Most had tragic themes. The gang members or homies described fathers who had been incarcerated with life sentences; fathers who had disappeared, abandoning their families; fathers who carried on whole separate existences involving other women and other children; and fathers who overdosed. Familiar, no matter which homie was talking, was an essential longing for a father—any father.

It was a longing Greg answered for many. We would sit in his office and talk after a long day in which men had trailed in to talk with Greg about their eagerness to leave gang life, their feelings of aloneness, and their enduring fears.

"You can just listen to them and understand that, somewhere along the line, they felt no one cared for them. No one cared about them," Greg mused. "That's why we have to be here for them. We have to care for them, because we know that our community—our family—is going to trump the gang. And maybe, just maybe, we will stop the cycle with this generation. We can teach them to be the fathers they never had, because that wound is deep."

I nodded as I listened. In interviews, I had discovered that many times a homie made the decision to leave gang life when he had a child, most notably a son. They were determined to raise their children in safety and repeatedly told me they wanted to see their children grow to adulthood. It was the turning point that changed their lives.

"I never had a dad," a boy who looked like he could barely shave told Greg. "I wanna be one to my son." After he left, Greg sighed. "We've gotta help him. I buried his father—he was shot and killed before this kid was born. His girlfriend was seven months pregnant at the funeral. The father was a nice kid too. Wrong place, wrong time."

But he was not the only one. Greg saw many who had experienced similar losses that had never been resolved.

"Everyone longs to connect," Greg would tell me. "Everyone longs for kinship, for attachment—to belong." At Homeboy, proof of his words was offered during the hours of operation. For days on end, I watched as heavily tattooed, angry men collapsed when they started talking with Greg. In fact, the angrier the homie, the greater the likelihood of a complete breakdown. Whether fourteen or forty, these men—brown or black—clung to Greg with an affection that bordered on desperation. They unfailingly referred to him as "Pops," or "my father, G." He referred to each of them as "my son" and often remarked, "If I were your father and I had a son like you, I would be *so* proud." At those words, even the most hardened gangbanger would break down in tears.

Watching their reactions invariably filled me with awe at the depth of their need for that bond. These men—who routinely used guns and dealt drugs and brutalized women and went to prison and had no clue how to father their own children—needed first to be fathered themselves. The depth of their loss and the needs they expressed also implied a question they rarely posed directly, but managed to communicate: How can I ever be a father? Because of Big Mike, I was about to become involved with a group of men who wanted desperately to learn. But as far as I knew, there was no teacher, no guide, and no training manual. I had no idea what I was getting myself into.

There was one thing I knew for certain: what I had learned by watching Greg—about loss, connection, and community—would surely inform what I was going to try to be part of at Jordan Downs. Every man longed for a father. I wanted to get to know the experiences of these men. Did they have fathers of their own? How did they feel about what they had experienced in their lives? And, more than anything, how did that affect the ways in which they acted towards their own children? I knew I did not have the answers, but I was in a place where I might find some. I was going to Watts, where much of the adult male population spent a great deal of time engaged in criminal activity or locked up because of that activity. I was going where there were more "absentee fathers" than there were in any other parts of Los Angeles County.

All of this was on my mind as I was leaving Homeboy Industries after interviewing homies to meet Big Mike at Jordan Downs. As I walked out the door to leave, Keeshanay, a wiry little lesbian gangbanger, intercepted me.

"Where you goin', Mama?" she asked.

"I'm going to Jordan Downs. I'm gonna have a meeting with Big Mike."

"Be careful, Mama." She looked at me more sharply than usual. "It's tricky down there. I don't want anythin' to happen to ya."

As her unofficial parent of choice, I hugged her close and reassured her.

"I'm cool."

At that moment, it was hard to square Keeshanay's anxiety with city-wide statistics, which indicated Los Angeles was experiencing its lowest crime rate in forty years. At the county level, the crime rate was the lowest it had been in fifty years. These are not minor numbers with negligible impact. The population of the city of Los Angeles is almost four million, while the population of Los Angeles County nears ten million. But in Jordan Downs in the past week, there were four murders, all gang related. When Keeshanay tells me things are tricky, I am certain she knows plenty about why the gangs—or neighborhoods—have suddenly turned so violent. But none of this matters. All that matters in this moment is that I am going home. To Watts.

THREE

Neighborhood

The only father I ever had was the neighborhood.
—Trayvon Jeffers

A week has passed since I drove down to Watts to spend the evening with Mike and another former gang member and community interventionist, Andre Christian, hatching plans for the fathers' group. Big Mike's warning that I slow down has proven prophetic. Before we can actually organize any meetings for Project Fatherhood at Jordan Downs, Andre, Mike, and I are required to participate in trainings at CII—Children's Institute, Inc. We are among thirty people at the first session, straining to hear the man who is speaking to the group.

Hershel Swinger's voice rarely rises above a whisper. He has plastic tubing inserted in his nose and a small, portable oxygen tank by his side. Yet his raspy tones can't disguise the urgency of his message. Swinger is dying, but he is using—literally—every breath in his body to get the point across.

"The most important thing," he offers, "is that we get these men to connect to their children. We know from research that children whose fathers are not around suffer more, do poorly, and—more often than not—wind up in prison, part of the cradle to prison pipeline."

After the training session, the three of us go out to lunch. Andre is excited about what the training covered.

"You know, I've always *known* what Dr. Swinger said in there—even though I couldn't put it into words. I never knew my father when I was growin' up. And most of these men in Watts tryin' to raise children, they never knew their fathers either. I wanna learn to be a father —a lot of men in the community do—but we don't know how. That's what Dr. Swinger is talkin' about. We gotta use this information to help ourselves."

"Amen," Big Mike intones. "This is the most important thing we can do."

"Do you think there are men ready to do this?" I am thinking about the requirements that Dr. Swinger laid out for the group sessions—topics to be covered, issues to be discussed.

"Think? I *know* they're ready to do this," Andre insists.

Big Mike and Andre are a study in contrasts. One grew up in a fairly conventional household and, despite his gang ties, was always more a businessman than a gangbanger. The other found his family in the gang, and his commitment to the neighborhood nearly cost him his life.

In recalling his childhood, Big Mike described being raised in Watts in a happy home. "I spent a lot of time with my grandparents—my dad was never around. But I wasn't much different from all the other kids at the time. No one's daddy was around." Everything changed when he attended Markham Middle School. He remembered being "jacked" at lunch—his sandwich stolen—on the first of day of school. From then on he relied on his gang for protection. However, high school took him down a different pathway. He had grown into his manhood, and he enjoyed life as a football star, tipping the scales at 350 pounds, playing tackle, and earning the moniker "Big Mike."

"I was good," Mike recalled, smiling. "Once I was set up in community college, I was heavily recruited. I coulda played football anywhere, but drugs were a way to make money, and that attracted me. I got caught up in the lifestyle." He manufactured PCP, and even now can readily list the combination of chemicals needed to create the drug. While building up business, he joined a neighborhood—the Grape Street Crips—to expand his drug territory. Business was booming, both legitimately and otherwise. "I was making a lot of money," Big Mike told me when I first got to know him. "I had a towing business that I started in 1984 and I was dealing drugs. I used the drug money to buy more tow trucks. It was goin' great. I used to have twelve tow trucks—I owned all of them," he recalled.

"What happened to them?"

"Went up in smoke—and I mean smoking crack. Gone. I sold everything so I could smoke crack."

That version of Big Mike is unimaginable to me now.

He detailed his alliance with "Freeway" Ricky Ross, a notorious drug trafficker who built an empire in the 1980s, and his cross-country trips with "product." When his drug use accelerated, he lost his tow trucks, his friends, his family, and very nearly his life. It all ended when he was busted and sentenced to three years in jail. While incarcerated, he sent his mother multiple requests for money.

"I wanted to get drugs; I wanted to plan a party for when I got out —so I kept asking my mama for money. Instead, she sent me scripture and said she was prayin' for me. I got so angry, but as time passed, I started to read the scripture and the Bible, and when I got out, I was a different man."

Eventually Mike married Sauna, had a daughter, and became an ordained minister. "I was never goin' back to the life. I was done. You know, I wasn't around for my other two kids. But this time I was gonna be different. When she was born I held her up to God and said, I give her to you, Father God, and I knew right there I was going to be a father—a real father—to my daughter."

He went back to his old job, working for another tow company until he earned enough money to buy a new tow truck—but only one. He returned to Watts, struggling to make a living as a tow-truck driver while the community continued its downward spiral into violence. In 2000, a young boy, nicknamed Little Donut, was shot and killed in the area right next to Jordan High School. Recalling his own experiences at Markham Middle School, Mike began to see the need for a Safe Passages program staffed by former gang members who helped escort children safely to and from school. This blossomed into his work as a community interventionist. "Now my life is beautiful," Big Mike observes.

Andre, unlike Mike, experienced a childhood filled with trauma and pain. Soon after Andre was born, his father abandoned the family and his mother remarried. The household was always in turmoil, and his stepfather routinely beat his mother. When Andre sought out his father and described what was going on at home, his father promptly provided him with a sawed-off shotgun and told him to deal with his stepfather.

"I never used that shotgun," Andre recalls, "but one day, before I knew what happened, I had jumped on him. I was beatin' him up. My mama told me to stop, and then he told her she had to choose between him and me. *And she chose him.* She told me to get outta the house. I left that day. I was twelve years old. I went to live with my granny. I started gettin' into trouble, gettin' into fights, and I went to see my Daddy again and asked him what to do. He gave me some brass knuckles and told me not to run away from any fight. I didn't have a daddy, and I didn't have a mama. So my neighborhood became my family."

In the end, the Grape Street Crips embraced Andre. They fed and cared for him, and baptized him with his street name—"Low Down." From inside the gang, he wreaked havoc throughout Watts. His street credentials involved criminal activity and shootings that twice had left him close to death. The first time, he was shot three times and promised God he would leave the gang, but he fell back into the life, bolstered by the Grape Street belief "We don't die; we multiply." Grape Street was the only family he ever knew, though somewhere along the line he tried to be a father to five—one biological daughter and four stepchildren.

Two years after he was first shot, Andre was caught up in gang war and shot ten times. He came to believe the most recent shooting represented "three for the first time and seven for not upholding your promise to God." After this, Andre began to realize "the stuff you do comes back on you," and his attitude slowly changed. But there was always the pressure from the neighborhood to remain "Low Down"—an active and important member of Grape Street. It took ten years for Andre to truly leave the gang. He devoted his life to making peace. Project Fatherhood is one part of that commitment.

"What Dr. Swinger talked with us about is the truth. It *is* about the babies—the next generation. We have to make sure they don't follow this lifestyle." Andre is insisting on this in between bites of a sandwich.

"I know you're right, brother. It's important for us to do this for the men," Mike reinforces.

"Mike, you know, there is a real impact of fathers not being in the home," Andre says. "We are also gonna have to educate the women on why having fathers present is important. Even if Mom doesn't like Dad, she needs to try to include him!"

I instinctively trust these two men. Their intervention work involves them deeply with active gang members, as well as with men just out of jail and prison. They work to counsel them and find them jobs, rivaling Sisyphus in their efforts to complete their task. Every morning Mike and Andre roll the "reentry" stone uphill. But with the employment crisis America is experiencing, it is almost a certainty that stone will roll right back down.

"These men want jobs. They want help, because they know they gotta be responsible to their families," Andre continues. "If we are gonna stop this cycle of violence and prison, this is where it's gonna happen. With the father. Our women can't do it by themselves."

He is not alone in this belief. Like budget cuts and jobs programs, fatherhood has endured as a favorite topic of politicians and policymakers—and the latest crusade, led by the Obama administration, is no exception. Even in polarized Washington, DC, an effort to "strengthen fatherhood" and "hold deadbeat dads accountable" unites politicians from both sides of the aisle. But this is neither a new development nor a novel focus.

In 2000, President Bill Clinton announced his commitment to strengthening the role of fathers in families and unveiled his "responsible fatherhood" initiative, with its explanatory motto, "Fathers work, families win." Ten years later, in 2010, President Barack Obama introduced his own Fatherhood and Mentoring Initiative, described by the White House as an effort to encourage "responsible fatherhood" nationwide. Overall, for the past two decades there has been no lack of masculine pledges, roundtable policy discussions, self-help books, and even popular sitcoms—all focused on the importance of fatherhood and the need for absentee or otherwise missing fathers to play an active role in their children's lives.

While the phenomenon of absentee fathers and "deadbeat" dads transcends class and culture, research reveals that the vast majority of men defined as such are poor, of color, and all too frequently involved in the criminal justice system. They are the focus of many fatherhood initiatives. But somewhere there was a gap. In all of the initiatives and plans and ideas to promote responsible fatherhood, one expert group has never been called to testify in front of Congress, offer their insights, or serve in a leadership role: the missing "irresponsible" fathers themselves.

I thought about this from time to time in passing as I followed the lives of gang members struggling to change their identities, prisoners waiting on death row, parolees trying to find jobs, and addicts self-medicating their traumas. So many of them expressed their frustration and their rage at a system that judged them, incarcerated them, and then—while it talked about rehabilitation—never gave them a clue about how to reenter mainstream life. I wasn't paying much attention to any of this when I first worked as an anthropologist in the streets, hanging out with gang members. At that time, I was really more interested in finding out why people joined gangs and in understanding the life gang members were living—what they did as part of it, how they got out of it, what their internal struggles were. I hadn't been prepared to discover that there was another story. Everyone interviewed—whatever their color, their criminal past, their prison record (or "jacket")—expressed dreams and anxieties about the children they had left behind. And when they spoke, so many of these men would painfully wonder: *How can I be a father when I never had one?*

All of this was running through my head at lunch that day.

"How can you be so sure the men are gonna show up?" I ask Andre.

"Young lady," Andre teases, "you're forgetting somethin'. Remember what happened at the picnic tables?"

In 2008, while politicians were discussing the finer points of responsible fatherhood, far from Washington, DC, in Watts, a small group of former gangbangers gathered. Andre "Low Down" Christian, Michael "Big Mike" Cummings, Willie "Elementary" Freeman, John "Reddy" Bailey, Fred "Scorpio" Smith, and Wayne "Honcho" Day pooled their finances and, under the umbrella of the nonprofit organization Watts United, had set up shop at "the picnic tables at the park"—three forlorn concrete tables set at the edge of a weathered playing field next to the projects.

Word went out through the Jordan Downs community that you could get a haircut and some barbecue at the tables every Wednesday.

But this was more than an open-air barbershop. The de facto community organizers actually wanted to engage, mentor, and even father the younger men in the community who were involved in gangs and crime.

"Remember what happened at the picnic tables?" Andre repeats. "We wanted to help the young men who showed up. I didn't want any of these youngsters to end up like me—in the neighborhood, doin' dirt, winding up in the pen. We wanted to give them some direction, too. We told them they needed to work—to get a job and start raisin' their children. The streets were raisin' their children. And the county. Now they needed to be fathers and really help their kids to grow up strong. The men knew that, too, so they kept showing up."

The group gathered at the picnic tables grew, but the meager earnings of the organizers were not enough to feed everyone. On top of that, during the Los Angeles rainy season there was nowhere to go. Andre and Mike both knew that the men needed a space to come together to talk about themselves and their families, and about the lives they were trying to remake. They had no idea that a few miles away, at the Children's Institute, Hershel Swinger was getting ready to expand his work with Project Fatherhood. In 2010, these two movements were brought together by the most unlikely of matchmakers: the Housing Authority of the City of Los Angeles, or HACLA as it is commonly known, the agency responsible for overseeing all of the housing developments, or "projects," in Los Angeles.

In the first decade of the twenty-first century, the three housing projects of Watts—Jordan Downs, Imperial Courts, and Nickerson Gardens—were synonymous with violence in Los Angeles. Jordan Downs and Nickerson Gardens, in particular, had served as the backdrop for lethal gang crime in the late 1980s and early 1990s, the accurately named "decade of death" when the number of homicides in Los Angeles topped a thousand or more per year, as police and policymakers decried a gang "crisis." The war between the Grape Street Crips of Jordan Downs and the Bounty Hunter Bloods of "the Nickersons" claimed many lives and decimated families. Even up to 2010, these two housing developments were viewed as dangerous for anyone who entered, including families who tried to carve out a normal existence living inside the cinderblock walls. The residents of Jordan Downs, especially, felt neglected and doomed to inadequate housing and hopeless lives. To make matters worse, HACLA had invested funding in repainting and restoring Nickerson Gardens, while Jordan Downs continued to decline.

But in 2010, everything changed. Attention shifted in a new direction with the announcement of the redevelopment of Jordan Downs. HACLA launched a splashy media campaign designed to trumpet the good news and—of almost equal importance—override negative attention the agency had been receiving. Reports in the news told of parties at city expense and other flagrant misspending; there was enough corruption to make a Mafioso jealous. HACLA was desperate for a positive headline, Swinger was working against his final deadline, and a small group of men from the community was longing for change.

Through its policy director, John King, HACLA brought the pieces together—Big Mike's leadership, Andre's community engagement, and the agency's plan to "build human capital" at Jordan Downs. As a team they would apply for funding for Project Fatherhood from CII through a nonprofit agency HACLA had created, Kids Progress Inc. All they needed to qualify for money was one thing: a social worker to assist with the program.

"We are all in this together, Miss Leap," Andre drawled. "You gotta have faith."

"It'll be fine," Big Mike added. "Y'know, folks in Watts—they might start out suspicious, but they'll come around."

"And we'll keep at it." Andre then added what was about to become a mantra: "Watts is worth it."

FOUR

Are You Gonna Leave Us, Too?

Sometimes I wish I didn't have feelings because I don't like to feel emotions. But I feel emotions. And I'm compassionate not just for my children but for the community that I was raised in. I love Watts.
—Terrance Russell

In November 2010, Project Fatherhood makes its debut. Big Mike and I are waiting in the "conference room" of the Jordan Downs community center. We sit in what is really an oversized closet with no windows. There is a table with twelve chairs jammed around it and a whiteboard.

Fifteen minutes later, exactly two fathers have shown up. Mike and I talk about the purpose of the group, pass around an outline of topics we will cover, and ask the men if they will refer others. Mike is upbeat. "Next week we will go through the outline in detail, and we will start talkin' about what you all want from the group. We'll see you then."

Afterwards we meet with Andre—who has been leading a women's group—for what Mike refers to as a "debrief." Andre sounds like the hood version of Old Mother Hubbard as he reports, "There were so many women and kids there for the group that I didn't know what to do." I am concerned that we are attracting women and children, but no fathers. The women's group is part of the Project Fatherhood program: under the mission of strengthening fathers, it is critical to provide support for the "significant others" and their mutual children.

The word "wife" is rarely heard. "It doesn't matter if no one is married, or if the men aren't livin' with their women. We gotta be respectful," Big Mike explains. "And we gotta teach these men to be respectful towards their significant others."

No one is more respectful towards his significant other than Big Mike. His relationship with Sauna, a majestically beautiful woman, differs from the relationships most active and former gang members experience for many reasons, including the fact that they are legally married. Sauna is a quiet but constant presence, along with their daughter, Emonni, whom Mike invariably refers to as Booboo. Sauna and Booboo are Mike's do-over family. "This time I am gonna get it right," he once explained to me, and all signs show that he is fulfilling that commitment. Mike has adult children from a past relationship, but he rarely talks about them.

The debrief ends with everyone pledging to recruit more fathers to come to the next session.

A week later, six men show up, including two brothers, Sy and Ben Henry. Mike immediately perks up. "Sy is one of the elders of this community," he tells me. "And Ben is strong. This is a good start." He passes out more detailed information sheets and tells the men what Project Fatherhood is designed to do, saying it will help them with their children by, among other things, teaching them good parenting strategies. The men sit quietly, staring at the information sheets. I wonder if they are literate. No one ever wants to admit he can't read. Instead, I have learned, men in the neighborhoods help one another devise strategies around this barrier.

Mike suggests that I review the content of each session. The men all laugh when I refer to a future discussion of "baby mama drama." But they are quiet and look away when I try to make eye contact. No one is connecting, and almost everyone is keeping his head down. My anxiety is shooting through the roof. What if no one else shows up? What if the group doesn't grow or bond or accomplish anything? Mike breaks into this internal second-guessing and utters two words that evoke the first real enthusiasm these men have shown.

Gift cards.

No one was more aware of the challenge of attracting men to the group than Swinger. He knew exactly what Project Fatherhood was up against, in terms of suspicion and mistrust. To encourage attendance, he devised an incentive for program participation. Each time a man attends four sessions of Project Fatherhood, he receives a twenty-five-dollar supermarket gift card. There is no checking up on how it was spent. When Mike tells the men about the gift cards and adds that each meeting will start with a free meal, all six enthusiastically tell us that they will return and that they will bring others. We do not debrief afterwards, as Mike and Andre are attending a candlelight vigil for a young man who has been shot and killed.

The next day I am back in Watts, talking to Andre, trying to figure out why we don't have more men coming to the meetings. Andre is laughing at me.

"Young lady," he begins, "are you gonna tell me after all this time you still don't understand Watts? Come on now—you know what this is. They're trying to see if we are *for real*."

I start laughing because I don't know what else to do. I am not sure I am ever going to understand Watts. I am constantly learning things, even as I become interwoven with the community fabric in unexpected, funny ways. Mostly I feel like the white mascot of Jordan Downs. A week earlier, while I am interviewing a young homie named Squeak inside his grandmother's unit, another homie—Zero—bursts in on us screaming, "Miss Leap, Miss Jorja Leap!! There's some white woman here in a minivan—what does she want? You know her. You gotta talk to her."

"Zero, I don't know every white person in LA. Why did you interrupt me?"

"You gotta talk to her—we don't wanna talk to her. She says she knows you."

The woman turned out to be a *Los Angeles Times* reporter working on a story about the redevelopment of Jordan Downs. I wound up introducing her to several community members. I thought of all this while I was talking to Andre.

"You mean they don't trust us? Even you? You've been here all your life. So has Mike!"

"They're testing us. They wanna see if we're for real. You gotta wait."

Waiting had never been my strong suit. After Andre leaves me to meet with some gangbangers he is trying to sign up for an intervention program run by the mayor's office, I walk across the street from the community center to kick it with Little Damien and Squeak, two homies who cannot conceive of a world beyond Watts. They are both under twenty-one and up to their necks in gang life. While Squeak is not a father, that situation may change; his current girlfriend thinks she may be pregnant. Little Damien has fathered two children already, and one of his rotating group of girlfriends is six months into another pregnancy. "It ain't mine," he tells me. Neither one of them is particularly worried about the fluidity of their situations. "It don't bother me," Squeak elaborates. "I wanna have kids. Now's as good a time as any. I gotta make sure I leave something behind—when I'm gone." Gang members are natural fatalists and set out to have children as quickly as they are able. They aren't allergic to birth control—they just want to ensure that they have at least one son before they die.

I am eager for both of them to come to the group, but LD laughs out loud when I suggest it. Between Andre, Little Damien, and Squeak, I am catching on about why the early meetings have failed to attract many of the fathers. There is suspicion of the group's purpose. The men also mistrust each other. On top of that, no one wants to go inside the community center, a place no gang really controls.

"We aren't goin' in that buildin', period. I don' trust anyone in there," Little Damien tells me.

"No way," Squeak adds.

"What about your children? Don't you think this could help you with them?" I ask the questions halfheartedly.

Little Damien starts laughing.

"I don't need help with my children. I need help with my court case."

"What's it about?" I am mentally reviewing the possible offenses— assault, drug dealing, weapons possession—when my checklisting is interrupted.

"One a' my baby mamas is haulin' my ass off to court for child support. How am I supposed to pay her child support? I ain't had a job for three years. I think she's stupid—what's she gonna get from me? And if they lock my ass up, then what? Does she think she's gonna get money from me while I'm in county jail?"

There is nothing for me to say, although I do regard it as a good sign that the court date has nothing to do with criminal activity. Little Damien is a small-time drug dealer who occasionally gets busted for selling nickel bags of marijuana. I am glad to see he has escaped detection. He is, however, juggling three baby mamas and two—potentially three—children. Project Fatherhood is tailor-made to fit his needs. I resist saying anything like this, but I mention the gift cards. Little Damien and Squeak both start laughing.

"You think my baby mama will try to—whadyacallit—attach the gift card to my case?"

I shake my head, adding, "I'll see you there." Both boys laugh as I hug them then walk away. I'm not holding my breath that they'll show up.

But word about the gift cards makes its way through the Jordan Downs grapevine—a communication system more effective than Facebook—and the next week the room is filled to bursting.

Sy Henry raises his hand. "What I wanna know, aside from all of these topics and all of these ideas, is how long are you gonna be here?"

"We got a one-year grant."

"Only one year, huh?"

"Yeah." Big Mike repeats, "We got a one-year grant from the Children's Institute."

"And then, after a year, what happens?"

"I don't know, brother. We're gonna try to still be here."

John King, representing HACLA, waits for Big Mike to finish and begins to speak, very smoothly. (I can never think of him as anything other than by his full name, probably because the men in the room refer to him that way.)

"This is part of a larger program, something the city is doing through the Housing Authority. We are building human capital. Do you know what that means?"

The men look at him blankly.

"John King," Sy starts, "what are you talking about?"

"We are investing in people in the community. We want to build programs—to help build up people in the community."

"You don't know what we have had to deal with." Debois is disturbed. "Here we go again with another program."

"We hear a lot of promises—alla the time."

"Dr. Leap knows—" Mike begins.

"I know," I say. "I remember the Watts riots."

"Shit, you too young to remember the Watts riots."

"Are you calling Dr. Leap a liar?" Big Mike is beginning to get agitated, but I recognize the comments for what they are. This is just the fathers' way of relating. It has taken me a while to catch on to this in South Los Angeles, but I understand. The exchange of insults is one of the most common expressions of intimacy available in Watts. Still, I was touchy when they got into my not being ghetto, but I accepted things for what they were.

"She should know the history," Sy offers.

I decide to take him up on this.

"So tell me."

"You know how many times we heard these promises? Do you know? Every time there's a riot or a problem or violence, here they come again. So after the Watts riots they built the hospital—Martin Luther King. Look how that turned out—it's closed now, after everyone who went there died 'cause they had such bad doctors."

I knew this well. I had worked at Martin Luther King when the hospital was known throughout Los Angeles County as "Killer King" and had very little problem living up to the reputation. When it finally closed, in 2007, after failing a federal inspection, the hospital left behind a thirty-five-year history of mistreatment, inadequate care, and wrongful death. There were stories of patients in the ER who literally died on the floor or on gurneys in the hallway waiting to receive medical attention.

"Then, after Rodney King and all that, they said they were gonna open businesses in the community. We *still* waiting for those businesses—where are they? Now we're hearin' they're gonna rebuild Jordan Downs. Well, I believe it when I see it."

"We're not mad at you—understand?" Leelee speaks up. He is shrewd. "We're just wonderin' . . ."

Sy clears his throat.

"What I want to know is . . . are you gonna leave us too? I don't really care about human capital. I've heard a lot in my life. And my daddy heard a lot in his life. The programs came and they were here a minute and then they left. And they never came back. I think you might be one a' those—a program that comes and goes. Or are you gonna stay?" The men in the room are all nodding.

Big Mike and I insist the group does not have an end point.

"We are here for a minute and then more. We are committed to Project Fatherhood," Mike offers. The men listen carefully. A minute is the hood equivalent of a long time. Big Mike is promising more than that. The men appear interested and several promise to return, but over the next three weeks, attendance is inconsistent. There is an overflow crowd one week sandwiched between two sparsely attended weeks. The entire time, the women and children show up with great enthusiasm. Mike, Andre, Reddy (who runs the children's group), John King, and I now routinely meet afterwards to debrief each session of Project Fatherhood.

"I don't understand how long it is going to take to get these men to trust us—what do they want, a sign from God?" I say, only half joking. Under the funding requirements, each Project Fatherhood site must have at least fifty men signed up over the course of a year. The plan made sense; out of fifty attendees, a core group would eventually emerge. At the rate we are going, I wonder how we can meet the numbers. As a seasoned bureaucrat, John King shares my concerns. But no one else is alarmed.

"The women come," I continue. "And we're overrun with children. But the fathers aren't coming. Not in any regular way."

"This is the way it always is—the women show up, the men don't come," Big Mike despairs.

"You know, you are both—what's the word?" Andre thinks for a moment. "*Unrealistic*. Highly unrealistic." He looks proud of himself. "Doncha remember what we are dealing with here? I keep telling you this, young lady." Andre winks at me before continuing.

"These are very, very suspicious people. They are afraid we are gonna go away after a few meetings. They want to see if we are gonna stay. I heard what Sy asked. And you gotta realize, *every program they have heard about has left*."

His words sink in. Everyone is too familiar with the long line of initiatives, each of which seemed to begin with the identical announcement that it was "offering the real solution to the problems that have so long plagued Watts." The programs disappeared before any problems had actually been solved. Often, such initiatives left things worse than they had been before. This had been happening as far back as Lyndon Johnson and the Great Society. These men are asking the right questions. I am thinking about promises made and broken, not just involving fathers and their children, but involving an entire community.

"Andre's right. We *have* to show up week after week. And we've gotta believe the men will eventually show up." I want to sound confident, but I've got nothing to go on but blind faith. I am clueless about how this will play out.

A few weeks later, the weather is threatening rain. Nevertheless, the meeting is well attended. Some of the men have now come enough times to qualify for gift cards, which will be distributed at the end of tonight's session. But the atmosphere is tense. Big Mike is upset that not enough food has been provided. And the topic du jour is a lulu: "How do you, as a father, deal with domestic violence?"

I am worried about how to introduce this, so Big Mike and I agree the direct approach is best. He will simply pose the question. Mike starts the session by asking, "How many of you have hit your woman?"

The room goes quiet, but I feel strangely relaxed. Anxiety silence is a staple of group work—it's the group-process equivalent of playing chicken. You've got to wait and see who will blink—or in this case, talk—first. No one likes the discomfort of silence, least of all these fathers. The gap does not last very long. A father named Terrance speaks up.

"Everyone in here has hit their woman—maybe not now, maybe not with the woman they got now—but at some time, y'know, we've hit our women. I'm not ashamed to admit it. I left my two sons' mama because that woman made me crazy. And I knew if I didn't leave her, I would kill her."

The men all nod.

"And I remember my daddy. He hit my mama whenever he would come around. That's what I remember, the cup on the table and his fist ready to go. You know, we all saw our men beating our mamas," Terrance continues. "We all grew up with the cup on the table." He gestures with a paper cup and elaborates about how men—his father, his stepfather, other men—would "sit and drink forty-ouncers and then get up and routinely beat their woman."

"Sometimes a woman needs to be hit," Sy speaks up, then starts laughing.

"You're just scared of this." Terrance goes right after Sy. "We need to talk about it. We're not supposed to hit our women. We've been doing it for generations, and it's wrong."

"Why do you think you do it?" I am genuinely curious when I ask.

The men all start talking at the same time.

"She cheated on me."

"She lied to me."

"She disrespected me."

"She disrespected me *in front of my kids*."

"I don't know why. I don't—she just yells at me and is always givin' me grief, and I couldn't take it. I didn't want to listen to it anymore."

"My daddy hit my mama, and my stepdaddy hit my mama. I guess I was used to it."

"Yeah—we just came up that way."

"And the women expect it."

"They do—and they do it too. They can hit us." The man saying this—Big Bob—is huge. Just eyeballing him, I am certain he tips the scales somewhere north of two hundred pounds.

I am more interested in what the men are not saying. Every single thing these men bring up is straight out of the domestic violence research literature, but they have left out one crucial factor: substance abuse.

I am about to mention this, when the door opens and two men enter the room. There is a stillness that I know not to pierce. One man wears a lilac-colored coat of Naugahyde that hangs down below his knees. When it flaps open I see he is carrying some kind of weapon. I don't look too closely—I know that it's time to keep my head down and shut up. Someone has a weapon, and he is wearing the color of the Grape Street Crips.

This is the home team, the gang that has controlled Jordan Downs since the 1980s. The two men silently walk up to each man sitting around the tables, stare directly at them, and then either shake their hand or extend a fist bump. They ignore me. It is as if I am invisible, not in the room. They shake Big Mike's hand but say nothing. It is a silent visit full of meaning. As soon as they are gone, the conversation resumes. It's as if someone pressed pause on a DVD and then decided to push play again.

"Y'know, you are talking about the way we've always done things here," Debois says. He is half laughing, half challenging.

"Sometimes our women are just askin' for it."

"I don't know." Aaron, one of the few Latinos in the group, speaks quietly. He has come consistently and talked to me before group about problems he is having with his wife. "My father told me it was wrong to hit a woman. So if I hit my wife, I feel like I am disobeying my father."

"My father never told me nothin'."

"My daddy told me sometimes a woman deserves it."

"I don't know, Aaron—how you gonna keep her in line?"

"It's hard. Sometimes I want to hit her—so bad—but I just can't do it." Aaron is almost gasping for air.

"It's okay." Sy reaches over and pats him on the back.

"I am telling you all now, I am never ever going to hit my girlfriend or my significant other. It's just wrong."

The men go silent. In sync, they all turn towards Matt. He is eighteen years old, a senior at Jordan High School.

Matt rarely speaks during the weekly sessions. He just quietly chews on his dinner and listens to the men's exchange. He has golden-green eyes and mocha-colored skin, and he dreams of being a biologist. I have checked on him at the high school. He is an honors student, a transplant from Chicago, living at Jordan Downs with his auntie. I wonder where his parents are.

The men are growing restive and want their gift cards. Big Mike brings the session to a close, asking the men to think about their relationships and their significant others. A few of them come up afterwards to reassure me, saying "I'm not gonna hit my wife, Dr. Leap." I hug them and say, "I hope not."

No one says a word about our visitors.

Afterwards, during the debrief session, the denial of what occurred continues. It is breathtaking. There is absolutely no discussion of the interruption in the meeting. When the men leave for the evening, I raise the subject of the visitors to Big Mike, but he cuts off my questions. "We need to leave that life behind—we're not part of any neighborhood. It's really not the place to talk about it." I have learned, through trial and error, when not to pursue certain topics. Big Mike signals to me that our conversation is finished, saying, "Come on, Jorjaleap. I gotta walk you out to your car." It doesn't matter that I have parked right outside of the community center—Big Mike insists on escorting me to the car and making sure I lock the door. I call my husband, Mark, before I leave. There may be a forty-year low in crime, but as they say—Watts is different.

FIVE

Brothers

I already did your jail time so leave it alone.
—Sy Henry

It is a good sign that the Henry brothers are part of Project Fatherhood. Each week, both appear long before each session starts. They help set up chairs, make sure the room is in order, and ask me if I need anything. Ben in particular is neatly groomed; he often comes straight from work. Sy does not talk about working anywhere. He has a twinkle in his eye and a memory for detail. Both of them have deep roots in the Watts community, and I spend some time learning their stories.

As Big Mike told me, Sy is clearly the elder. Early on, I notice the other men turning to him for his opinion on disputes. He remembers being "raised right here in the Jordan Downs housing projects, in unit 365. I can remember just growin' up playing and doing things and dealin' with the neighborhood. I was able to go from grade school to high school and get a high school diploma. But instead of following up, goin' to UCLA through the Upward Bound program, I was in jail. I had committed a robbery with a friend of mine and shot the person."

What Sy fails to add is that the person he shot died.

Sy is a legend in Watts, the hood equivalent of a "made" man: eighteen years old, high school graduation in June, jail in July. Because of his age, he was sentenced to the California Youth Authority (CYA)—what homies like to call "baby prison"—and released when he was twenty-five. Sy laughs easily and says, "So that's how my little history started. Then I was in and out of jail for the next twenty years. But I finally got out and stayed out. I never been back since because jail just wasn't for me. Even though I ended up in there, it wasn't for me. It's for no man, if you ask me."

When Sy was released from CYA, he was into "all kinds of illegal stuff, because you need to understand, black men can't even get a job out here. The police try to grab you young, you get your criminal history, and then it's hard to get a job. So we were doing other things to make money. We weren't hurtin' anybody, trying to kill nobody or nothing like that. We were just tryin' to survive and take care of our kids."

I have heard the same words from many of these men. Whatever the method, they were going to provide for their children.

"When I became a father, the whole world changed for me. I was focused on what the babies need. I was always out in the streets, always trying to take care of them. I'm nobody's loser. Because each and every time I went to jail, it was for just trying to feed my children. And you gotta understand, *this was the only way we could take care of our families.*"

The family Sy and Ben grew up in was not dysfunctional. According to Ben, their parents "were both in the house." But the streets were calling, and answering the call brought trouble with law enforcement. From an early age, Sy in particular remembers, "There was always the problem with the police—they always wanna mess with you for nothin'."

Both Sy and Ben remembered everything in Watts changing after cocaine and crack hit the streets. People disappeared—they were on drugs or in prison, or they simply vanished, running off to other states to avoid arrest. Over time, Sy married twice and fathered five children—four sons and a daughter. (The daughter, fifteen, is the youngest.) There have been several women in his life, but the children are a constant. He lived with his first wife, Annie, for sixteen years, but now lives with his current wife, Cherise. Sy is proud that his four sons do not have any criminal history and that he has always emphasized education in his children's lives.

"I tell alla my children, 'I need you to go to school. That's your only job. Get an education, stay academically sound. Me and your mama, we'll get you whatever you want. Graduate high school. Try to take it farther if you can.'"

Sy is adamant that even though he pursued a life of crime, he wants to instill different—and better—values in his children. "They need it, and Watts needs it," he tells me. While Sy is talking, all I can think about is the idea of family and community strengths. This is not to glamorize Watts—the community is poor, under-resourced, and violent. But Sy is highly invested in bringing his sons to manhood in Watts, as part of the community.

"With my boys, it's all about love. If I argue with one of my sons, trade words before we separate, I have to have a hug, and I have to tell them to give me a smile before I get up out of there. I let my sons know, 'I love you'—no matter what just happened, I still love you. I think that kept them out of a lot of trouble. Because I used to tell them before they walked out the door, 'Henry boys are not followers. We lead, we don't follow. I respect you more if you get in trouble by yourself, but if you out following somebody getting in trouble, I'll be disappointed.' I think that's why my boys never been to jail or nothing like that, 'cause they always were able to make the right decision, just walk away and leave it alone. I used to tell 'em, 'I already did your jail time so leave it alone. I got you. Daddy all right.' They know what I mean when I say that. Daddy all right. I am proud to say that my sons went a different way. They went the way I wanted them to go. We chose for them, instead of what the streets chose for them."

Ben is much quieter than Sy and less of a jokester. Born five years after Sy, he speaks openly about their past.

"I don't know if you could say gangs were in the family. My dad was in the Sons of Watts—they were men from Watts who wore burgundy dashikis with 'Sons of Watts' on the back. He wouldn't call that a gang. But when I was growing up, gangbanging had taken off. My brother Sy got into the Grapes first—he was faster. I was a square. He was always out doing stuff with his boys—riding, robbing, whatever he did. I was a little mama's boy. I just did kid shit—make kites, learn how to do flips on the ground, swim. I wasn't really out there, like some of my partners my age."

Ben finally got into trouble in middle school. "I thumped my teacher, and they said that was assault. I ended up going to jail, and my dad—he beat my ass for that one." Despite his father's efforts at discipline, in high school Ben quickly got into selling weed and other drugs, attracting the attention of the police.

"I was just getting my little money. Growing up in the projects on 103rd, you had the clinic, you had the parking lot where all the hustlers and players would hang out. You had Bob's liquor store. If you're going to the liquor store, you gotta pass through the parking lot—you see these dice games, pretty cars, guys dressed nice, three-piece suits, tailored suits. Your neighborhood plays a big effect on your life growing up. You going to do one of two things: either you in or you ain't in. The majority is with it—they're in."

Although Ben was involved with Grape Street, once he went into the drug business he "put gangbanging to the side. I would work with the other hoods." He reminds me of another homie I have known for years, Dennis Payne, who grew up in Nickerson Gardens. Even though he was part of a Bounty Hunter Bloods clique, Payne could negotiate in Jordan Downs.

Ben confirms this experience. "When crack came out, there was ways to get money. Your neighborhood might have this drug and their neighborhood might have that drug. They might be your enemies. They could be the Bloods, but there's a few cats over there that you get along with and you deal with. And y'all form a bond, because you're not on the gangbanging trip, but rather on the money trip. That's how certain guys can go to certain projects. Even though they're from here, their reputations are good. For me, that's how it goes."

I see this in the group. Ben is agreeable and rarely argues. Everyone likes him, even the group members who don't get along with each other. But Ben is one in a long line of men from the neighborhoods who told me that no matter how agreeable things were on the street, in jail everything changed. "You gotta push your linc in jail, because they'll try you."

Ben remembers Grape Street nostalgically. He is no longer active, no longer involved, but there are facets of the gang he views in a positive light. He believes the neighborhood formed part of the strength inside of him. He sounds a lot like Andre when he tells me, "One thing about Grape Street—we're not scared to go anywhere. If it's on the moon and we got a way to go there, we are going. Certain gangs are limited. They only gangbang in their neighborhoods. But Grape Street—anywhere they havin' something we feel like we wanna be a part of, we going."

While all of this is in his past, Ben does not deny Grape Street is still part of his identity. "It's nothing to glorify," he tells me. "It's a piece of my life. It's things that I've done seen. I ain't proud of it. But, shit, it's part of my history."

Despite his gang ties, Ben never was particularly violent. All of his prison time was related to drug dealing. But he fell prey to the same demons Big Mike did, using as well as "slanging"—dealing drugs. He was in the streets for eight years. Ultimately, his parents kicked him out and he had nowhere to go. But all along, he says, he "did whatever I had to do to get another hit."

Ben looks back gratefully and admits, "I thank the Lord that I'm here." Prison served as his rehab. "When I was in there for that time, I kind of got my sanity back. I got back to who I was, the person my mom and dad raised. When I finally got out, I'm going back to the same neighborhood, but I know I can't get caught up in the same thing, as far as smoking the dope." With the help of a girlfriend, he stayed straight for several months.

But Ben could not resist the lure of the streets, and he started selling dope again. He didn't fall back into addiction. As he tells it, he just hooked up with his "partners and started getting some money, real money. It was good." He was caught in a dope-house raid and ended up going to jail, sentenced for drug possession but not distribution. Even so, the sentence was five years, including rehab, but he ended up serving only fourteen months in Adelanto State Prison.

He returned home, but the relationship with his girlfriend had changed and they split up, though Ben insists that to this day they remain "the best of friends. If I needed something and she had it, I know I could call her. If she needed something, she can get it from me."

Unlike some of the men in the group, Ben doesn't feel embittered. Instead, he moved on and "had a little job, renovating the projects, doing lead and asbestos." He met and married his wife and they had their first child. "At the time, I didn't think I could have kids," Ben recalls. "I ended up having my little chocolate daughter, and things were going good."

I am hoping against hope that the story ends here. Ben is a good man. He reminds me of my father, my brother, the boys I grew up with. But he is a convicted felon and I know far too well the struggle for money and for employment that so many men have endured. Fighting to make a living, Ben got back into the game, selling drugs. Then his story took a strange turn.

"I did a guy a favor, one I thought it was cool to do, because he was my partner. Didn't do it for a profit or nothing, I just did it. The whole time he was working with the FBI. Some people warned me, but I couldn't believe it, because he was my partner. You know how that goes. You gotta trust and believe in people. So, I did the favor for him. Eighteen months later, the Feds end up calling my house at four in the morning. Long story short, I went to jail."

His daughter was barely two years old. Ben grows quiet, then re-members.

"Whenever I was out in the streets, her mama would call my cell and let me talk with her. 'Daddy, come get me,' she would say, and I would tell her, 'All right, I'll come get you.' She was my little ride-or-die buddy. Y'know, we say that in Watts, it doesn't mean you're gonna die; it means you're loyal, you stick with your buddy through thick and thin. And I knew my daughter loved me. When I went to jail, after all the process-ing, I called home. My little baby said, 'Daddy, come get me,' and I cried like a baby. I knew it was gonna be a while before daddy could come get her. She didn't understand; she was only two. I cried, because that hurt."

That was Ben's turning point. He did his time and came home and has been straight ever since. He is certain he will never deal drugs again.

Ben is one of the few fathers who is employed full-time, working at an auto-parking service near Los Angeles International Airport. He has held the job for over seven years. He explains, "I'm just being the man I knew I could be." I am thinking about Greg Boyle when Ben tells me this. Greg often likes to say that the process of healing takes place as an individual sees the truth of their lives.

Ben tells me that life is a struggle. "It ain't good, it ain't bad. It's in between. You've got to just hang there. I don't let anyone deter me. I just do it. Rolling the clock back, of how I grew up in the projects—it was a real learning experience. I've seen life, I've seen death."

Ben is not exaggerating.

I done actually been to bottom, where people don't give a fuck about you, only your loved ones. And they care because they hate to see you in a position you in, knowing you could be better, you wasn't raised like that. It done took me a while. The Lord still lets me be here. So I thank him for that, all day every day, you know? I love it here, and I care about Watts. There's places worse than Watts. We ain't had no mass killings, even back in the day. We had civil unrest, but it's worse in third world countries. We ain't had no one walk into an elementary school killing twenty kids and teachers. No one walked to a high school and killed fourteen to fifteen kids. Nothing like that here in Watts. You get real-life lessons here. I wouldn't trade it for the world, I always wanna come back. Got out of jail, took that long-ass Greyhound ride coming up the 10 from Arizona. I seen downtown Los Angeles and smiled like a baby.

SIX

Abuse

I got whupped and I turned out okay.
—Robert "Bobby" Windom

The next week the room is full. I am trying to figure out if this is related to the unscheduled visit we had the week before—has Grape Street given its blessing to this endeavor? I don't want to ask too many questions. Instead, I listen to the men complaining before the meeting starts up.

"My boy—he has homework I don't understand. I need a tutor so I can help him. What are we gonna do about it?"

"That's nothing. The school kicked my girl out for fighting. They didn't even call me or anything—they just sent her home. When I went to see the teacher, she was so disrespectful, I couldn't even believe it—who they hirin' now? I just left. There was no one to talk to. They said they was gonna kick her out. Now what am I supposed to do?"

"I got an appointment with DCFS. I need you to go with me, Drjorjaleap. What am I supposed to say to them? They gonna take my kids away. My girl is upset."

"The electricity is out in my unit. Can you tell Mrjohnking that?"

"I need money."

I look at Big Mike and start laughing helplessly at the deluge of announcements and questions. It is chaos as usual; this signals the beginning of every meeting. Big Mike and I fight for order by first reassuring the men that after the meeting Drjorjaleap would deal with each of these matters. I was, after all, the "master social worker." We then valiantly try to introduce a topic for the men to discuss. In his training sessions before the start of Project Fatherhood, Hershel Swinger had explained that the topics were designed to help the men understand more about parenting and to encourage them to share their experiences. Today, it is obvious Dr. Swinger had never met the fathers of Jordan Downs.

"Why do you bring up these crazy topics? Can't we just talk?"

"I got something I wanna talk about. I got problems with my—whatcha call it—significant other—"

"I got a problem. I caught a case—"

"I think my two boys got their girlfriends pregnant—"

I didn't need the Project Fatherhood training manual; I needed a whistle. The men are all screaming. Sy looks on, smiling, and then announces, "Maybe you ought to let me run the group."

I start laughing, but right before the meeting begins, another father—Mel—takes me aside and tells me *he* really ought to help run the group. He had already raised two teenagers and they had turned out fine, although he's not sure where one of them is right now.

Even as they periodically express interest in leading the group, the men *always* want information—and resources. When was HACLA going to demolish Jordan Downs? Could they get a job? I should come to a party at their unit—could I bring food? Would I give them my laptop computer—they needed it more than I did. Their questions were constant and shameless. I was amazed at the ideas they brought up. Nothing was off-limits.

Until this meeting. This was the night we hit the third rail of Project Fatherhood: child abuse.

California state law divides child abuse into three main categories: neglect, physical abuse, and sexual abuse. I was not new to this game. I started my career as a social worker at Martin Luther King Jr. General Hospital in Watts, investigating child-abuse cases. However, despite my experience, I was not nearly the expert these men were. Every single father had been directly or indirectly involved with the Los Angeles County Department of Children and Family Services (DCFS). Or, as the fathers referred to it, "the County," or "Social Services," or "those motherfuckers in Protective Services." I had been one of the county officials, and I had been on the receiving end of threats—with knives thrown or guns waved—when I ventured into the projects alone for a home visit.

When Big Mike brings up the topic of child abuse, I feel like I have entered the twilight zone. The antipathy and suspicion I encountered over thirty years earlier is alive and well in the room. I feel defensive. I know DCFS is a mess, but some noble men and women I know work for "the county." They are compassionate and responsible professionals, and they get a bad rap from policymakers, the media, and the men in this room. Trying to navigate around my own defensiveness, I ask the fathers how they feel about the first of the three interrelated parts of child abuse: neglect.

No surprise. The men have lots of thoughts about neglect, and they all run along the same line of reasoning: because not one father is the primary caretaker for his children, this is viewed as the women's responsibility.

"Takin' care of my kids—that's my baby mamas' job. All of them," Leelee begins. "They wanted the kids; they got 'em."

"Didn't you want them?" I ask.

"Yeah, I wanted them. I wanted alla my kids, but that's the way it was. The woman—she takes care of them."

"That's the woman's job," Debois adds. "We all know it. That's the way God intended it."

I am trying to forget my father telling me that my brother didn't have to clear the dinner table or wash the dishes because that was women's work. I am also trying not to recite the changes that have occurred after three decades of feminism, while Debois patiently explains—as if he is talking to a five-year-old—exactly what God intends for women. Big Mike steps into the discussion.

"Now listen, it's everyone's job. You're a father, and you as a father are supposed to take care of that child, even if you don't live with him or her. I know I gotta keep a roof over my children's heads and food on the table and the heat on *even if I don't live with them.*"

The room is silent as Mike's voice booms out. I decide a slight addition may be a good idea.

"One of the major causes of all child abuse, especially neglect, is using drugs and drinking—substance abuse."

The men all look solemn. Drinking and drugs are not an abstract. They are a problem at Project Fatherhood on a weekly basis. Several fathers routinely appeared at early meetings drunk or high, treating the evening as a social gathering. The group generally reacted with benign neglect unless someone grew disruptive. On those odd occasions, Big Mike would ask me to go get Andre, who would then escort the offending father from the room. The week before, a new father had shown up and refused dinner. "I think he's high," I whispered to Mike, and about ten minutes later the man confirmed my suspicions, going into a nod. When his head bobbed up right before the meeting ended, he stood and left the room. I found him outside sleeping next to my car. I gently nudged him into consciousness and he quickly responded, apologizing and promising to come back "straight" the next week. One of the most articulate fathers, Scorpio, had recently gone missing from meetings because he was in rehab, dealing with his substance abuse problems.

The men do not argue tonight when I tell them that drinking and drugging were the major reasons children wound up in "the system."

"If you use, your baby's gonna lose."

"That's true. That's the real problem."

"That's why I never wanna have a baby with a woman who gets high alla the time. I might wanna go with her, y'know, but I don't wanna have a baby with her."

"The truth is," Terrance begins, "I know a lot about neglect. My mama was drunk or high so much of the time, she didn't take care of us. I saw my baby brother run over right in the street because she was high and she wasn't watching him. That killed him and that nearly killed her. She was drinkin' and usin' drugs even more after that. And then social services came—they said she was a drug addict. As if we needed them to tell us that! They tried to take us away. We wound up living with my granny."

"My kids all live with their granny. My girl can't take care of them."

"That's because children's services tries to keep the kids all together and in the family. It's called kinship care," I explain.

"I know that—but why they gotta meddle in our affairs?"

I whisper to Big Mike that all the state wants to do is protect children. Through trial and error, I have learned it works better if I suggest ideas for him to put forward. He paraphrases and adds on beautifully. He is better at communicating with the fathers than I ever will be. The men listen to him.

"Until any child is eighteen, the state of California is legally required to protect them from harm. The state also protects adults from domestic violence. But as fathers, don't we want our children protected?"

There is enough antigovernment sentiment in the room to make a Republican blush.

"I don't want the state tellin' me how to raise my kids."

"It's none of their business."

"They only do this to black folk and brown folk. They don't do this to white folk."

"That's completely untrue," I pipe up. "In my own family, I had cousins taken away from their mother and father. They had to go live with their auntie until the mom and dad got help, because they were drug addicts."

The men eye me suspiciously.

"Well, maybe they did that to your cousins, but they do it a whole lot more to black folk than anyone."

"I got something to say."

Everyone stops talking and looks at Fudge. He is recently out of prison, and both Big Mike and I are worried he is institutionalized, meaning he is so accustomed to the structure of incarceration that he doesn't know how to function within the ambiguity of everyday life.

"The child welfare people—they want to take my kids away. Well, I don't know if they're my kids, but I feel like I've raised them, so they're mine. Anyways, a neighbor called on us. They said my girl has been whuppin' the children, and they reported it. So now I got social services makin' these home visits, and my girl is going crazy. She says she's not gonna let her babies go. Now, she got reason. My girl grew up in the system, and not with her granny raisin' her up—with some foster family, no one she even knew. And they fucked her up bad. The foster father went and molested her. Y'know, she's always been crazy. That foster father fucked her up."

The room is silent. Aaron starts talking, and his voice wobbles.

"The same thing happened to my wife. She was in the system, and she got molested in a bunch of foster homes. She doesn't hit the kids or anything. She is just so depressed. She doesn't even get outta bed a lotta days in the week. I don't know what to do to help her."

"Those guys that do that—molest kids—y'know what they ought to do to them." Sy is very clear.

The men are all nodding. Several bow their heads and look at the ground. I can't figure out what it is—shame, embarrassment, rage? I will bet money someone in the room has been sexually abused, but this is neither the time nor the place to discuss it. What is clear is that when it comes to sexual abuse—incest and molestation—the men are in complete agreement. Leelee, one of the fathers who has emerged as an unofficial leader within the group, opens up.

"We don't wanna talk about it. But we gotta talk about it. My uncle did that to my sister, and it fucked her up for life. She's never been right. She's forty years old now, and she's still not right."

"It is wicked. There's no two ways I see it," Sy adds, then Leelee continues.

"I think of what that—that—excuse me—that sick fuck, Michael Jackson, got away with, and I want to kill him. I'm glad he's dead. People say 'greatest black entertainer.' Lemme tell you—he was a sick, sick guy."

"That's why they gotta isolate the child molesters in the pen—we woulda killed them."

"I understand, and that's why we have to always observe boundaries with our kids and also watch for the warning signs when it happens." I am trying desperately to facilitate at this point. Big Mike has fallen silent.

"I don't need no warning signs. I catch anyone doing that to my kids, I will kill them. You can come visit me in the pen, Drjorjaleap, and bring me a cake," Sy retorts.

The men all start laughing. But I won't let go.

"You don't catch them. People who sexually abuse children are very careful. They don't want to be caught."

"Well, then, if they so careful, how do we watch out for our kids?"

"You need to watch how they behave."

"Like what?"

"If they're usually happy around you, are they all of a sudden acting depressed? Or are they not doing well in school? Or do they seem like they're jumpy or afraid?"

The men are all looking at me blankly. I realize I am describing the daily existence of many of the children at Jordan Downs. The warning signs are useless—for them, for everyone. A drop in grades? It might be sexual abuse, or a learning disorder, or boredom, or a bad teacher. There was plenty of fear about sexual abuse, but this was not helping. I was not Dr. Jorja Leap, lecturing to a group of undergrads worried about grades and letters of recommendation. This had to be practical. Real life. I start again.

"You need to make it so your kids are able to talk to you—so they feel like they can come to you with anything that might be bothering them. You've gotta be someone they see as strong but who they can talk to. And . . . this means that you can't hit them. Because how can they talk to you about one kind of abuse when you might be subjecting them to another type of abuse—physical abuse?"

I am in the midst of a culture that believes beating a child was not abuse. In fact, most of the men in the room believed you *needed* to beat your son or daughter from time to time. I had my own cultural baggage; I knew about families in the Greek community who pushed the envelope in this particular area, and I always found this information disturbing. In my own family, my father was very contained. He slapped me one time when, as a teenager, I called my mother a bitch. The next day he gave me a card in which he had written an apology and told me how much he loved me.

But there are other reasons I won't let go tonight. In my professional life, I had seen far too many gang members and "career criminals" who had endured severe abuse, both physical and sexual, as children. I keep thinking about José Rodríguez, whose mother had beat him on his back so badly that he wore three T-shirts to school because he didn't want kids to notice that he had bled through the first two.

"No doubt, you a kinda zero tolerance, zero compassion person with this child abuse stuff," a gang member had once observed, mixing the terminology. But his meaning was clear. I had warned him that I was going to personally turn him into the county if I ever caught him hitting his children.

And now I was up against an immovable force: the men in this room.

I had my personal issues, but I was also professionally responsible to the mandate laid out by Hershel Swinger and CII. The grant funding that Project Fatherhood received was predicated on the ability of these groups to strengthen fathers and *prevent child abuse*. I had already spent a long time talking with Big Mike about how we had to examine child abuse, in general, and the difference between discipline and abuse, in particular. Now that the topic is finally in play, these fathers are offering a very specific idea of just what constitutes physical abuse.

Leelee announces what rapidly becomes the consensus policy. "There's nothin' better for a child than a good whuppin'." Craig McGruder quickly joins him.

I ardently admire McGruder, a lifelong drug abuser who turned his life around and is determined to make up the parenting he failed to provide when his children were younger, when he was lost to addiction. He brings his two teenaged sons to every group meeting. I am not prepared for what he is about to say.

"How do you think I get these two to come to Project Fatherhood? I tell 'em I will beat 'em if they don't come."

His words immediately tie me up in an ethical and emotional straitjacket. As a social worker, I am charged with reporting any suspected child abuse. But I want the fathers to trust me. This is not going to happen so easily.

"We gotta be careful because Drjorjaleap is a social worker."

"Yeah, she'll be reporting us to the county if we don't watch ourselves."

They are half joking, half strategizing. I am sitting next to Big Mike with a poker face.

"Well, I think what we gotta do is just speak hypothetically, y'know? Maybe we can talk about what someone we know is doing."

I am being manipulated, and I can feel it. There is no way I am going to shut up now, even if they don't like me or don't trust me or don't want me in the group anymore. I have had enough.

"Your little plan is just fine, but if I suspect any one of you is abusing your child—physically or sexually—I am gonna turn you in so fast your head is gonna spin right off your neck."

The room is silent. But I am still furious.

"And aside from the county and what they do to you, I am gonna personally fry your ass."

"Man, you goin' gangsta on us, Dr. Leap." Ben Henry is half laughing, but I know a compliment when I hear one.

"She is. She is gangsta. I am standing right next to her, ready to help. You know there is such a thing as hood justice." Mike is very clear.

"And we gotta be accountable for our actions," Leelee adds.

It is clear the group is in no mood for political correctness. Instead, for the next half hour there is an unabashed and uncensored discussion—with total conviction—of how children should be beaten. Leelee leads the charge, invoking the adage "Spare the rod, spoil the child." There is nostalgia for the "good old days" in the neighborhood when— the men claim—they were beaten, not only by their parents but also by other folk in Watts.

"I would get beaten at one end of the block and then get beaten at the other. But they taught me *respect*," insists Delvon Cromwell, whom the men all called Chubb. This is too much for me, and I bring the room to silence when I ask, "Was this because of the beating, or because they gave you attention?"

The men wait a beat and then start again.

"Probably both."

"You don't understand; you're not ghetto," Sy begins.

By this time—after years working with active and former gang members—I am used to people telling me I don't understand.

"Let's just agree: I'm a stupid white girl from the West Side who doesn't understand, and you need to educate me."

Sy starts laughing.

"You know we love you."

I am insecure enough to be glad he said that, but I am still pissed. I listen.

Another father, King Spider D, or KSD, insists that both his grandmother and mother had beaten him at the same time. "They did it because they loved me, and I loved them to death." Two fathers—one black, one brown—tell similar stories about loving the stepfathers who raised them, who beat them whenever they got in trouble. One of the fathers, Adrian, declares in halting Spanish, "I wish I could have been his biological son." For each person, it is as if having a father, *any father*, is all that matters—even if the man beat him.

Big Mike is silent throughout the discussion. He appears angry and tired, but whatever is going on, he isn't talking. Fudge finally speaks up and begins to describe his struggle.

"Alla you talkin' about wishin' your stepfather was your father— well, I'm tryin' to raise a child, like I told you last week. But now my girlfriend told me to leave it to her—that it wasn't my child. I still feel like I gotta do something." There were problems on top of problems: Fudge's girlfriend knew that if she beat her child and protective services returned, the daughter might suffer her same fate—foster care and molestation. But the daughter continued to act out.

"My girlfriend told me she's gonna give that girl a whuppin'. And sometimes, I'm thinkin' the girl needs it. One of my homies thinks she's a woman—he told me he wanted to hit on her, and I had to tell him she's twelve years old. I don't know if I should say anything. You're probably gonna report us."

I laugh uneasily and say, "No, I cannot report this." Still, the entire discussion is making me uncomfortable. I don't know where the boundaries are. Sy speaks and plunges me further into confusion.

"With my own children, I've always had a plan, because I never wanted them to go through what I been through. My father was always puttin' his hands on me. My boys didn't have to go through none of that with me. Never put my hands on them. I probably whupped them a few times. One got a whuppin' two times and one got a whuppin' one time from me. Other than that, I kinda get them with my voice. And I always know, and I would always remember, the same thing I used to tell their mama: Just act like they smarter than you! You know what I'm sayin'? You got to trick them! We could trick them into doing whatever we wanted them to do. I always been strong on that. You know, like without them even knowing it. Didn't really have to go there with puttin' hands on them. If they don't wanna do it one way, we'll have them do it this way—a way where they enjoy it and get more fun out of it. But it's basically what I wanted you to do in the first place."

I am trying to figure out the difference between a whuppin' and putting hands on children. I am certain this is not spelled out in California state law.

Then Debois speaks up.

"I don't whup my kids. I just use fear. Fear and love. I think they need a balance. And I don't think discipline—not a whuppin' but physical discipline—is such a bad thing."

"I agree," John King starts, and I can barely contain my shock. He always seems separate from the fathers—the HACLA bureaucrat attending the meetings in his carefully pressed shirt and tie. But not now.

"My dad was a Marine, and I guess you could say he believed in discipline. He was really tough, really strict. When my mom started reacting to him, not agreeing with him, not getting along with him, he kicked her out. He was the one who raised me. And he would beat me. He believed he was doing it for my own good. I don't know. He raised me right. But I couldn't beat my own child, maybe because she's a girl, and girls are less trouble. I don't know. But the beating didn't help."

The men are silent. Most of them are in awe of John King—he is something they aspire to be and cannot imagine achieving. And yet, he shares the same experience. Matt ventures into the conversation.

"I wanna have a kid—and I am never gonna beat that kid. Never. It's not good."

The men all rebel.

"You say that now, but you just wait—"

"You'll be back here next year sayin' you agree with us—"

"That child is gonna test you—"

Matt listens but keeps shaking his head in disagreement. I finally lose patience and turn to Big Mike.

"Do you hit Booboo?" I ask. Big Mike is on the spot.

"I've never hit Booboo. Maybe Mr. King is right—girls are less trouble."

"No way—girls are *more* trouble."

"I was way more trouble than both of my brothers, but my dad believed that girls should never get spanked," I announce.

The men are laughing at me—and I am quick to add, "But of course, I'm white. I'm not ghetto."

"That's right," Sy reinforces.

But this is my opening.

"Do you know that almost everyone on death row in the United States of America has been physically or sexually abused? You say, 'spare the rod and spoil the child,' but it's the exact opposite."

The men are quiet. There's no counterargument.

"I've seen what this does." I am emboldened. "It hurts people. It causes depression and PTSD."

Fudge looks at me intently and then announces, "I gotta say something. I was beat when I was a youngster—by my stepdad—and I'm still fucked up from that."

The men are silent. The session is running over, and they suddenly notice how much time has passed.

"You don't understand," Ben tells me. "This is our culture. We been whuppin' children for generations."

"It's not just your culture. It's my culture too. It happens in Greek families just the way it happens in black families."

But Ben insists my experiences are not the same, telling me that "white children are different." This isn't a fight I want to have, and I start to back off. Do they really believe white children are different? But I won't let go.

"Can we at least agree you don't hit a child on the head?"

"Yeah."

"Yeah, okay."

I think the men are as tired of fighting about this as I am.

Half an hour later I am pulling out of the parking lot and I see one of the fathers fighting with another man. I go looking for Big Mike but cannot find him. Instead, I find Michaela—a woman on the community center staff—who comes outside to see the father dropping to the ground dizzily.

"Get in your car, right now," she hisses. "Keep your mouth shut. We'll take care of it."

It is getting dark. There is no sign of Mike or Andre. Even though I want to intervene, something tells me I had better listen to Michaela. I am barely through the door at home when the cell phone rings. It's Big Mike, asking me if I'm okay. The words come tumbling out.

"I saw the fight and I looked for you. When I couldn't find you, I wanted to try to stop it, but I didn't. I should have just taken care of it."

"You did the right thing. Sometimes things get settled by street justice," he says.

"We're not supposed to do things this way."

"I know, but y'know some of the men—they're not there yet. Some of them are struggling with the P-stuff."

"PTSD."

"Yeah. And that's what came out tonight. You gotta be patient. You know that."

I am speechless. And I am worried about the group. Not about the numbers—in fact new men show up every week, attendance is good, recruitment is working. The men appear, they discuss the topics, they argue their points of view, and they collect their gift cards. But something is missing. It's as if the group is somehow less than the sum of its parts. The men are there, but they are not coming together. There is no core. The fathers are talking about different ideas, different ways to deal with their children, but I don't know if the new ways of thinking about things and acting are sinking in. This adds to my concern. I don't know what to do, and I am itchy. I cannot sit back and wait patiently, as both Mike and Andre have often counseled me. I make a plan to do something on my own. I am going to talk to Leelee.

SEVEN

Leelee

We're crazy, but we are strong.
            —Leelee Sprewell

"Who you waiting for, lady?"

I pause for a moment. I can't think of Leelee's real name.

"Lee Sprewell."

"He on the phone, says he's on his way."

"Thank you."

I am at the Watts Coffee House, which, despite its name, isn't competing with Starbucks. It is the only sit-down restaurant in Watts. There is no drive-through window and no fast food, although you can order takeout. The place is full of customers who wait for tables, read the menu, and set themselves up for delicious honey biscuits, fried steak, and brisket. While I sit, I think about Matt, who hasn't shown up for the past two weeks and hasn't been to school. Some of the fathers are concerned about him, while others are focused on business as usual.

Leelee arrives breathless, half an hour late, and immediately announces, "Well, I am here, CP time"—insider code for "colored people time." Before I lay out my concerns, I ask Leelee how he's feeling, and he confesses, "I feel like I abandoned Watts. I gotta do something about it."

"I don't know what you mean."

He explains that he has moved to Inglewood to protect his sons, who are living with him. He wants to find a way to keep them in private school, away from any kind of outside negative influences. He knows all too well what these influences are. Leelee was born and raised in Watts after the riots, one of six boys and one girl, although his two younger brothers had a different father.

"But even if they were different, they were the same—the fathers weren't around," Leelee tells me. "This is what is plaguin' us here in Watts. Alla our men get sent to prison, alla our boys grow up without fathers. And we gotta change it. But you gotta understand the Watts mentality." I know Leelee is a natural historian. He explains how things used to be.

"I grew up in Watts. It's part of me. My mom still lives right on Grape Street. I was raised there all my life, and I knew all the people who claimed Grape Street—backstreet niggers and project niggers."

Today, the Grape Street Crips remain a predominantly black gang. They wear blue or purple to represent Grape Street, and Michael Jordan basketball earrings turned upside down to signal Jordan Downs. Where Grape Street and 103rd Street intersect is regarded as the core of Grape Street territory, an area that includes the Jordan Downs housing projects and Jordan High School. Leelee talks a great deal about the early days, when the gang or neighborhood was referred to as the Watts Varrio Grape and comprised both black and brown gang members. However, "prison politics ruined that," he explains, as the Mexicans fell under the control of Sureños. In prison, Latino members of southern California gangs united behind the Mexican Mafia (la Eme) as "Sureños," or "Southerners," while members of northern California gangs united behind Nuestra Familia as "Norteños," or "Northerners." This created a schism within Watts Varrio Grape.

As a result, the group split into the South Side Watts Varrio Grape Street 13, a Latino gang whose members considered themselves allies of what ultimately became the all-black East Side Grape Street Watts Baby Loc Crips. The Crips count the Bounty Hunter Bloods—with whom they had engaged in a bloody gang war—as their long-term rivals. But a peace treaty negotiated in 1994 involving the Grape Street Watts Crips, the PJ Watts Crips, the Bounty Hunter Bloods, and the Hacienda Village Bloods—all Watts gangs—was still holding as Project Fatherhood met.

"Y'know, some people say that the treaty was based on the Egypt-Israel cease-fire," Leelee tells me. "But I think we're doin' better than the Jews and the Arabs."

Prison is as familiar to Leelee's family as Grape Street is. He has a brother who has been locked up since 1989, one of the first men in Watts sentenced under the policy of mandatory minimums. Leelee says that several men in the group continue to carry the prison mentality with them. "You know, Miss Leap, if you are locked up, your instincts kick in and you need to listen to them. Fear keeps you on your feet; hope and the good Lord keep you from getting too badly hurt. The cops lock you up in the dorm, so you fight each other, and then when you're beaten, the guards throw one of these things in there—it's like a grenade and it shoots rubber pellets. So it's not enough you're locked up and fighting each other, the guards are makin' things worse. And you can't talk about it. Now, you gotta understand, you got men in the room at Fatherhood, they've been through all of this, and they've got that post-traumatic stuff going on. They can't trust anyone, not even themselves."

I know what Leelee tells me is accurate. The men in Project Fatherhood—without exception—have been incarcerated at one point or another. But that is not the only trauma they have encountered. They grew up in South Los Angeles, where children routinely navigated dead bodies on the way to school and babies slept in bathtubs to avoid bullets. In the past, I had heard cops refer to the Watts housing projects as "self-cleaning ovens," where law enforcement at one time did not want to engage, preferring to let rival gangs kill each other. There was trauma everywhere I looked, and I was uncertain how to help heal the wounds. I ask Leelee how he deals with what he has seen and experienced.

"Well, you know I've been raised with the Lord. But you've got to understand the Watts mentality. The Watts mentality is the same whether you are born on the backstreets or the projects—it is deeply embedded. You walk the same, you talk the same. If you grew up in Watts, you know how to fight. You learn to be proud of what you've gone through. The Watts mentality is the people there. They're comfortable not having cars, not having slippers, being in the store with no bra, their titties hangin' out, and they don't care. We all drew strength from growing up in big families. We're crazy, but we are strong."

I am beginning to hear what Leelee and others have been trying to say to me.

"I was exposed to a lot of stuff through having a big family. When I got out of the sixth grade, Mom didn't want me to go to school in Watts.

But you know, I thought I wanted the high life, I wanted to be in the neighborhood. I wanted to be part of the action. And you know where the action got me—locked up and facing a murder charge."

When he was in his twenties, Leelee was charged with a capital crime: homicide with premeditation. The pain of that experience is written on his face.

"I didn't do it, but that didn't matter. I knew I was going to do time. I give complete credit to the old white lawyer who got me a deal—a manslaughter charge and two strikes. I didn't know if I should take it, so my lawyer said to think about it. And I'll never forget, there was this guy named Woolf—he had a similar case but didn't take the deal. He told me, 'They ain't got nothin' on me, and they offered me manslaughter. I didn't take it. My lawyer told me we're going to court and then I'm goin' home.' So he goes off to court a few weeks later, and he came through the door back to lockup late, three o'clock in the morning with his head hung down low. He told me, 'They messed up with me—I got twenty years to life.' Soon as he told me that, I started thinking. They had offered me somethin' similar. I was already in for three years in county jail and I was tired. So I took it. They gave me eleven years for involuntary manslaughter and a year and three months for the robbery, and another year for something else. My sentence was thirteen years and four months. I went in '89 and came out in '97. I did a little close to eight years—seven and some change offa that—then I came home and ran the parole out. But my sons were babies when I went in, and when I came out I felt like they grew up without me."

Leelee tells me he has never recovered from the regret of missing those years. His children are adults now—both graduated high school and live productive lives. But Leelee emerged determined never to let that happen again.

Although he did not settle down with one woman, he fathered several children when he got out of prison—two daughters and two sons. Now he has another child on the way. Leelee recites birth dates, bloodlines—all the details of his children's lives. He is determined to be an active father, and is devoted to all of his children, speaking to them on a daily basis. I ask him how he felt about his own father.

"Oh, my father left early on," Leelee explains. "He couldn't take what my mother was issuing out. She was tough—she raised seven kids alone. But there's one thing my mother did— even if she didn't wanna mess with my father or his people, she always kept a number for us. She told me, 'Whenever you want to go see them, I got the information.' I never saw my daddy, but when I was eighteen I wanted to know where he was, and my mama—she gave me the number. Now I talk to him from time to time, and I understand him. But I know from him not bein' around that I want to be around my kids. That's why Project Fatherhood is so important. I got no idea about how to be a father—but now I am learning."

Over the past decade, Leelee has lived a relatively stable life. But his children are the still point in the turning world. Women are more complicated. He lived with one woman for five years. When that relationship ended, he moved home to Watts. Now he has a girlfriend whom he loves, but he wants to "keep a space, just for me and my boys."

Leelee laughs and tells me there is only one challenge in his life, and it is constant—he has never been able to find steady work. Instead, he has often resorted to the moneymaking activity of choice in Watts, drug dealing. For men out of prison—unable to find work, unable to make money—the main option continues to be the drug trade. Of course, this inevitably backfires, as it did for Ben and for Leelee. "I've been to the pen one more time," Leelee recalls. "It wasn't a strike case. Nothing violent, no assault. It was drugs—00.44 grams of cocaine. I did two years exactly off of that, and I swear to you, Miss Leap, I am never gonna deal drugs again. I just gotta find me a real job. That's what I need."

We never get around to discussing my concerns about the group, but it doesn't matter. Just talking with Leelee has helped me gather my thoughts. His discussion of the solace that he has drawn from his family—that he continues to draw from his mother—is significant.

There is strength within these men, and within the Watts community. These are the family strengths that Hershel Swinger urged all of us involved in Project Fatherhood to build upon. I feel like I am dealing with a world rich in natural resources. Still, there is one small problem: how could I help these men to recognize what they had inside of themselves? Just how was change going to begin to take place? I am not sure how to facilitate this. But part of what Sy Henry said to me about getting children to overcome their reluctance to do something keeps running through my mind. "Sometimes, you've got to trick them. If they don't wanna do it one way, we'll have them do it this way—a way where they enjoy it and get more fun out of it. But it's basically getting you to do what I wanted you to do in the first place."

EIGHT

Fatherhood

*Family is everything. I already knew it but Project Fatherhood
reinforced that fact that sometimes we ain't all perfect, nothing is
perfect. Anything that we come up against, we have to deal with it,
and it's the way we deal with it. Through love, we'll win everything.
Because love is love. If it ain't love, it ain't nothing.*

—Elementary "Ele" Freeman

I have obeyed Mike and tried to forget that I saw one of the fathers
fighting after the last meeting. But I feel like the group is acting more
white Anglo-Saxon Protestant than black in its complete denial of any
problems. And I am still trying to figure out how to help the men bond.
Despite my concerns, the next week the room is jammed. The turnout
emboldens both Mike and me. We decide, spontaneously, to discuss the
big question: "What makes a good father?"

The men all begin talking at once and their responses vary wildly.

"How should I know? I thought you were gonna tell us!"

"My father was never around—"

"I didn't have no father—"

"What is this group about—"

"Drjorjaleap, *you* tell *us*!"

I usually defer to Mike, but this time I am determined to make sure
the men face why they are here—together.

"I've been talking to a lot of you one-on-one," I begin. "And you've
all told me you want to be there for your children. You want to be good
fathers. But first we have to talk about just what it takes to be a good
father—in your own words."

I look pointedly at Sy, and he responds.

"As a father, I guess I try to show the example and be the example, you know, of the things that come out of my mouth, so my kids can see that he's not only talking, he's living it also. Especially around my own boys—try to show them some things that they don't need to be doing, you know? You can't just talk the talk; you need to walk the walk also. And I practice this all the time."

Chubb follows Sy. He is shy and hasn't said much, but he has steadily grown more open. When he speaks, his voice is low and barely audible. He sounds vulnerable. "I don't know what it takes to be a good father. I never had a father. So I always wanna be the protector. And I can really go crazy. I wanna say, 'I love my baby, you ain't gonna hurt her!' But you gotta understand, that's not the way to handle business. Kids play. Let's say one of the kids hit my daughter. She come back crying. That's the hardest thing to get past, 'cause you wanna do something, but it's kids. It's children. They just wanna play; there's gonna be a little roughhousing, whatever. So you gotta just let it pass."

I am listening to Chubb, thinking how difficult it must be for someone whose idea of problem solving has always been gangbanging or listening to big homie, and now he's here, in the group, trying out a different role.

He continues, "I just sit back and watch from a distance and see how she handle things, just so she won't always be reliant on me to be involved in certain situations in her life. She'll be able to handle it on her own. Later on I might tell her, you know this is what you do, and you don't do that, but I want her to try first. How does that sound?"

Ben looks thoughtfully at Chubb.

"It sounds like wisdom to me."

Chubb glows. Ben is his big homie, someone he looks up to. The praise means more coming from him than from anyone else. Ben then adds, "You gotta be able to love them—love your children, unconditionally—even when they're doin' something you don't understand. We need to have love. None of this hood, gangster mentality. Just love."

Willie Freeman follows Ben. He has just started showing up for the group. Most of the men call him Ele—short for Elementary. He is quiet and thoughtful.

"You gotta protect your child. And provide. And listen." Ele is on a roll. "You know, I think that you gotta be a listener. That's why if you just do that math—God gave us two ears and one mouth, to do less talking, and more listening. It's simple mathematics, ain't it?"

Sy echoes what Elementary says. "Ele is right. You gotta be willing to listen at everything, listen to everyone's opinion. I mean, if it help your opinion, then use it. Once people see you're a good listener, they know you're a good learner. If you talking all the time, they know you ain't—you don't know nothing. Just be able and willing to learn."

"I think we're missing out on something simple but important." Leelee has joined the conversation. "It's time—we need to spend time with our kids. We all sit here and say we never had a father. It's not that we didn't have a daddy—we all know our daddies—but they didn't spend time with us. That's really what we mean. They weren't around. And we gotta be around for our kids."

"We've really gotta be around for our sons." Debois focuses in. "The father is like, basically, the king of the house. Without a father, the queen, you know, she's kind of like empty. You know, there's no fathers teaching here in Watts; it's just women teaching. You know, women can't raise a man. There is no one that can love a child like a mother, but no one who can teach a boy like a father. And you gotta be real. Any father, in trying to raise kids, if you still go back to the streets and try to raise kids—to me it don't fit. It's never gonna fit. You tusslin' with two different things, so I knew once I had them, I had to let a lot of things in the street go—the gangbanging, the selling drugs. With them, all that was gone before they got here. It was like, you know, it was a thing of the past. Especially our sons, they need me—they need us. The statistics show that, without me, without a father around or a father figure, for boys the odds of succeeding are low. I think that being around, teaching—that's the most important thing a father can give."

The men are more animated than I've ever seen them. Big Mike and I don't have to push; we just need to make sure everyone's voice is heard. At times they become excited, interrupting one another. Then Mike quietly says, "I think Twin is next." Men like Sugarbear and Chubb, who have never spoken before this session, are trying to express their opinions. What is most striking is that the men are not arguing—they are turning to one another, listening, asking questions.

"I haven't talked yet," Ronald James—Twin—begins, "but I got somethin' to say. Don't act like a deadbeat. Don't act like the baby's not there. Don't act like you ain't a part of that. You know? Act as a father should act. Do as a father should do. Be what a father should be. Take that role. Don't let someone else take that role for you. Because it's no greater thing than being there for your kid and he's there for you. Especially when they grow past that toddler age and you can call and they come to you. Or they call you on the phone. You should always take that call."

I am thinking that this is different than the previous collective wisdom of the group—that raising children is the woman's job. But I wasn't about to point that contradiction out. Maybe that was what they had seen as children. It didn't matter. What mattered was the way all of the men were talking about fatherhood.

"We are all just sitting here giving our own opinions about our way of parenting. But I think we've got to think about something new." Sy waits a beat and looks around seriously at all of the men. I am thinking of how he recalled telling his sons, "Henry boys are leaders." Sy is a leader. But what he says next is a revelation.

"I don't just have my way of parenting. I have to look at a lot of other folks' way of parenting, 'cause I've always learned from other people on what to do. You know, I always had older people to talk to in different situations that I didn't understand. I always had someone I could go to fifteen years older than me, to put what I was doing in perspective and let me know what to do. And it always works. We can't just do it alone."

Big Mike steps in here. "Sy Henry makes a good point. Some of us older fathers, we gotta mentor the younger fathers. And I think we need to listen to what all of us are saying. We can learn from one another."

The men are nodding.

"We can really try to teach one another," Ben Henry adds.

"I think we have to look at what we are talkin' about tonight and commit to this." Leelee wants to make a plan. "We can't just say it; we gotta do it—talk to each other, call each other, be there for each other. Not just in the group but outside of it."

"We are part of this, and we are all strong." Mike looks at me carefully. We had talked about reinforcing the men for their strength, and now he is doing it. The men are nodding, agreeing. Project Fatherhood has a hint of a Baptist revival meeting to it.

"I think we are strong," Big Bob says. "But no one is telling us that. So we gotta tell each other."

"We gotta remember—we want the same things," Sy says. "I just want to see my kids grow up and try to be successful in life. That's the big challenge to me: getting my children to be better than me. That's the whole thing with being a good father. You tell your kids, 'You have to be better than me. You have to be better than Daddy.'"

After Sy says this, I want to cry. Several of the men say, "Amen," and Leelee quietly urges, "Preach, Sy." He is voicing all of their dreams for their children.

"I wish I had someone like you, Sy," Matt says quietly. The men in the room all turn to look at him. "I never had a father. And my brothers are all the same way. All of us—except one—we have the same father, but he was never around. He was a drug addict. So was my mom, and they were never around. We raised ourselves. I never saw my father. And I mean never. He was just gone. So I came out here to be with my auntie—she raised me. Then one day I got a call, my dad was coming to see me. All the way from Chicago. He came out here to Jordan Downs. He visited me. We spent the day together. The next time I saw him was at his funeral."

The men are shaking their heads.

"That's rough," Sy says.

"I feel for you," Terrance adds.

"But you gotta know, Matt, you're still a youngster—and we're all here for you." Big Mike looks around the room as soon as he finishes this statement of reassurance.

"You're better off than me. I never knew who my daddy was," Fudge says. "I want to be a good father. And all I learned about how to be a good father was to be the opposite of him."

"I knew my daddy," Andre offers, "but it didn't help me at all." The women are not meeting this week and Andre has joined back in with the group. "But I think part of us being good fathers is making peace with our own fathers."

The men all consider this. Andre continues.

"I was angry at my father for a long time, because he wasn't around. And then I realized that before I could be a good father myself, I was gonna have to forgive him."

"So you're sayin' what makes a good father is forgiveness?" Sy looks closely at Andre.

"I think so."

"I got one more thing to say." Debois is talking now. "I think to be a good father you have to always give your support. Support is not just buying shoes and stuff like that, but also being there when they need you. Your kids—they have their days, too, where they won't be so happy. They need you there. I ran into that situation, where one of my twin boys had a rough day at school, so I had to go up there. I sat with him to find out what was going on. He was all right. He had a rough day, but I think he just wanted me at the school. I'm not there at the house as much, so I think he's feeling strange. I went down there to the school and talked to him—just reassured him. Later, I called the teacher and she said he had a good day."

The other men listen closely as Debois tells this story. One by one, they praise him for what he did.

"This is what we need to do for our babies," Big Mike intones. "We need to go to their schools and talk to their teachers and find out what they need. Not just on back to school night. How many of you know the names of your kids' teachers?"

The room is silent.

"Well," Big Mike sighs, "we've got work to do."

"But Mike," Debois begins, "you know this has been a problem for black families. Some families, you can have a real good role model. We need to be role models and help each other. Like—my oldest brother is here—Big Bob—and he's been a lot of support for me. I think in here we need to be role models for each other."

"I hear you, brother. I think you ought to summarize things, Debois," Big Mike says.

"To be a good father, you've got to be prepared for change. Kids change you, you know. As a young person—like you, Matt—you're probably not ready for change. So it's easier for you, as a young father, to walk out on that situation."

"I'm not gonna be that way." Matt is on the defensive.

"Well," Debois continues, "it's time-consuming to be a good father but a good kind of time-consuming, because it changes you as a person.

Like I said, lot of young guys round here have babies and they're not ready for that change. They still wanna run the streets and still wanna hang out. They leave their baby fatherless. And the woman, she's there alone, raising the kids. It's one of the struggles we face around here. It's one of the ways we need to all be together on this, help each other and help the young kids who are gonna be fathers for the first time—the ones in our group and the ones out there who haven't come in yet."

"And we've got to do this ourselves. We can't rely on other people to do it." Ben says this quietly, but Leelee immediately picks up on it.

"You are right—we gotta do this. 'Cause all we got are all those politicians and social workers that keep makin' promises and showin' up and askin' for votes. But they aren't telling us how to do this. They promise us—they're gonna bring this to us. But that's not the way to do it. We gotta do it ourselves. We gotta be the fathers here. In our families. And in our communities. Isn't that what we been sayin'? We gotta show that, black men and brown men, we *can* be good—no, *great*—fathers."

I am not talking during any of this. There are three about-to-be fathers in the group. Except for Matt, they have listened to the discussion and barely spoken. It doesn't matter. The group is finally beginning to gel. They have found their purpose. They will father each other. Mike brings things to a close.

"We gotta remember, we are all gonna help one another—we are fathers together."

Big Mike looks out at the room. For the first time, he asks the men to bow their heads. "Let us pray."

NINE

Daddy's Girl

*What's hard for me to do is to maintain my sanity, face problems
from my background and how I used to live. You sometimes wanna
revert, and some people will take you there, but you weigh your
situations and you know not to. Being a father has actually kept me
sane. It helps—it kept me on the right path. Instead of just going
doing what I used to do, it gave me tunnel vision. I know that's my
baby, I'mma have to stay here and be here for my daughter. And
take care of her.*

—Delvon "Chubb" Cromwell

Over the past weeks, I have been thinking a great deal about my own
father. The men who come to the weekly meetings possess something
in common with him that I am hard-pressed to describe. It is a deep
and abiding sense of sadness, an unnamed loneliness. It springs from
something they share, black and white: the father wound. I remember
my father, who adored his mother but always felt separate and quietly
troubled in his feelings toward his own father.

I recall very little of my father's parenting methods, save a few
things. He was a creature of habit, careful and dignified. I never saw
him wearing pajamas. In 1971, when the Sylmar earthquake shook all of
Southern California in the middle of the night, he magically appeared
fully dressed. He cooked homemade pancakes every Saturday, biscuits
on Sunday, waffles on Wednesday. In his drawers, his personal articles
were neatly arranged; the "emergency money" rested next to the con-
doms. Most significantly, he was unfailingly loyal—to my mother, his
brother Jimmy, and his sisters, Katie and Ernestine. He was the rock of
the family, inexpressive and strong.

Over time, particularly after he was diagnosed with cancer, I came to understand how he had struggled as a parent. His father was distant, un-available—working six days a week and sleeping all day Sunday. There was no "father-son" relating, although this certainly was not unusual among immigrant men. The emotional absence of his father was never openly acknowledged, but occasionally he would admit to having had doubts about his ability to be a good father. The words haunt me.

"No one was really a father to me, so I wondered how to be a good parent," he told me. The deaths of his mother and then his father, one year apart, brought out the confessor in my father. For the first time, he told me things I had never known about his life. With all the zeal of a true believer, I asked him if he wanted to go to therapy.

"Don't you think it would help you to talk about your dad to some-one—a therapist?"

"No, not really. I talk to your mom and I talk to God."

"But maybe someone who's not involved—who could help you?"

"Why do I need help? I pray. It makes me feel better."

There was no gift card for my father, no enticement. When cancer came, he even dreamed that he was talking to God and that his Heavenly Father was going to help him. But he also told me he felt very alone.

I think of my father now with my own sadness. When I was a child, my family promoted the idea that I was a daddy's girl, but this had not turned out to be the truth. Instead, he and I shared a loving but diffi cult relationship. I am not sure my father ever truly understood me, but somehow that didn't matter. The irony remains that without being able to fathom what I was about, he was there—a steady presence in my life until the day he died.

He was the child of two immigrant parents, raised by a doting mother and a man who truly had neither the experience nor the desire to serve as a loving father to his son. In certain ways, my father struggled with the same issues the men in Watts did: how could he be a father when he never really had experienced one? But that struggle ended with him. I had plenty of demons, but I never endured a father wound. I had no knowledge of what these men went through.

While my relationship with my father had never been idyllic, there was no doubt in my mind that he loved me. And yet his love was part of a deeper contradiction. My father neither understood, nor even liked, the young woman I was growing into. I was too loud, too inquisitive, too restless. "You ask too many questions, Jorja Jean," he would offer, and there was no joy in this observation. I was the child who was difficult to stomach—rebellious, angry, and provocative. As a teenager, I smoked pot, grew the hair on my legs, and appeared at a Greek wedding braless, wearing a tie-dyed bedspread, while he stood next to me in a suit and tie. I don't know if he wondered how he spawned this wild child. I certainly did. I felt separate from him, alien. And yet, there was never a doubt in my mind that if a crisis were to arise, he would be there, whenever I needed him. He was the father you called in the middle of the night when the car broke down or a boyfriend was too drunk to drive. And when I was troubled and unhappy, anxious and unstable, he was the one who arranged for me to go to therapy. The whole concept of therapy and dependence on a therapist—a Jewish one at that—were equally difficult for my devoutly Greek Orthodox father to stomach. Yet he paid for my weekly sessions, telling me, "It's my responsibility. Mom and I did something to create this problem, and we need to take care of it."

What could be a better example of love than a father who did not completely understand his daughter but still supported her and paid for her to do things that might threaten him (going to college) or that he did not believe in (going to therapy)? While often questioning the choices I made and the life I was trying to live, my father took complete and unconditional responsibility for me. At times I felt his disapproval, but I still felt deeply loved.

When I was in my first year of college, my father was diagnosed with cancer—islet cell carcinoma. It's an unusual form of the disease, although well known now as Steve Jobs's cause of death. But thirty-four years before that—before liver transplants and genetic mapping, when chemotherapy and radiation were crudely delivered in mega doses—my father was unspeakably brave as he endured all that 1970s oncology and hematology had to offer. He had one major surgery to remove part of his colon, his spleen, and part of his pancreas—but the bad news kept coming. The cancer had metastasized to the liver. The surgeon, a brilliant but humorless man, told my father to get his affairs in order. Instead of resigning himself to his fate, my father volunteered for and endured a six-month trial of chemotherapy, augmented by radiation. The treatment, arduous and experimental, bought him four years of good health.

I was suspicious and frightened, already stuck in the anxieties of my first year of college, when all this began. I decided what I needed was backup—lots of it. There was my beloved Theo Pete, who already served as a second father and an intellectual role model. But I needed someone to call in the middle of the night, someone who would act as a wiser balance to all my angst and rebellion—even someone who could set a limit on me when no one else could. I needed boundaries, borders, fences. I needed more than a little psychological discipline. My Theo Pete had four children of his own. While he and Thea Adrienne always served as an emotional horn of plenty, I still knew—deep down—it was not fair to demand that they take care of me as well. I needed a father of my own.

Dr. Joseph Rosner, whom I would ultimately call "Papa," was unlike anyone I had ever known. First of all, he was probably the proudest Jew I had ever encountered. (This was an immediate issue. Despite the profound tolerance practiced within my immediate family, most of my extended family was somewhat anti-Semitic.) Here was Papa, born in New York, raised in Harlem, full of life, opinions, and therapeutic instructions. He spoke the magic words—"You can call me twenty-four hours a day"—and meant it. When I tried this out once at 3 a.m. (I wanted to leave a party without my date, who was getting more stoned as the evening progressed), he answered the phone and began yelling at me to quit worrying about what anyone thought, go home, go to sleep, and forget about it. "There will be other parties—you have a long life ahead of you," he barked. That was what I needed. The day my father died, I was comforted by Papa and by Theo Pete. In that moment, I was covered on all fronts. But I still feared the future.

The need to turn to a father never goes away. The men in the group all knew this. I certainly knew this. It has been over forty years since I met Papa. He is *still* the father I know I can turn to if the need arises, even in the middle of the night. (I try not to do this, as he is now ninety-two years old.) I still laugh when I think about how people close to me have quit trying to understand our relationship and have accepted his place in my life. Mark knows he is part of me, and Shannon thinks of him as a grandfather. I am lucky they understand. I still need that one person who holds my personal history and understands it better than anyone else on earth, who remembers me as the girl I once was—and still act like from time to time. I needed my father, just as the men in the group needed their fathers. The problem was that for them, there was no Papa, no Theo Pete, no Daddy. There was going to have to be another strategy. The men's promise to help each other—especially the older fathers' desire to serve as role models for the younger men—was a start.

One man determined to fill the role of father was Debois Sims, who never knew the presence of a father. Instead, he tells me, "these streets were like my father. I had a lot of issues growing up. Trying to not be rejected, that was a big problem—like you wanna fit in. So you get caught up doing in things, because you like the response from it. I would have liked to have a father growing up. Little kids, especially a little boy in the house, he needs his father. Without a father in the house, I think it really hurt me in ways, but also it made me strong. For a while, the gang was like my family. I had one brother in the gang with me, but our other brother went down a different path."

Coming of age in Watts, Debois got into gangbanging as a way out of poverty. But the story sounds painfully familiar. Trying to make money, he engaged in illegal activities and was incarcerated. Like so many of the men in the group, he is reluctant to share his history. They do not want to dredge up the past. The men use it strategically—for credibility with youngsters, when they are trying to give advice—but it's clear they don't want to glamorize the gangster lifestyle.

"I was incarcerated; I was involved with the Department of Corrections," Debois says. "I had a few cases that, unfortunately, I had to go down for. I did my time; then I came home. I look at it now and I know, no one wants to be selling drugs or gangbanging, but it's so hard to try to get in on the other side—working. And it's not just gangbangers. We have people that go to college and get degrees and they can't even get a job. There are things we need to change. But for me, I guess I had to go through that experience to change. I was twenty-four years old when I first went to pen. Not too long after I got out from my first case, I went back in. So it's like they said—that revolving door? That's all true."

Debois sold drugs to take care of himself. But he struggled with the aftereffects of incarceration, along with depression. "I went into the closet. I didn't wanna be around anybody. I wanted to be by myself. But religion really helped out a lot, as far as dealing with that. Both depression and religion—really opened up my eyes to a lot of things."

While Debois was caught in the revolving door of incarceration, he had his first child, a daughter. Her birth wasn't planned. "I think for us around here, basically, a lot of babies are just made out of lust," Debois explains. "Maybe that's what happened to me, but I ended up having a beautiful daughter. I love her to death, she's my pride and joy. Now I have two twin boys, Rasheed and Rashad. They're my pride and joy, too. I love them so much. They are ten years old and getting bigger. But it's different raising them. Who I was then, I'm not now. I didn't spend as much time as I wanted with my daughter. The boys, they get all my time because I wanna support them. I know things now that I didn't know that helped me out a lot, as a father."

Debois, like so many other gang members, both black and brown, faced a turning point in his life. He says: "I had a lot of close friends die violently. It hurt. To me that was the very focal point right there, me wanting to change. I didn't wanna die. I knew this when I was around twenty-three. And this is before I had kids."

When his sons were born, Debois felt he was already on the right path. He wanted to work, wanted to fit into society and do the right things. But the twins reinforced and even accelerated his efforts to change. "When the boys got here, I was already goin' the right direction as far as bettering myself. But when they got here, they helped me sharpen up a lot faster. I had to be sharp—helping them read, write, do things that normal kids should be able to do. To me, that's the joys of life right there, witnessing that right there, your creation. Being able to function as a family." But Debois turns thoughtful. Despite the happiness he feels at fathering his sons, he is filled with doubt and uncertainty.

"It's a start, you know. I'm still here in the ghetto where a lot of things happen that you have to be cautious of, as a man here, to not get caught up. So that's a struggle within itself, just trying to stay on that straight path. And it's a struggle to be a good father."

For Debois, one of the most important things he has to accomplish is to "just leave the streets alone. You know, some friends are good, that you don't wanna leave alone, but it's for your best interests to not associate with them as much as possible." In certain ways, Debois feels he is betraying childhood friends, but he adds, "You just hope they get in and change too." He wants to set himself up as an example, "so someone can say, this guy changed; he's not in the streets no more."

In the first year of the group, Debois emerged as one of the success stories of Project Fatherhood. Early on, John King worked with Big Mike and Andre to enroll Debois in the WeBuild job-training program, which offers pre-apprenticeships for construction workers. After completing the training, Debois tried to find a job. He repeatedly consulted Craigslist, to his great frustration. "I was on Craigslist just trying to look for work. I had finished the construction class. . . . I didn't want to let anyone down and I wanted to put myself as an example for Project Fatherhood. I never got a job through Craigslist, but I went to the high school up here that is getting rebuilt. So the company up there hired me." He is grateful to be working as part of the construction crew. "I really feel supported by all of the guys in Project Fatherhood. We can get into our little disputes in there, but it's helpful."

For Debois, the biggest challenge now is trying to save enough money to buy a house, which is his dream. Even in the group, he often seems surprised with himself and admits, "Wow. I didn't think I had it in me. . . . I never held a job this long—seventeen months now. It's a good point in my life, where I can say it's not a big one, but a small goal has been reached."

It's very important to Debois that he serve as an example for the fathers. "You know a lot of people, good people, come up out of here. I wish they could come back and show these kids the accomplishments they have achieved, 'cause what we are missing is a lot of good role models around here."

As I listen to Debois, I think about people who abandon Watts. There is such strength among these men—they want to lift the community up. Why do others want to run away? As if reading my mind, Debois tells me, "There's good people here in Watts that keep you balanced. A lot of people think it's nothing but bad people around here—that's not true.

To me, that's what keep me striving on the path I am—people that's on that path too, the good people that surround me here. Their strength—and I think we have strength for each other, against the odds."

As I listen to Debois and hear the depth of his commitment to his children, I know that the obstacles my father confronted had been personal. He had not had the added stresses that race and poverty inject into the already difficult task of being a good father.

I keep thinking about what Michelle Alexander articulated in *The New Jim Crow*—how "hundreds of thousands of black men" couldn't be good fathers—not due to any lack of commitment but because they were incarcerated, many of them due to the ill-fated and ineffective "war on drugs."

The effort wound up overcrowding prisons through sentencing inequities based on color, while producing no gains in controlling illegal drug trafficking in the United States. The evidence is overwhelming and is especially notable in documenting how patterns of incarceration have contributed to a form of social apartheid—with an underclass of the formerly incarcerated economically segregated from mainstream society. According to the Sentencing Project, a nonprofit research and advocacy organization that—among other activities—works to address racial and ethnic disparities in the criminal justice system, Latinos and blacks tend to be sentenced more harshly than whites for drug crimes. This pattern holds for individuals convicted of high-level drug offenses, including large-scale distribution.

But the disparities extend far beyond the damage wreaked by the "war on drugs." Nationwide, on a state-by-state basis, both African Americans and Latinos convicted of crimes are far more likely to be incarcerated, even when there are sentencing alternatives such as electronic monitoring and restorative justice. On top of that, young men of color consistently receive longer and harsher sentences than their white male counterparts do, with more time spent in state prisons rather than in local jails. Worse, unemployed black males—like some of the men who surrounded me—are subject to more severe sentences than are unemployed white males. There are also differences in the impact of past criminal records: blacks and Latinos are sentenced more severely than whites with the same or similar criminal records. Another disparity, this time connected to the race of the victim, is that black offenders who victimize whites are sentenced more harshly than blacks who victimize other blacks or whites who victimize whites. This leads to a picture of black men who are locked up for longer periods of time in prisons that are farther away from their families, with more stringent reviews guiding their release, as well as the conditions of their probation or parole.

When I read statistics like these, I am in awe of the strength it took for Debois to overcome these obstacles, to stay close to his children, and to try to serve as an example to his community.

TEN

Baby Mamas

We all have troubles with women.
—Ben Henry

It is 2011. After a year at Project Fatherhood, I am increasingly aware of the complexities the men confront. Most of the men in the group could probably make good use of an organizational chart to keep track of their women and children. As fathers, they operate within a sort of extended family constellation that includes children, elderly relatives, and significant others who can be their wives, their girlfriends, or their baby mamas. But rarely does life proceed on that single level. In addition to coping with issues relating to poverty, drugs, prison, and crime, the men are often caught up trying to manage their domestic realities. With few court orders and no child support demands in the group, the biggest problem the men confront is time management—doing the calculus of who is to care for whom, when. A few fathers end up temporarily withdrawing. "When I think of my responsibilities—my kids, I don't know which one of them to look at first," Shug, a father who has just started coming, tells me. "So I pretty much don't look at any of them. But the ones who really drive me crazy are not the kids; it's the baby mamas."

"I'm not so good at it," Fudge adds. "When my girl is driving me crazy, sometimes I think about getting locked up just to get a rest."

Fatherhood in Watts is much more nuanced than I ever had imagined. When the men are on the outs (dealing with life outside of prison), they are just overwhelmed, making their reentry even more of a struggle. Their existence swings between two extremes: they are either incarcerated, locked away far from family life, or they are enmeshed with domestic complexity that few people could ably manage.

And then there are the women.

The men's relationships with their wives, girlfriends, and baby mamas are complicated and often freighted with conflict and pain. This is never more apparent than when they talk of multiple, tumultuous relationships that intersect. "I need a big map for alla your women," Bob complains, when Kyle laments the stress involved in dealing with "four baby mamas."

"No one told you to get involved with so many women, K," Debois starts in.

"Yeah, you can't manage your women, don't get involved with 'em," Sy snaps.

Mike shushes the group, telling the men we are going to start the "check-in," a new practice that has been added to each meeting. It's a moment to offer a quick update on their lives, and on any given Wednesday, the men present a grab bag of achievements, sorrows, and dilemmas. Tonight Ben, who rarely speaks, asks Mike if he can share first. The words come waterfalling out in Ben's tortured voice.

"I don't know what to do. There's no good way to say it, so I'm gonna come out with it. My girlfriend had a baby about two years ago. No one knew—I didn't tell anyone, and I told her not to tell anyone. My wife didn't know, my kids didn't know, my friends didn't know. And, y'know, I was excited. The baby was a boy, my first son."

At this point, the group breaks out in applause.

"A son, man, that's great."

"Good."

"Congratulations."

Ben waves the enthusiasm off.

"But my girlfriend called me last night—I got a burner just for her so she can call me anytime. She told me that lately, when she was talkin' to the baby, he wouldn't respond. She thought he might have no hearin'— he might be deaf. So she took the baby to the doctor. And the doctor thinks the baby may be—what's it called—autistic."

The room is silent.

"I don't know what to do. I don't know what to do." Ben's voice is shaking. "I don't even know—should I tell my wife? She knows something is wrong, but if I tell her she is gonna kill me. I was with this girl,

and she caught me and she told me to never go with her again. I promised. I really did, I gave her my word. But I just couldn't do it. And sometimes I feel like God is punishin' me for goin' with another woman."

"Don't beat yourself up."

"No, we all been there."

"That's deep, but we gotcha."

"What am I gonna do? I don't even know how to be a father to regular kids. And if my kid is sick . . . ," Ben's voice trails off.

"What you need to do is get some resources. You need some resources."

"We need to get you some help."

"Aren't there some referrals?"

Several of the fathers make suggestions at the same time. Then they
all shift their eyes towards me, as if they are participating in an Olympic
event: the synchronized stare.

"Drjorjaleap. You gotta have some resources."

"Yeah, you need to find him some help."

"Some doctors at UCLA."

I quickly agree, making notes, but the fathers are not finished with
their efforts at case management. It is another sign the group has bonded
strongly.

"Now, you know what you gotta do," Leelee begins, looking around
at the other fathers. They all nod their heads.

"It's gonna be hard," Sy adds.

"It's gonna be a bitch, it is." Tiny joins the chorus.

"You gotta tell your wife. Everything."

"And then you gotta tell us what happened."

"Do it this week. Do it tonight. Then come and tell us what happened."

The men all nod their heads. Andre clasps Ben's shoulder. Ben quietly says, "Thank you all," while bowing his head. The silence is quickly
broken.

"I got a problem I want to talk about," Aaron blurts out.

"Go ahead, brother."

"My wife, when I met her, she had a little girl. She wasn't mine,
but I raised her like mine, like she was my own," Aaron carefully

begins, speaking in lightly accented English. He is one of the few Latino members of the group, and he has been attending steadily since the
second week. "Now she is sixteen years old. She's a good girl, and we're
proud of her. Straight As. She wants to go to college. She does not run
around with boys." He is the picture of fatherly pride, when the story
takes a turn.

"Now she wants to go meet her real father. She told me and my wife.
I don't want her to go. What's gonna happen if she meets him? He has
money. He has a house. *What do I have? What am I?*"

The group issues a collective moan. Ele hangs his head and begins
shaking it back and forth, muttering, "That's deep."

I carefully ask, "What are you afraid of, Aaron?"

He wastes no time in answering.

"I am afraid she is gonna love him more than me. I am afraid she is
gonna forget all about me."

"That's not true, Aaron. She is your daughter. You raised her. She's
not gonna forget about you," Big Mike reassures him. The other men
in the group do not appear to be as certain. Some of them look away
uncomfortably. There is so much going on in this room, all of it unex-
pressed. Many of the men had "abandoned" children of their own when
they went to prison. Those children were raised by others.

Andre Christian begins to talk.

"I was with someone. Well, I don't want to say this, but I am gonna—
she was a tramp, excuse me."

I am always amused that the group members don't want to use certain words in my presence. The men rarely say the word "fuck," and
when it happens, they apologize profusely. Personal derogatory terms
also are never used, with the exception of "nigger, my nigger," which
is for these men a street term of endearment. Language etiquette has
never been raised as an issue, and no prohibitions have ever been laid
down. Yet Big Mike and Andre both tell me, "Bad language should never
be used in front of a lady." Perhaps it is a throwback to mores they in-
herited from the South.

Though language was never discussed, early in the group's development a core group of fathers set down rules to deal with issues like
showing up on time and being respectful. Despite these basic efforts,

the men continually struggle with group process. They have trouble taking turns, and certain fathers have a tendency to monologue. But their vocabulary is invariably G-rated. When a curse word slips out, they usually apologize. Sometimes members warn the group a profanity is coming and apologize.

Andre is clearly uncomfortable with the term he has used. He continues.

"Before we had a baby together, she had three children by three different men, but I didn't care about that. I raised them like they were my own. One day, one of my daughters—'cause they *were* my daughters—came to me and told me she wanted to meet her real daddy—"

"Why?" Aaron interrupts.

"Maybe she wanted to see what he looked like, so she could see why she looked the way she did. Maybe she wanted to just talk to him, get to know him. I told her, 'You go see him, we'll be here when you get back if you wanna talk about seeing him.' That's what you gotta do. My significant other . . . ," Andre stumbles over these words, "she didn't want her to go. I stopped her. I told her, 'No, you wait. That's her daddy. Let her go see him.' She saw him and she came home satisfied—she met her daddy. She talks to him from time to time, but she calls him by his name, and she calls me Daddy. I know I'm her father, when she needs something. That's all that matters."

Andre is secure in a way I can't begin to imagine. Aaron looks at him like he is speaking Swahili, and continues with his plaint: "I can't do that. I don't wanna do that. She's gonna love him and forget about me."

Big Mike quickly whispers to me—"I gotta build him up." Then he starts booming in a louder voice.

"Now, you know that's not true. You raised that little girl from the time she was a baby. She's not gonna forget about you. You are a great father. Where's the Aaron who was on TV, who was interviewed on Channel 7 news? Everyone in this community knows what a great father Aaron is."

"Thank you, Big Mike. I appreciate what you are saying. That means a lot to me. I just want to be a good father."

"You are a good father, Aaron," Sy reinforces. "Just don't forget it."

At this moment, the discussion veers, becoming a verbal referendum on women and how they undermine the authority of men. Andre starts shaking his head. He continues with the story of the woman he once lived with.

"She was hardheaded, that one. I had trouble with our communication. But when she didn't listen to what I wanted, I took away the money. I stopped giving her anything to spend. That way I could stay in control. Men need to stay in control."

The issue of control is tricky. I can't take much more of this. Many of the men in the room talk with me—when we are alone—about how women bedevil them. This is the hood version of Freud's query: What do women want?

I start to explain, "But we all know women need to stay in control too. And everyone here knows what women do to have control. I'm a woman, and I know. Please forgive me, but I'm gonna say it right out in the open: women control sex."

The men all start to laugh.

These sexual politics are universal. My grandmother used to advise me to "make him sleep on the couch" when I complained that my first husband was trying to control our mutual bank account and my spending habits. Her admonition was based on experience. When my grandmother discovered her husband's late-night attendance at Communist group meetings—a dangerous activity for an immigrant in pre–World War II America—she immediately moved his blanket and pillow to the couch. My grandfather's political involvement ended the following morning.

Andre, however, adds a twist to my analysis. "Yeah, you are right. She would do that. She would take it away, tell me she wasn't gonna give me any sugar. But I could always go find something else for myself." The fathers are all laughing, but right now I think Andre sounds pretty hardcore and controlling.

Paternity often is another bargaining chip in the struggle for control. Fudge starts speaking, and everyone in the group leans forward, straining to hear his soft voice. He is just out of prison after serving fifteen years on a murder charge. When he speaks, Fudge has the sensibility of a poet.

"I had a woman once," he begins. "We had three children together, and I don't even know if they were mine. She would tell me they were mine, but she would lay with everyone—excuse me for sayin' that." It is street chivalry again, this knee-jerk politesse. "Even after we broke up, she kept havin' children and puttin' my name on the birth certificate. I feel bad. I don't know what to do." The men in the group all nod. "My dad was not around, and I didn't wanna be like my dad. I wanted to be around for my kids. But what if these aren't my kids? And then I think, 'It doesn't matter. I wanna take care of them.'" Fudge looks up helplessly.

The problem of parentage is a constant here at Jordan Downs. DNA tests are a luxury, and they have about as much relevance to life in the projects as cosmetic surgery. If parentage were to be determined, what would be the point? These men are not celebrities with inexhaustible incomes being asked to pay child support. Assigning parentage is a woman's way of laying claim to a man and potentially enlisting his emotional support in the raising of the child. Many women also look for someone to blame. Too many times I have listened to mothers scream at a misbehaving child, "You are just like your daddy!"

It's strange that even though the men struggle with being fathers, they rarely seek out proof that they have biologically fathered a child. They feel responsible for the children of any woman they are with. The strength of their feelings of responsibility was often unacknowledged in the political concern with "absentee fathers," but it was powerful. Even though most of the men in the room feel this way, they feel defeated by their women who, in Leelee's words, "just can't be satisfied. They wanna control everything!"

"The system has given women the power," Sy observes. "I always felt like the system is not geared towards young black men, young Latino men, period. But it's geared towards our women. You see it every day. You go to the big office building, look through the window. All you see is women. Women have all the jobs. It's been like that ever since I can remember. But there's other problems with our sisters. They don't feel like we are the men of the house, because of the things that's been taught to them by the system. One way I pointed out to them is with public housing—it stops the black man from being a father. Look at public housing. I got three babies by you. You move in the projects, they tell you that daddy can't move in. That's a problem. How am I gonna raise my children? You know, so the system has always been part of the problem and causin' the situation that a lot of black men are in today."

I am stunned at how effectively Sy analyzes how public policy has failed to support responsible fatherhood, and in fact conspired against it. Leelee then adds history to the equation.

"We all have troubles with women, and it goes back to prehistoric times," Leelee begins. I am bracing myself for the latest lecture on male superiority. Leelee is smart, enterprising, and insightful. He is also, like so many men in the room, an unrepentant sexist. "You know that men have always been superior, physically and mentally. So women, they had to find ways to compete. They used everything they could—their looks, their land, their children—and we're in the same place now."

All of the men nod in agreement. I surrender. This is not the hill I am going to die on.

I am worried about Fudge. After the meeting I talk to him briefly about how I might help him with the Department of Children and Family Services. He promises he will call me if there is a home visit. When I walk outside, a knot of five women comes walking towards me. Every week, the "significant others" group lets out about ten minutes after Project Fatherhood. I am a sitting duck for the women of the group, who simultaneously start asking me for help with their men.

"I need money—"

"I think he's cheating on me—"

"Tell him he better come home tonight—"

"You gotta talk to the men. They listen to you," one of the women, Danise, implores. Being viewed as the conduit to the men in the group makes me uncomfortable.

"Talk to Anthony, he will listen to you. He needs to come home," she continues.

I don't have the heart to tell her there are rumors that Anthony has a girlfriend. I have to draw boundaries, but when I tell Danise I can't talk to her baby daddy—that it won't work—she accuses me of always taking the men's "side." I try to explain that I am not on anyone's side, but she keeps repeating, "Just talk to him." I feel helpless and frustrated.

The next day I am back at Jordan Downs with Andre. But this time, instead of talking about the men, I tell him what transpired with the women the night before. I ask what is going on in the women's group. Andre shakes his head.

"You gotta understand, neither side knows how to talk to the other side. It's like one of them is speaking French and the other side is speaking Japanese—they don't even have the same letters in common." His analogy is apt. "The women want the men to be home with them, supporting them, helping take care of their children. They want emotional support. But then they want money, too. They want it all. And the men—they don't know which way to look first."

"But don't the women understand all the trauma these men have experienced, what they have been through? That they are trying to reenter the world after having been locked up? That they don't know what to do with themselves?"

"Yeah, but these women, they've been through trauma too. You *know* that! Come on! This is crazy." Andre starts laughing.

"What's so funny?"

"I'm arguin' the women's side and you're arguin' the men's side. We got both sides that have lots of trouble, lots of trauma, lots of need—and not enough help to go around. So they start fightin' each other."

"And there's abuse on both sides."

"Yeah. The men hit the women and the women hit the men."

"And no one wants to talk about it," I add. An idea hits me. "Do you think they should meet together? Maybe we should get the two groups in one room." As I suggest this I am trying to imagine the men and the women in the same room. Andre quickly cuts into my thought process.

"I don't think it would be a good idea right now. It would just end up with a lot of screamin'. You know—he said, she said. Alla that. I think Project Fatherhood is workin' right now because the men feel they have a space just for themselves, a place where they can talk about their concerns that's just for them. Together. And they're just startin' to feel that way. You don't want to interrupt that process. I'm learnin' about group process, and you don't want to interrupt the group bonding."

I am always amazed by Andre—his intelligence and his curiosity, how he is constantly learning. I tell him this, but he brushes my compliment aside.

"But you know what would make this better? For everyone—for the men, the women, and the children?"

I am longing to hear what Andre has to say.

"There needs to be jobs and money. Nothing is gonna changed until these people have a steady income, until the fathers have a way to provide for their children."

ELEVEN

Men at Work

Even beyond the need to comply with the conditions of parole, employment satisfies a more basic human need—the fundamental need to be self-sufficient, to contribute, to support one's family, and to add value to society at large. Finding a job allows a person to establish a positive role in the community, develop a healthy self-image, and keep a distance from negative influences and opportunities for illegal behavior. Work is deemed as fundamental to human existence in many countries around the world that it is regarded as a basic human right.
> —Michelle Alexander, *The New Jim Crow: Mass Incarceration in the Age of Colorblindness*

How can I be a father if I don't have a job?
> —Juan Scoggins

In late April 2011, Guillermo Cespedes, the Los Angeles mayor's office gang "czar," stops by Project Fatherhood. He wants to build support among the men for the Summer Night Lights (SNL) program, a mayor's office initiative that takes place from June to August. Funded by the Gang Reduction Youth Development (GRYD) program, SNL brings softball tournaments, barbecues, and other family activities to gang-impacted zones throughout the city. It is an innovative strategy to combat the recurrent summer increase in gang crime and violence. Guillermo wants to ensure it is a success this year. As he discusses plans for this year's SNL program, the fathers perk up. Several ask if they could work at the local Jordan Downs site. Right now they aren't the least bit interested in crime prevention—they want to talk jobs. This is no surprise. The unemployment rate in Los Angeles is 12 percent; in Jordan Downs, it is 53 percent.

A few days later, I am on the twenty-second floor of City Hall talking to Guillermo about Watts. The phrase that runs through our conversation is a mantra in Los Angeles: "Watts is different." Guillermo shakes his head and says, "Don't I know it." Through the GRYD program, which he runs, the mayor's office funds gang prevention and intervention organizations citywide to provide "anti-gang programming." This effort works both to control gang crime and to strengthen communities. Watts is the only community out of fourteen gang "hot spots" that does not possess a single nonprofit organization qualified to provide such programming. In Watts, the mayor's office must run the intervention program itself. I have been working with Guillermo, conducting ethnographic research to reinforce the mayor's office efforts.

Guillermo is mulling the discussion at Project Fatherhood.

"A summer job in Jordan Downs? At Summer Night Lights?" he asks, sadly incredulous. "Is this all they think they can do? Is this all they think they are capable of? I can't believe they don't have a vision beyond that. These are smart guys. They could do more than Summer Night Lights."

"But they want jobs," I say. "That's what's gonna make them feel like fathers—and part of the community."

"I know that, but I gotta believe they're capable of more than employment in a three-month summer program."

In fact, about a third of the group is working at some type of job. However, the benefits of these jobs are limited to a paycheck—no health care, no pension. Four of the men work for the City of Los Angeles as street interventionists, or as part of the Safe Passages program. One father is the janitor at the Jordan Downs community center. This is all "soft money," dependent on city funding and programming. I know that Ben Henry has a steady job working at a parking service near Los Angeles International Airport. But the rest of the men are question marks. While I am not quite sure what he does to earn a living, KSD insists that he is an entrepreneur and that he knows enough about tax write-offs and business to set up as a CPA. But the remaining men work inconsistently. Virtually every man in the group is interested in getting a job in construction. Failing that, they want to become gang interventionists.

I had been talking about this with the gang interventionist I am closest to—Kenny Green—earlier in the day. We were eating sandwiches at the Sandwich Saloon in San Pedro, a restaurant Theo Pete owned with his son-in-law. Kenny and I discussed the latest gang wars in the harbor, wondering how to end the violence. We both agreed with Greg Boyle's now two-decade-old statement, "Nothing stops a bullet like a job," but jobs are a huge problem for the men Kenny has been trying to help leave gang life.

"You know and I know that intervention has represented the only employment option for these men," Kenny reminded me. "It's about all they can do and earn something of a living, but even then it's no good. There's no way they even think about the future."

"This is the space labor unions used to fill," I said, and Kenny nodded.

In the past, unions afforded the working poor some protection—health benefits, pension funds. The gang interventionists represent a group of the working poor who will never have any protection or security. Despite this, they are grateful for the jobs and the wisps of professionalism surrounding them.

"How can these men talk to others about making a life plan if they don't have a plan themselves? Do you know how many gang interventionists ended their lives in poverty? They didn't even have enough money to pay for burial. And the fathers—they probably want to be gang interventionists because that's the only job they think they're qualified to do." Kenny is always worried—about the future, about changes.

"Can I have a dollar, Kenny?"

A small Latino girl, not more than six or seven, stopped at our table as she passed by. She smiled to reveal several missing teeth. Kenny sighed and took two dollars out of his wallet, telling her, "Bring me some good grades," as he gave her the money.

Talking with him forces me to think about the interrelated problems of self-efficacy and self-esteem. This is the big fat elephant that has taken up permanent residence in the room at Project Fatherhood in recent weeks. The men all want to work and they don't know what to do.

They attend job-training programs and job-readiness seminars. Their resumes are in order. They have role-played job interviews. And still nothing. Which causes them to feel like nothing—inadequate fathers, partners, and men.

The single biggest obstacle for each man seeking work is his prison record, his "jacket." Along with lack of education, this is what prevents a man from working, or from advancing if he does have a job. This obstacle leads to greater issues. In *The New Jim Crow*, Michelle Alexander gives voice to the reality that is woven into the lives of these fathers: their inability to find work is all too frequently connected to both depression and violence. So many of these men have been identified as felons, convicts, or criminals since late adolescence. In underfunded middle schools they were placed in "leadership classes" or offered "opportunity transfers" to other equally marginal schools. High school is all too often a lost cause, and the men ultimately "graduate" to overcrowded county jails or state prisons. Then they confront a double dilemma—the educational system has failed them in terms of knowledge and job readiness, while the criminal justice system has condemned them to "check the box" on job applications indicating their felony records. If one of these men wants to work on his own—as KSD does— he finds it difficult, if not impossible, to secure a union card or a business license due to his criminal record, even if the criminal activity is completely unrelated to what he wants to do.

In the group, some of the fathers' lives now span two generations "stuck" in the Watts mentality, unsure of acceptance, let alone success anywhere else. Their joblessness is supposed to be temporary, just like living in the projects is supposed to be temporary, but the entire situation has moved beyond the acute and taken a left turn at chronic. It is now a permanent reality.

Many of the fathers resort to their tried and true defense, turning a negative into a positive—the hood version of a "glass half full." Shug proudly announces, "I've been in Jordan Downs all my life. This is my community and I love it. I don't have a real job, but I find odd jobs around here. I do outside plumbing; I help out folk. It works out." But Debois is not so philosophical. Like so many fathers in the group, he is

angry, proud, and—more than anything—uncertain about how he is going to make a living. "I got a record. I've been in the pen a buncha times
and no one wants to hire me. I say I love Jordan Downs, but sometimes
I wonder if it's 'cause I'm stuck here. And then I'm thinkin', 'How am I
supposed to be a good father if I'm not a provider?' I wanna work, but
no one wants to hire me."

A day after my meeting with Guillermo, I am back at Homeboy
Industries to see what more I can find out about expungement, a legal
process to seal records of an earlier criminal conviction. Elie Miller, director of Homeboy legal services and the unofficial godmother-attorney
for Los Angeles gang members, starts laughing when I ask her about it.

"Okay, I am going to make this as simple as I can but, you know, the
American legal system is complicated. If someone wants an expungement, first I need to know about their criminal convictions. Then I need
to see a court docket or criminal rap sheet."

I interrupt Elie here. "Why do you need those?"

"I can determine if the person is even eligible for an expungement.
If they've got an active case or a post-conviction matter, I have to give
them the bad news that they're ineligible for expungement and offer
some advice about how else to clear things up."

"But if they are eligible for expungement?"

"If someone *is* eligible for the expungement, then the forms I have to
complete are online," Elie continues. "There is a Petition for Dismissal,
an Order for Dismissal, and the prosecutor needs to be served with a
copy of the petition. That all requires a payment every time a motion
is filed, but you can request a fee waiver. Then I prepare a declaration
based on what they've told me about their life and what changes they've
made since the convictions. The judge decides whether to grant or deny
the petition, so the declaration helps to make the client's case.

"But remember," she adds, "expungements are for employment pur-
poses only—they don't wipe the record clean. There are still situations
where they might have to reveal or admit to the conviction—if they run
for public office, win the lottery, or apply for a state or local license. If I
go to court with the client, I sometimes have to educate the judge about
the law or explain why he or she should grant the client's petition. You're

not the first person to ask me this question and, believe me, the clients aren't the only ones who don't understand expungements."

No wonder the Project Fatherhood men don't often pursue expungements. I am already exhausted by this conversation.

Jobs are still on the agenda at the next meeting of Project Fatherhood. Three months earlier, Big Mike had arranged a six-week job-training course at a local community center, which ten fathers enrolled in and completed with great enthusiasm. There's a waiting list for the next training session, and the entire group shares a sense of hopeful anticipation. This hope soon turns to disappointment, however—then rage. Six weeks after the course ends, the ten fathers are fully trained but unable to secure jobs because of prison records and drug use, and because they lack a high school degree. Big Mike decides to take on HACLA and sets a goal. He wants the men of Project Fatherhood, along with other male residents of Jordan Downs, to be guaranteed 50 percent of the construction jobs created for the development of the "new" Jordan Downs.

"We are gonna get this guarantee," he tells the men. Then he adds, "But there's one thing you gotta do. You gotta stop smoking bud. They are gonna drug test you—they have zero tolerance for drug use. Drjorjaleap, can you talk about how they have to stop?"

The men listen intently to what I have to say.

"Here's the biggest problem: marijuana has a very long half-life. That's what you call the amount of time leftover drug stays in your system. If you smoke bud tonight, you have to wait a month before it clears your system. In other words, you can't smoke bud tonight and then go take a drug test in the morning."

I don't tell the men the other part of this, although I am certain most of them are aware. Methamphetamine and heroin clear the system more rapidly than marijuana. Many of the fathers had told me previously that they smoked pot, or bud, at night just to relax and calm down. To make things even more problematic, I actually support their behavior. I had been guilty of the same practice before I became a mother. Having always believed that pot is safer "recreationally," I had spent my daughter Shannon's high school years advising her that if she was going to party and *if* she was going to indulge, it was probably better to smoke marijuana than to get drunk.

Despite all this, if they wanted a job, the men were going to have to stop using. Most of the men treated this as a huge inconvenience but not a major problem. "I'm just gonna have myself a beer instead of a bump," one father tells me. But there were four or five outliers. I already suspected that these were the fathers who continued to carry more serious drug problems. Two had been in and out of alcohol rehab.

For most of the fathers, drugs were not really used to get high. Instead, most of the men were self-medicating. They had seen too much, done too much, and were afraid of too much. Some had trouble sleeping, others had memories of pain and loss and violence. Drugs seemed to me a reasonable response to environments—whether gang zones or prisons—that were filled with threat, intimidation, violence, and uncertainty. "If I weren't using," one father had told me, "I'd be screaming 24/7." I understood. I'd probably be using too if I lived such a life. The trouble was that employers wanted a clean drug test.

Along with the inability to test clean, there was another hindrance for some fathers: they stoically accepted that they were not employable. "I've killed people," one man announced. "No one is gonna wanna hire me. What do you think?" I had no answer for him, but the fathers had a pragmatic response. A groundswell of interest arose in starting their own businesses. This was wrapped into the mythology of Watts—that there was always something new around the corner, that Watts and all of its residents would be revitalized. (Their renewable optimism was another strength these men shared.)

A few weeks later, there is a full house at Project Fatherhood. Mike has produced Ted Hiatt, a special projects manager for the California Small Business Development Center. The men listen to him with rapt attention. Ben and Sy sit together, wearing matching shirts and looking like bookends. Debois Sims and Donald James flank them. Donald has been joyful lately—De'Shawn, the nephew he refers to as his son, is a basketball star at Jordan High School and he's been scoring plenty of points. But tonight, Donald is full of questions about business.

As I listen alongside the fathers, I wonder if these men can actually

get something going. As Hiatt talks about small businesses and how to
get started, the men remain silent. They look both interested and overwhelmed.

What did the men have to draw upon? It is so different from my
own experience. My upbringing had been both typically immigrant and
quintessentially mainstream. Small businesses that employed exclusively
family were the foundation of the Greek community. In my grandparents' and even my parents' generation, everyone was entrepreneurial.
It was the means of upward mobility. While there were exceptions,
it took until the next generation—the grandchildren of the original
immigrants—for things to shift. We were expected to attend college,
although even then higher education was viewed as a pathway to earning more money and contributing to the family business rather than an
opportunity for self-knowledge and intellectual growth. It was *The God-
father*, without the Mafia and bloodshed. Many Greek men I grew up
with played the part of Michael Corleone. Although these men enter-
tained the fantasy of an outside career, they ultimately joined the family
business, whether it was a restaurant or a liquor store or wholesale food
distribution. I had uncles and cousins who made a small fortune opening
full-service liquor stores, which traced their roots to the two small stores
my grandfather Jimmy Skrumbis and great-uncle Pete Ballas opened in
South Los Angeles, next door to Watts.

Stashed away in my hope chest are black-and-white photographs
of my grandfather—or Papou—at his store. A small Greek man with a
neatly pressed dress shirt, bow tie, and long white apron, my Papou is
pictured standing in front of the cash register. His grocery store pre-
dated the wide-aisled supermarket; it was a "mom and pop" business
serving all needs.

My other Papou—Tony Manos—went into business with his
brother-in-law, Pete Koulos. (The Greeks were not the most original
culture, with personal names or commercial enterprises.) Tony and Pete
opened a diner with the prophetic mission statement: "Stewarts Coffee Shop, A Little Something Out of the Ordinary." Inside of Stewarts,
extended-family life played out with antic and unintentional consequences. Tony fought with his sister-in-law, who sued him several times.
And, in a real-life example of what *My Big Fat Greek Wedding* satirized,
Papou employed his daughters as waitresses, while his sons were allowed

to run free. Yet, despite all the conflicts, Tony remained the workhorse; he was not so much entrepreneurial as driven to labor. Family lore has it that he was robbed at gunpoint one morning as he prepared to board the bus that would take him to his restaurant. As his assailant held a gun to his head and asked for his wallet, all my grandfather could say was, "But how will I get to work?" His business meant the world to him and he was devoted to keeping it running.

Understanding the mindset of the black fathers I was getting to know was proving to be a different matter altogether. They shared an entrepreneurial spirit—they were proud, independent, and scrappy. The trouble, pure and simple, was that their small-scale business experience involved drug dealing. For almost all of the fathers, drug activity belonged to their past. But others talked openly about how—even now—when they were running low on cash, drug dealing was the direction they turned. It was the Amway of the hood, the way to make a little pocket change. ("I only do it when I, y'know, need a little money on the side," one father explained.) But when I spent time alone with one man or another, I heard stories of major drug networks some had participated in during the late 1990s. These men clearly possessed the transferable skills that would enable them to set up a business. They had acted as accountants and knew their way around a ledger. We had lengthy discussions of profit and loss, even marketing, while I carefully avoided asking them specifics or even identifying just what the product we were discussing was.

But it never went any further than this. Setting up a business remained a half-baked fantasy for the men. I listened to ideas that never resulted in any sort of specific plan, and I felt frustrated, unsure of how to help. "Don't come to me about investing in any of this," my husband half laughed, half warned, as if he knew what I was thinking.

When Andre Christian approached me to discuss his plan to set up a coin-operated laundry, I felt excited. There was a small strip mall under construction a block and a half from Jordan Downs. It was on the "right"—or Crips'—side of the railroad tracks. The fact that this aspect of the location was even part of our conversation reflected the general Watts craziness. Andre had long ago denounced his gang affiliation, but old habits die hard. I was no better. In my own mind, I invariably described locations as being on the Crips' side of the tracks or the Bloods' side of the tracks, even though a gang truce had been in place for twenty years.

Andre wanted to include the men of Project Fatherhood in his business plan, as part owners or employees. The first step was to obtain a small business loan to set up the coin-operated laundry in the strip mall. The site had a ready-made clientele—very few people in the projects owned washers and dryers. This was something I had never thought about, further evidence in what I felt was an ongoing case for my insensitivity and lack of consciousness. Thirty years earlier, when my first marriage was just beginning to founder, my grandmother turned a deaf ear to my concerns and announced, "You take everything for granted. You've got nothing to complain about. You've got an automatic washer and dryer in your garage. *You don't appreciate what you have.*" Now I was too self-absorbed to understand that no one in the projects went to use the Maytag on their back porch to wash clothes. I knew I would never learn everything I needed to know. Malcolm Gladwell insisted an individual required ten thousand hours of experience in something to be considered an expert. In Watts, it was going to take me a whole lot longer.

I thought Andre was smart and motivated, and I thought his business plan would signal a breakthrough for the fathers. It would reinforce the idea that *you could actually start your own business.* But when he brought the plan up at the next Project Fatherhood meeting, it was greeted with a combination of suspicion and barely concealed scorn.

"Just where are you getting the money for that?"

"Who's setting you up?"

"Are you using the money from Project Fatherhood for that?"

Andre was furious.

"Why do you all gotta talk this way? Can't we all help each other? Why are we always so suspicious of each other? Y'know, in Koreatown, Korean families—they all get together and start their own businesses, they help each other. They don't worry about where the money comes from—they put all the money in a pot. We—here in Watts, we can't get out of our own way."

Andre was right. In Watts, small neighborhood businesses were often viewed as the outcome of some underhanded activity. Nothing is

ever legitimate: anyone who opened a new endeavor was accused of using money from questionable sources. I had heard rumors of individuals
starting mainstream businesses using the proceeds from drug sales. At
first, I told everyone who would listen that I found this idea ridiculous.
Every business? Before his death from cancer, one of the most effective
gang interventionists in Los Angeles, Bo Taylor, sat me down and told
me the facts of life.

"What do you think happens here? No one finds an investor. Come
on—do you think we go to Bank of America and get a business loan?
You gotta get your hustle on, make some money, start a business. That's
what our young men learn." I bring this conversation up at Project Fatherhood, after Andre presented his business plan, and the men all nod
their heads.

Sy unintentionally echoes Bo, explaining, "We know if someone
gets something started that's legit, y'know it got started with something
shady on the side. You don't understand—it's ghetto. You're never gonna
get that, Jorja. You're from the other part of town."

I got it, although I was keeping my mouth shut. If someone starts
a business or succeeds in moving away from the projects, it is rarely
viewed as the outcome of hard work. It is the Protestant work ethic
turned upside down. If someone is getting ahead, they are definitely
fucking someone else over. Or doing something illegal. Or both. But I
wasn't sure this was true.

Big Mike had started—and restarted—his tow-truck business honestly. But I had my doubts about how "hood" he actually was. Despite
his claiming Grape Street and his time spent as a guest of the California
state prison system, Mike's real allegiance is to his family and himself.
He is the quintessential entrepreneur, with a record of personal success
and achievement that sets him apart from the other fathers. Even now,
Big Mike is always thinking money. He wants to hold a fund-raiser for
Project Fatherhood, and he wants to get a grant to build a Boys and
Girls Club. He is beginning to think that he might want to start a new
program for youth, near his home, out in the Moreno Valley. Unlike
many of the fathers, he is hopeful enough to have a vision. Many of the
fathers are still letting the past get in the way of their future.

TWELVE

Job Creation

*It doesn't matter who we are—black, brown, old, young, OGs—
we want to work. It's the only way we can get any self-respect.*
—Craig McGruder

In the midst of all the talk about jobs and the pending redevelopment of Jordan Downs, a twentieth anniversary commemoration of the Watts Truce between the Bloods and the Crips is organized by Aqeela Sherrills, a local activist. The men in the group were ambivalent about this event. They planned to show up at the celebration wearing their Project Fatherhood T-shirts, but as late as three days before the event the group was still arguing about the whole idea of commemorating something that involved gangs.

"All those neighborhoods did was kill a lot of people," Ben offered.

"You gotta remember, we've had peace 'cause we negotiated that treaty," Big Bob countered.

"Yeah, yeah," Ben laughed. "But you know, sometimes I wonder if in the hood we should talk so much about negotiating. Isn't that sorta like approving of the violence? What is it they say—negotiating with terrorists?"

Ben was unknowingly channeling Greg Boyle, who strongly believed the truces were useless. Greg often insisted, "We are giving oxygen to gangs when we negotiate with them." But civil rights attorney Connie Rice believed the truces were catalysts for what became a period of calm, as Los Angeles witnessed its lowest crime rate in forty years.

The men remained divided as they dissected the history of the bloodshed. Many insisted that the root cause of the Bloods-Crips war could be traced to the fact that a member of the Grape Street Crips had mistakenly shot one of their own and then blamed the homicide on the Bounty Hunter Bloods. As usual, the evening ended with everyone in disagreement and nothing resolved—except that the fathers agreed they would show up wearing their T-shirts. I went to the anniversary celebration with some degree of trepidation.

There were all sorts of community leaders and folk from the churches and city government—a strange combination of the usual suspects from the mayor's office and advocacy organizations, along with women from the community, who signed people in. Children helped pass out T-shirts and goodie bags. The event was guarded (supervised? watched over?—I wasn't sure quite what) by young black men and women dressed in a style that was vintage Black Panther—black berets and reflecting sunglasses. All of this created a festive, yet slightly strained, atmosphere.

As a member of the local nonprofit social service agency Shields for Families launched into the usual riff about collective efficacy, Lennie Dawson, a community activist, leaned over and whispered to me, "There's never going to be any redevelopment. They don't have any money yet. No one knows if the federal government is going to come through on this."

The message was just preposterous enough to be true. Over the past few weeks, as visitors arrived and departed from Jordan Downs to talk blueprints and renderings, I kept wondering just exactly who was funding the redevelopment. The federal government? A public-private partnership? The HACLA folk were holding meetings, reviewing elaborate plans, and trotting out contractors. But it was mysterious and worrisome that, in the midst of a crippled economy, no one was talking about where the money was coming from, or when it would arrive. The *Los Angeles Times* ran editorials. Every once in a while a reporter would show up and word would spread through the neighborhood. Some reporters, particularly Kurt Streeter from the *Times*, came back repeatedly to understand the social and emotional climate in the community. Others made only one visit, then wrote a superficial article about "the ongoing problems in Watts."

Jordan Downs was in redevelopment purgatory, awaiting demolition. I continued to wonder if there really was going to be a redevelopment. I was jolted from my reverie at the truce commemoration when

John King rose to speak and began proclaiming that "big changes" were coming to Watts.

"We are investing in human capital," he told the people assembled, "and when the redevelopment starts, there will be jobs in construction. And when the building is complete, there will be small businesses that you can work in, or maybe even own. The community is going to change."

"Do you think this is really going to happen?" Chubb asked me. We were hanging out after the celebration. Unlike some of the other fathers, Chubb is still trying to sort through his feelings about the hoods and life at Jordan Downs, and about his past. He is one of the younger, quieter members of Project Fatherhood. Chubb has lived his whole life at Jordan Downs. "Whether it feels good or bad, I've always been a part of it," Chubb tells me. In his mid-twenties, he turned his back on gangbanging, trying to help improve Watts. "I've lived on both sides of this area. Our biggest problem has always been lack of resources, so that the only way of getting by was joining into a gang. Back in the day—it's strange—gangbangin' was more family-oriented, and the gangs provided provisions for each other. We all helped each other out. That's how I ended up gangbanging, period."

Chubb was part of the juvenile justice system at the age of fourteen, when he was caught carrying an illegal firearm. He constantly had to both report to and endure home visits from his probation officer and the LAPD. Eventually, he was detained at juvenile hall for various crimes, but he never experienced a long-term stay at probation camp. As an adult, Chubb was arrested and incarcerated. Now he carries the same emotional scars from jail that some of the other fathers do. For many of them, county jail was worse than state prison. But Chubb tried to gain as much education as possible, even while he was locked up, and he speaks thoughtfully about his experiences.

"It's different than in the streets. Dudes that you might not like on the streets, in jail, it'll be the brothers that protect you. Jail is divided up in races, and you gotta stick with your race. Whatever that's going on during that time, your race will have your back."

Chubb's father was heavily involved with drugs. Chubb saw him periodically, but to Chubb, the gang was his father. "I've been in Grape Street all my life. Yeah, my whole family is a part of a gang. Like, individually, my household is Grape Street. But I have family from Bounty Hunters. I have family from PJs. I have family from all the gangs from Watts, but we never knew each other just because of gang ties, and the separation of the neighborhoods. I know it's confusing, but that's life in Watts."

His family existed at a subsistence level. Chubb rationalizes why he committed crimes. "You just have to fend for yourself. You have to do what you have to do to survive. I had to deal with my struggles head-on—whatever it took for me to get past that moment, to cross that bridge—and I did it."

Chubb became a father for the first time at eighteen. He was living in what is called "suitable placement," a sort of foster home for youth in the juvenile justice system who the court determines cannot return to their families. The woman who ran the home sought and received permission for him to remain with her until he was twenty-one. But, Chubb says, he was "young and dumb, and I left. I left at the age of eighteen and stayed with my baby mama during that time, and that's when she got pregnant. My first child. I didn't want no child at the time. I denied it, denied it, denied it. But I knew in my heart that that was my baby. And I was very, very scared. I was like, whoa, wait, I can barely fend for myself. I needed help—I still need help." Chubb now has a second baby with a different woman. He is slowly growing into his role as a father. "My life is full of ups and downs as a father. I mean you have your good moments, you have your bad moments, but all the time you love every moment of it."

Recent days have been difficult for him—his younger daughter went with her mother to Bakersfield. "We don't get along," he admits. His other daughter is in Texas. Still, Chubb feels close to them and credits them with changing his life. "When you have no kids, you really live reckless. I was pretty much reckless, but now I have mouths to feed, and I want to make sure my girls are prepared for life, so I can't run around doing the same ignorant, stupid stuff that I used to do. It's time to grow up and be a man and make sure that this new life that you brought into the world is capable of dealing with life's situations on their own once they get old enough. So the thought process is pretty much more on a positive move."

Chubb rarely speaks at meetings. But he is attached to the older fathers and seeks their counsel on an individual basis. "All the fathers, they actually helped me emotionally to go through certain struggles, because I'm a new father. Certain situations you don't know how to deal with, and by these brothers being fathers for as long as they've been, they have different routes and different ways of handling situations. So they gave me a lot of knowledge through that and, physically, they helped me out with job leads and [a] better thought process on how to handle situations. It's more like a counseling session, I wanna say."

Conversations with fathers, especially Andre and Ele, have helped him.

"I feel like we all have similar problems," Chubb explains.

However, there is at least one way in which Chubb differs from many of the other fathers: few of the other men want to talk about the violence they have witnessed or the losses they have experienced. Chubb is the most open about this.

With all that he experienced, Chubb never expected to live into his twenties. "Look at we're all here at this anniversary. What surprises me the most is that I'm still here. Like, when I was younger, I always thought I'd be dead by the time I turned eighteen. And from eighteen, I thought I'd be dead at twenty-five. So now I'm thirty-four, and I'm feeling like the sky's the limit."

A few days later at Project Fatherhood, the men are all talking about the rumor that there is not enough money for the redevelopment of Jordan Downs. John King immediately tells them this is nothing but a few people in the community spreading gossip. He asks if the group will speak at a town hall meeting in support of a plan for new units. Despite their personal desperation, the fathers are cagey and demand a quid pro quo.

"If we speak there, at the town hall meeting," Tiny shouts, "are we gonna get jobs?"

"Who you talkin' about, Tiny?" Ronald Stringfellow asks. "You can't work no job."

Tiny was older and had diminished eyesight. He walked with a cane and required assistance from Debois, who always sat by his side and helped him get up and sit down. I was pretty certain that his impairment was enough to make him legally disabled. None of this stopped him from flirting with me every chance he got. It also didn't stop him from demanding a job be made available to him.

"If we get up and testify in front of that panel," Tiny says, revving up, "if we go, are they gonna create jobs for everyone? That paper you're writing there, Jorjaleap, it's gotta say jobs for the disabled and jobs for senior citizens."

I was doing what I always did when there was a public issue in play—writing down the list of questions, grievances, concerns, or whatever the men asked me to record to express how they felt. This had become my latest job at Project Fatherhood. I was part group leader, part big mama, and part court reporter. I would take down the fathers' words and read them back. Then the screaming would begin.

"No, *no, no!* We didn't say that."

God forbid I point out that it was exactly what they said. I learned quickly—when the fathers changed their ideas, they simply insisted that I had recorded everything wrong. Tiny's latest piece of dictation ends with me adding the clause, "Jobs to be created for disabled seniors." Just what job on a construction site might be available for Tiny remained a mystery.

"Yeah, Tiny," Leelee asks, "you gonna check their union cards?"

Despite the teasing, the fathers are deadly serious about their list of demands. Foremost among these is the insistence that at least one third of the jobs at the construction site be reserved for men who actively participated in Project Fatherhood. John King is enthused and announces, "I think we've got a good chance of getting this jobs idea through."

"I'm just glad we're havin' our say."

"Yeah, it's important our voices are heard."

"They really have to hear our stories—"

"We know more about this development than anyone. We the experts."

The following week, the men are discussing their appearance at the town hall meeting, where each of the fathers had read one of fifteen points the group wanted to make. The points involved matters such as demolition, relocation, and toxic waste, and included the demand for assurance that there would be jobs for the fathers. They are excited and optimistic that this may finally mean work for those who have been looking for so long. John King walks into the room and asks if he can say a few words.

"Well, all of you did great at the town hall. I think you are going to be really happy with what came out from the executive session that took place afterwards."

"You mean we get one third of all the jobs in the redevelopment if we're part of Project Fatherhood?" Leelee asks.

"Well, it's not exactly that."

"Not exactly" was pretty much the refrain of life in Watts. It occurred on a regular basis, and what it meant was that someone was about to get shafted. And that someone was more than likely a resident of Jordan Downs.

"Well, if it's not exactly that, what is it?"

"Well, they're gonna hold back 10 percent of the jobs for residents of Jordan Downs," King quickly says. "But that's good. It's better than nothing."

"*What?!*"

Tiny was screaming.

There was no good way to describe how piercing Tiny's voice was when he was really angry. You waited to hear an announcer declare, "This is a test of the emergency broadcast system." The trouble was Tiny did not stop after thirty seconds. He just kept screaming.

"*SO LET ME GET THIS STRAIGHT: IF YOU DON'T LIVE HERE, EVEN IF YOU USED TO LIVE HERE, EVEN IF YOU COME TO PROJECT FATHERHOOD EVERY SINGLE WEEK, YOU AREN'T GOING TO GET A JOB?!*"

"Yes, I'm afraid so," King answers. "The jobs are for residents only— your name has gotta be on the lease."

The room erupts, and I know exactly why.

"What about us?"

"We don't live here now, but we come every week, and we care about this community."

"You lied to us."

"I live in the community," Shug was screaming, "but I ain't got my name on the lease!"

This was the case for many men in the group who lived in the community. Only two of the fathers actually had their names "on the lease." The vast majority lived with women who had *their* names on the lease. This remains one of the ways that women in Watts exercise ultimate control. Men are either unable or unwilling to have their name on the lease. Some don't want the commitment; some don't want the police or any authorities to know where they are living. (Many people at Jordan Downs confided in me that they believed two of the fathers were still involved in intermittent criminal activity.) The general fear of authority extended to HACLA. One father told me, "I don't want my name on any piece of paper except my birth certificate and my death certificate."

King tries to be conciliatory. "Okay, let me see what I can do."

The men all start talking at once, until Big Mike hits his enormous palm on the table.

"Why don't you all be quiet and listen up?"

Aside from Ronald Stringfellow and Matt, every man in the group has served prison time. The men view the redevelopment of the community as their best and only chance to finally get the jobs that they need and seem to want desperately. Trying to advocate for an exception as residents or former residents is their high card. No one wants to hire a felon—it's that simple. And these men have serious records. I keep hearing the same words over and over: "I just want a chance," "I just want to get started."

Leelee asks for the floor.

"We can't keep waitin' on the redevelopment. We need a Homeboy Industries in Watts," he declares. "Why don't we have one? That place would be perfect for the fathers."

Leelee's assessment was accurate. At Homeboy, every individual got paid while enrolled in the HBI training program. It was an ingenious idea—pay people while they are getting trained to work and then gradually move them to jobs in Homeboy social enterprises and finally into jobs out in the community. But that's where things often fell apart. Employers *still* didn't want to hire felons, even if they expressed great admiration for what Homeboy was doing. In turn, the homies didn't want to leave the security and warmth of Homeboy—they were all institutionalized in their own particular way.

Institutionalization is a strange phenomenon. It's how people get to love the thing they hate. Serving long prison sentences, these men become institutionalized, gradually growing comfortable in the prison routine. Often, for the first time in their lives someone else is taking care of everything. There is a structure, and a bed, and meals. The violence, the deprivation, and the threats they experience in prison are all variations on a theme that many are accustomed to from the worlds in which they have lived. It's hard to grasp that prison is not completely alien to many of the men I know—and that it often is preferable to their everyday lives.

But people do not realize how, after a lengthy incarceration, a lack of structure makes life hard for men "on the outs." That is the aftereffect of institutionalization. And for anyone who participated at Homeboy and grew attached to the program, an institutionalization of sorts resulted. I certainly had my own form of institutionalization at UCLA. I was used to the structure, the passing of the quarters, the beginning of school, winter and spring break—it was how I marked time, how I understood life.

"Before you go that far, Leelee, let's see what we can do." John King is trying to appease the men.

"You told us to go to the town hall. We did what you wanted—now you got to help us." Donald is angry. "We need jobs."

"The problem is we can't just depend on the redevelopment. We gotta try to find jobs now."

"Let's see what we can do," John King repeats.

No one is mollified.

The men are unhappy. Leelee summarizes the feeling in the air.

"What else can we do? We gotta see what happens. And keep fightin' to work."

"We gotta have faith."

"We gotta support each other in this."

The men are bolstering each other.

"We've been through worse."

"We're from Watts, we can deal with it."

THIRTEEN

Big Mama

Why did I stick around? The answer is so hard because I swore,
I promised, and I said over and over I wouldn't be like my dad.
So I'm in a relationship. I know it's bad. It's toxic for myself
and this woman. But because of who my dad was, I would not leave,
because I was afraid of being so much like him.

—Terrance Russell

Big Mike is worried.

"You know, Dr. Leap, we gotta talk some more about the women—y'know, the significant others."

"I know. You're right."

"Really, Dr. Leap. Dr. Swinger said that in Project Fatherhood we gotta get the men to talk more about their relationships. We haven't gotten to it for more than a minute now, and we should. Please, Dr. Leap, we gotta do this."

With three "Dr. Leaps" in a row, I know this is serious. Big Mike is determined to get to the prescribed discussion on the Project Fatherhood topic list: "baby mama drama." But there are problems. First, he is insistent that the men not call the women "baby mamas."

"It's disrespectful," he says. "And it's hood. We gotta get out of that trap."

"Well, what word are we gonna use?" I ask. "I don't know how many of them are married."

"*No one!*" Big Mike laughs uneasily. "Well, some of the old-timers are married, but the youngsters—none of them are married. But we gotta call the women by a different name."

"We gotta use 'significant others.'" Andre is talking. "They like to be called that." Along with another gang interventionist, Ron Noblet,

Andre meets with the women every other week as a group and at other times one-on-one. Many of them approach him with their problems, and he then comes to me. Few of the women connect with me directly. They still don't trust me, believing that I help only the men. This whole process is turning out to be ineffective because the women's problems often explode before Andre gets to me so I can then obtain the resources or referrals they need.

I don't want to bring up the obvious: that the men have been so focused on jobs, we haven't really been discussing women. I share Big Mike's anxiety about the topic list, and I wonder if the men's difficulty in relating honestly with their significant others might be connected to their frustration in trying to find jobs. "I want to be a provider," Chubb had confided in me. "I feel like I can take care of my kids and stand up to my baby mama. But how can I do that without a job?"

Mike and I agree that we will try to neutralize the topic of significant others as much as possible. After check-ins, he announces, "We are going to talk about a new question: 'Women and relationships: How do you love?'"

The men have plenty to say in response to the question. The problem is that little of it concerns their significant others. Instead, their loving warmth is reserved for their "mamas." Whatever the circumstances of their childhoods, each man describes his own mother in the most idealized terms.

"I gotta tell you," Terrance announces, "my mama was a stone-cold drug addict, but I loved her and she loved me." It is somewhat breathtaking how among the men in the room—black and brown—*no one utters a negative word about his mother.* This is the protected territory of their hearts, the demilitarized zone in lives of conflict.

"I don't blame my mama," Terrance adds, "even though she was a drug addict. There were reasons she turned to drugs. She saw my brother run over in the street. And I was in and out of the pen alla the time. I don't blame her. Those drugs did terrible things to her, but I knew she loved us all the same."

"How do you feel about women—aside from your mama?" I am trying to redirect the conversation. "Debois—what about you?"

"My women? Which one?" Debois is laughing. "I can't even keep track—but they keep track of me. The woman I depend on is my mama. She's the reason I'm here."

"Why?"

"My mama told me I gotta quit messin' up and be a father to these boys. I never been a father to any of my kids, and now I gotta do this right. I made a lotta mistakes—some of the men here know—and I wanna make it right, by my kids and by my community. Just having a good moms, that's important. The women today—they aren't good moms so much—a moms who loves you and cares about you, we need that. I don't know where it went around here. But, you know, my moms is older; she's seventy-something years old. So she's part of the old school. Just having her and her wisdom around, that's good help to me, too, as a father."

The group members begin to nod their heads.

In talking about his moms, Debois inadvertently reveals part of what guides the purpose for the group: the men's mothers are part of their search for redemption.

I wanna do right. We've done a lotta wrong. It's time to change things at Jordan Downs. And my mama is the reasons I wanna change things. I don't wanna let my mama down.

Big Mike adds to what Debois is saying: "Along with your moms, D, the whole problem with families now is we don't have any more big mamas." I am wondering what he is talking about, while all the men in the room are nodding their heads.

"You know our mothers and our grandmothers—our big mamas, as we call them, Drjorjaleap," Leelee says, taking the lead, winking at me while he explains, "they're wise, and they are the better problem solvers. That's why Hillary would have been a better president than Barack. Ask a woman—she knows how to get things done. She is a real big mama."

"What's really wrong with Watts," Ben observes, "is that we don't have any more big mamas and grannies to take care of our kids. Women used to be the soul of the family."

"And you know Big Mama watched out for all the kids in the community—even if they weren't her own," Big Mike adds.

"I remember Mama Washington chasing me up and down Grape

Street with an extension cord, tellin' me she was gonna beat me if she caught me hangin' out, gettin' into trouble." Sy was laughing. Several fathers jumped into the exchange.

"They watched out, and they fed us, and they disciplined us. They was always there."

"What's happened? Why aren't there any more big mamas?"

"Because women are selfish!" Leelee is in a judgmental mood. "Alla these women now, they're thinkin' only of themselves. They're not thinkin' about the children; they're not thinkin' about the community. They wanna party. They wanna have fun."

"Big Mama would watch out for all of the children—and she would watch out for the community. You know that town hall we went to—we needed to have some big mamas there. They woulda been running that meeting."

I thought the community did have some "big mamas," most notably the community interventionists Kathy Wooten and Cynthia Mendenhall, whom everyone called Sister. Kathy and Sister had both lost sons to gang violence, and they worked through their grief by trying to stop violence at Jordan Downs and Imperial Courts. But the men were talking about a sort of general mother figure who watched over all the kids on the block. The men extolled the virtues of the community big mamas while expressing their great affection for their own mothers.

"We gotta help our daughters. They're the next generation of big mamas. We gotta raise them right," Ben suggests.

"We gotta watch out for our daughters—"

"Protect our girls—"

"I don't want anything happenin' to my girl babies."

As the men discuss their feelings, it's as if love skips a generation.

The men talked animatedly about their little girls and their big mamas—their thoughts and feelings are completely absorbed with their daughters and their mothers. Yet the ideas and emotions they expressed as they talked about their daughters and the young women in the community were full of emotion and conflict. In certain ways, their daughters served as a focal point for the men's ambivalence towards women. All of this surfaces when they talk about their daughters and other young women, nieces, and cousins. The men worried when their daughters resembled them, but expressed pride when one of their female offspring displayed any toughness. Near the end of the meeting, Ben proudly reports that he felt he had raised a good daughter, then adds he was mad but proud that his daughter had been suspended for beating up another girl at school. The men all nod, and a few express their approval. I am surprised by what Ben tells me, and I try to form an opinion about why his daughter, who is usually well-behaved, had been fighting. Ben listens to me stumble around seeking the reasons behind her actions, then decides to put me out of my misery.

"Let me tell you why it happened—it was about respect," he says.

"I don't understand what you mean by respect. I feel like you respect the big mamas, and you want to teach your daughters respect, but you don't have respect for the women that you have your children with."

"You don't understand, Miss Leap," Leelee begins.

"Again you're gonna tell me I don't understand!" But this time Leelee is right. The truth is I don't understand.

"These women now, they're not like Big Mama," Leelee continues. "They are thinkin' only of themselves—they are out only doin' for themselves—"

"I know women who don't only think of themselves—"

"Who?"

I wait a minute, then try to tell the fathers what had happened to one of the women I knew who lived at Jordan Downs.

Carmen and her baby daddy, James, had always represented a mini-resolution of the black-brown conflict: she was Latina and he was African American, but they were both devoted to their family. James swore he would never leave, that he would be there for her and for the children she delivered in rapid succession—two girls, two boys. James's own father had abandoned him when he was four years old. "I never knew my dad," he told me. "I want things to be different for my kids."

Carmen was pregnant with their fifth child, another daughter, and I helped to throw her a baby shower. Friends and family assembled at Athens Park, right outside of Watts, and covered the concrete picnic tables with pink paper tablecloths and baskets of pink candies and cookies. James was not there, but Carmen insisted he had gone to "pick up the cake." Three hours later, Mark left to buy a replacement cake while

I feverishly texted James. Something had to have happened for him not to show up. Carmen was terrified.

That night Carmen called me, crying, and asked me to come over. I drove to Jordan Downs. When she opened the door I could see she was distraught.

"That motherfucker's been cheating on me. Do you know why he never made it to the baby shower? He was with his girlfriend. I'm gonna fuckin' kill him."

"That's what happened," I tell the fathers. "And now she's alone, *waiting for her fifth kid!*" I am screaming. "Where's the respect in that?"

The fathers are all laughing. The more outrage I express, the harder they laugh.

"Miss Leap, Miss Leap—you've got all those pieces of paper with all those letters and you haven't figured this out," Leelee begins.

"Come on, you know the truth. She-e-e-t." Sy is the Greek chorus.

"You know—all men are dogs. We are all dogs." Leelee is smiling at me. He almost looks like he is going to lean over and pat me on the head.

"My husband doesn't cheat on me. I trust him with my life." As soon as I announce this, the men are laughing so hard they are gasping for air.

"Oh come on, you're gonna tell me your husband never cheated?"

"Never."

"Why not?"

"It's not in him. He's not that way."

"Do you have sex? Are you sure he's a man?"

I knew it was ridiculous to continue this line of the conversation. In the world of Project Fatherhood Jordan Downs, men were incapable of fidelity. Love and faithfulness were two different issues, never to be connected. I knew there was at least one outlier—Big Mike—but I wasn't going to expose him. I would bet my house he never cheated on Sauna. Perhaps in his younger days he had subscribed to this line of thought, but I didn't believe it was in his current worldview. But I also knew the men were telling me the truth. One of the fathers, Julius, was sixty-six years old and his forty-year-old significant other had shown up screaming the week before that he was running around with "young girls." So I decide to turn the conversation back to Carmen.

"Okay, if men are dogs and James has cheated on Carmen, and she's ready to have a baby, what do I tell her to do?"

"Shut her mouth, take his money, and don't ever have a child with that sorry motherfucker again."

For once I am ready to accept hood therapy. I don't have a better solution.

FOURTEEN

The Light Comes In

I guess there's gotta be a crack for the light to come in.
—Leelee Sprewell

By 2012, Project Fatherhood had become a fixture in Watts. The key men who had been in the group from the beginning had built a strong connection to one another. The fathers felt more involved with their families, and they had begun to participate in community events. Many said the group was an important part of their lives.

Then the funding ran out.

Hershel Swinger, the driving force behind Project Fatherhood, had died in May 2011, but his vision was very much alive. To further the work, Children's Institute had appealed to the federal government for more money. It was unclear when—or if—that funding would arrive. In the interim, Big Mike, Andre Christian, and I turned to HACLA, requesting the minimal amount of money needed to pay the three of us and keep the group running—about $2,000 a month. John King hemmed and hawed, explaining, "I just don't know how much money we have." I immediately announced I would forfeit my monthly stipend. King looked relieved to hear my offer. But Big Mike and Andre disagreed. I wondered why the bureaucrat who would truly want to ensure equity was not rejecting this idea, while the two men who had the most to lose *were* objecting—and strenuously.

"This isn't right," Andre started. "Listen, young lady, either we all get paid, or we don't get paid. We're in this together."

Mike was even more emphatic.

"No," he bellowed. I was surprised at the depth of his concern. "You gotta get paid," he insisted. "You got a daughter in college. Don't do that Jorjaleap. Don't do it."

One thing that always amused me about Mike was his penchant for calling people by their full names. It was not restricted to authority figures. Andre was Andre Christian. I was Jorja Leap—when discussing Project Fatherhood, it was *Doctor* Jorja Leap. The HACLA bureaucrat was Mr. John King. Mike would run the names together as if they were all one word: *Misterjohnking, Doctorjorjaleap.*

Mrjohnking had not blinked an eye when I said I would forfeit my pay.

"That's a good start," he mused. "If you do that, we might be able to find funds to keep Project Fatherhood for a few more months. But that's all the money we've got."

I was trying not to laugh. The annual budget of the Housing Authority of the City of Los Angeles was half a billion dollars. HACLA probably left enough change in the couch cushions to fund Project Fatherhood for several years. This was not John King's fault. I had learned, from the year I spent working in former mayor Antonio Villaraigosa's office, that this was the way bureaucracy operated: the city held on to money for dear life. It was a long trip from budget allocations at City Hall to the streets of Los Angeles.

I felt almost Republican in my belief that there was too much waste. I helped to review a proposed gang-prevention strategy that allocated $100,000 in services to a hundred kids who lived in one the city's fourteen designated gang "hot zones." A reporter writing a story on the proposed program asked me, "Wouldn't it be better if they just gave each kid's family ten thousand dollars and told them that they could keep the money if they stayed out of gang life?" I couldn't come up with a response. The idea made too much sense. At Jordan Downs, I seemed to have momentarily forgotten the lesson I had learned working for the mayor.

In search of outside funding for Project Fatherhood, I once again meet with Guillermo Cespedes. He is more than sympathetic, talking openly about how the city needs to invest in Watts in general—and in Jordan Downs in particular. But then he delivers the bad news: *there just isn't any money.* Guillermo insists that he is actively seeking funds for Watts programs, including Project Fatherhood. He asks if he can visit again. After we meet, I e-mail him possible dates, and we set his visit for early November. He tells me there might be news of funding by then.

Strangely enough, that November evening, all the stars aligned—in more ways than one. Earlier in the day, Guillermo had called to tell me an agreement was imminent between HACLA, the Los Angeles City Council, and the mayor's office—within the politics of LA, an unholy alliance if ever there was one. I didn't quite understand the bureaucratic terminology, but money could come to Watts through a PILOT program—and this didn't mean an experimental scientific design. In a PILOT (payment in lieu of taxes) program, the funding previously allocated for one purpose could instead be reallocated to another purpose. The city council motion Guillermo e-mailed me read like an elaborate, government-sanctioned Ponzi scheme. But it was completely legal. I didn't care about the details, as long as Jordan Downs got the money. Miraculously, along with funding for gang intervention and family case management, there was an allocation for the Jordan Downs "Fathers' Group" for a year. When Guillermo added that he was coming to Project Fatherhood that night, I was actually looking forward to the event thinking *this is going to go somewhere.*

But I was going nowhere. I got caught in traffic and arrived twenty minutes late. In that brief time, the wheels had begun to fall off the bus. The room was crowded with men, and they were definitely not members of Project Fatherhood. The LAPD had shown up, unannounced, wearing short-sleeved uniforms and carrying walkie-talkies and weaponry. While the fathers sat around the table, the officers rimmed the perimeter of the meeting room. None of the Project Fatherhood men were talking. Instead, the group was listening to a six-foot, blonde Amazon police officer, her hair pulled back tightly in a small ponytail. I knew by the stripes on the uniform she was a sergeant. The men under her command listened attentively. The fathers in the audience looked on with a combination of doubt and confusion. I took my seat between Big Mike and Guillermo and listened as Big Mike muttered under his breath, "They shouldn't be here. This isn't the point of Project Fatherhood." I leaned in and asked Big Mike if I should stop them. He looked at me plaintively and said, "In a few minutes."

At the opposite end of the room, John King looked like the cat that had swallowed the cream. The sergeant's message, which she repeated several times, was that the officers in attendance that night had been carefully chosen to serve the community. She assured the fathers that they would all work together to "make sure your community is safe," then added, "but sometimes we're gonna have to arrest people."

After a few minutes, I was developing whiplash trying to follow her. She was a combination good cop/bad cop all in one body. "We know that you're the good citizens of Watts." *Wait for it*, I thought. "But if any of you goes wrong, there will be legal consequences."

One of the officers stood up and began giving heartfelt testimony on his wish to "protect and serve" the community. However, after a few minutes, his cop speak began to give way to negativity. He started with "knucklehead" and quickly worked his way down into outright profanity. He slipped all protocol when he got to "motherfucker." I gave him the first dirty look I had ever overtly offered up in the life of the group.

"We really try not to use any profanity during our meetings. And I need to ask you to take one more question so we can move on to Project Fatherhood," I calmly declared. None of the fathers protested. John King started arguing that this was an important opportunity to "have a dialogue" about the LAPD's new approach to policing in the community.

"All due respect, Mr. King," Big Mike finally chimed in, "we have an agenda, and we gotta get the meeting started."

At this point, I was sick and tired of the born-again LAPD. This was not to take value away from the new Watts Gang Task Force–LAPD initiative, the Community Safety Partnership (CSP). While I believed in the focus of this initiative, I sometimes felt like the department had just discovered the community strengths that had long been apparent and at work inside Watts. Prior to the creation of the CSP, the LAPD had attempted to rule Watts with a combination of fear, rage, and derision. This wasn't going to be forgotten just because a whole new generation of multicultural cops—full of tolerance and pledges to partner with the community—had shown up. And despite the new methodology, the message remained the same: *we are in control*. Tonight, the tendency to be "badge heavy" had already led the LAPD to try to hijack the Project Fatherhood session. The sergeant had not been listening to the men so much as talking at them. I was distinctly uncomfortable. Guillermo whispered to me, "This type of discussion is more for a town hall meeting than a fathers' group."

"Are you here *with* the LAPD?" I asked Guillermo, wondering if this was a quid pro quo. He shook his head no, adding, "I had no idea they would be here."

John King backed down and Big Mike carefully read the topic of the evening from his syllabus: "How do I know I am making the right decision as a father for my children?"

The discussion began in a desultory manner. The presence of the cops was clearly having a chilling effect. Still the men tried to talk, but there was little of their usual bravado. Debois began gingerly, "I know I am making the best decision when I consider everything carefully and then decide what to do with my kids."

"You have to take your time and decide—it's what Big Mike said, 'Listen for a long time; answer in a slower time,'" Leelee chimed in.

The men nodded.

"I think we're all learning to listen to each other, tryin' to help each other do right by our kids."

Slowly, the discussion began to pick up. I decided it was time to turbocharge it.

"What about making the right decision when you are dealing with your significant other?" I asked. The conversation came to a halt. I was wondering what it was about my question that caused this response, when I suddenly realized that a train wreck was taking place in the middle of the room.

A large African American man, Ernie, stood up and gestured to one of the patrol officers. "I remember you. You messed me up. I wasn't doing anything, and you came in and handcuffed me up—in front of my kids—and locked me up. The next thing I knew I was serving thirteen years in the pen because of you." The cop stared at him, dumbfounded. Ernie continued; it is a primal scream of pain, but I wasn't sure if he had the correct cop in his sights, or if the man in the uniform was a stand-in for Ernie's rage.

"Whatcha gotta say to me now? I wanna know. You come in here and say you are gonna help the community, but I wanna know what about everything you did in the past?" The volume button was turned way up as Ernie's screamed. I looked at him carefully and saw a bulge near his belly button, which I suspected was a firearm. I was not even thinking about the topic of the day as the discussion quickly went sideways. But John King saw an opening.

"Let's open up this discussion—if that's okay, Dr. Leap?"

Why was he asking me this? I don't think he saw what was bulging from Ernie's belly. I was terrified there was going to be a shooting. King already knew the answer, but I made a big ceremony of looking at Big Mike, who nodded in agreement.

Sy stepped in and calmly began to defuse the situation.

"If I can just say—we've got a whole history in these projects of officers abusing men in the community and shaming them in front of their children. I realize you are not these officers. But you gotta understand what we've gone through."

The patrol officers nodded in unison—it was synchronized agreement intent on crowd control. Ernie turned and ran out of the room. Everyone stared after him in silence. Then a member of the LAPD stood up; the officer was Korean, and he was angry.

"We're trying to have a dialogue here, but this man says these things and rushes out, and now he's left my partner hanging."

It was the only part of the scene I liked. Based on the name tags, it was clear that the officers reflected the diversity of Los Angeles. The Korean officer's partner was a Latino officer who quickly slipped me his card. On it he had written: "Sorry for my language being inappropriate." The official print was punctuated with a happy face he had drawn. In spite of my own bias, I was having trouble not bursting out laughing. Maybe this really was the new LAPD.

"I just don't think it's fair," the Korean officer continued. "We were having a dialogue, and now we can't." Welcome to the new Jordan Downs, I thought ruefully, but the men in the room responded supportively.

"We're gonna go talk to him—that wasn't right."

"He shouldn't have said those things. It got a little outta hand," another father added. I couldn't figure out what is going on. They were actually being sensitive and reassuring the LAPD.

I was measuring the mood in the room, doing what any self-respecting anthropologist would call a climate survey. These fathers looked at the cops with a combination of suspicion and yearning. The men wanted to believe the community could be changed. They wanted to believe that their children would grow up in a place where violence was not the norm. I thought about what Debois said to me before the meeting: "I just want to raise my boys somewhere peaceful. I want them to be safe." He was thinking about his seven-year-old twins. For them, these cops represent a promise.

The fathers wanted to believe, but they were frightened. Leelee carefully asked, "Are you going to be the ones patrolling these streets?" The sergeant went into a lengthy discussion on community policing, but the answer boiled down to one statement: "Not all the time." There would be our super-duper, well-trained community police some of the time, but there would be other times when it was straight-out cops, locking the bad guys up.

Officer Tim Pearce stood up near the end of the session. The men all looked at him with respect. No one spoke. Pearce has paid his dues. His wife, Kristina Ripatti, a ten-year veteran of the LAPD, was gravely wounded in a gas station shoot-out in 2006. As a result, she is paralyzed from the chest down. In their courage, devotion, and resilience, the two represented the best of the LAPD. Pearce did not falter in this situation. He was the first of the entire group of police officers to offer a rationale—not just cop talk. He explained what is going on:

> What causes violence in the community is dope. And the people we want to lock up are the dope dealers. You all know this; I don't need to tell you. The dope drives the violence. We just want to make this a safe place for you and your kids. We're gonna try to do this by telling the dope dealers to stop. We want to drive them away. But if we can't do it that way, we're gonna lock them up.

The men listened, but did not comment. The session ended.

The results of the evening were mixed. After the group left, Big Mike sat down wearily. We barely talked, just made brief plans for next week's session.

On Friday, I spend the entire day with Andre Christian, walking around Jordan Downs, hanging out with homies, talking about what happened at Project Fatherhood. He and I agree that while we should have been asked or even just informed beforehand that police would be attending, the meeting was probably a one-off. The cops wouldn't be back.

We are both naïve.

At Big Mike's behest, I send an e-mail to Mrjohnking indicating that Mike, Andre, and I do not want the LAPD to attend Fatherhood, with our reasoning spelled out in (slightly academic) detail. John King responds agreeably but says this will all take effect *after* the cops attend the next meeting.

Two nights later, I arrive at the community center and it is déjà vu all over again—complete with fathers sitting at the table and uniformed police officers standing over them, manning the perimeter. The sergeant appears but leaves the room once the meeting begins.

"We're gonna pick up where we left off last week," Big Mike announces. "The question for tonight is, 'What is the most difficult decision you have ever made as a father?'"

But no sooner are the words out of his mouth than the LAPD officer who had given me his card and apology begins to speak.

"I wanted to tell you that I investigated that man's file—"

Everyone, including me, turns to him, dumbfounded, wearing identical expressions—the universal nonverbal "What the fuck are you talking about?" look. The silent question is so obvious that he quickly annotates his remarks.

"—The man last week who said I arrested him unfairly and then ran out of here," the cop offers helpfully. He looks at the men to gauge their reaction.

I didn't want to tell the officer what everyone in the room already knew: Ernie fled because he really had no reason to confront the officer. He probably even knew he had gone after the wrong guy. *Everyone in a uniform looks alike.* Most of the fathers had dismissed Ernie as drunk or crazy, or both, and had promptly forgotten the incident.

But the officer continued, holding up a manila folder. "I looked up his case, and I wasn't even working that day. I was off. *I wasn't even working that day.* I wanted to have a dialogue with him, but now he's not here, so I can't just talk to myself. I wanted to have a dialogue with him."

Big Mike briefly bows his head in the cop's direction and then says, "That's okay, that's okay. Let's just go forward." Then, in very pronounced and formal diction, he once again asks, "What is the most difficult decision you have made as a father?"

One man raises his hand and quietly says, "One of the most difficult things I have ever done as a father is to shut up and listen to what my significant other has to say. I have shut up and let her talk about her feelings."

The room is silent with disbelief.

"Will you talk to my husband?" I ask. Everyone starts laughing, and the tension is broken.

This is a lie—Mark always listens to me. I am never without a voice in our household, although it is a position I have fought hard to attain; it was not that way in the early days of our marriage. When I married Mark, there had been three wives before me who I suspect had been frustrated, angry, and acting out but who had still not succeeded in teaching him anything about shared authority. I already had one failed marriage behind me and I had no fear. I never wanted to lose Mark, but I was much more afraid of losing myself. But sometimes at Project Fatherhood, I kept up the façade of the poor, misunderstood significant other. It served me well here.

Big Mike calls out a police officer, who is standing directly behind him leaning on a podium, and asks, "What about you, officer? What is the hardest decision you have ever had to make as a father?"

The room is silent and the officer—black, portly, with a shaved head—speaks with the voice of authority.

"Within my home, I have made the decision to make respect the highest priority. I make sure my family is in compliance with respect. That means we have to show respect for one another. My son has to give my daughter her space—in the bathroom, when she goes to her bedroom. It's important we have respect—"

"Pardon me, officer—"

It is my voice, and the room is still. I have had a bellyful of this sanctimonious, nonrevealing bullshit—last week and now this week. I am pissed and I am tired.

"We aren't talking about your philosophy of life and your family. We are talking about a decision that was hard for you to make—that cost you something. These men talked about their significant others expressing themselves or finding out their kids are smoking dope. I'm sure they all want respect,"—and individual bedrooms for their children, I itched to add—"but right now they're talking about things that were hard for them to do. What was hard for you to do? What have you had conflict over—*inside of yourself?*" *You authoritarian asshole*, I added mentally.

"But respect is important . . . ," he sputters.

I see a few of the fathers with their lips twitching as they try not to smile.

"We all believe that," I begin gently. (I remember that I am supposed to at least act like a social worker.) "But what's been hard for you to do—even in terms of respect?"

"I guess, I don't know yet," he answers, befuddled, his mask dropped. "My kids are young. I guess I haven't gotten to that place yet. I guess I wanna learn from what I hear tonight."

I should be happy to settle for this small victory, but I'm not done.

"What about you, Mr. John King?" I turn to the other side of the room, where John sits with his white shirt and his tie, surveying the group. "What's been a hard decision for you?"

There is uneasy laughter in the room. Most of the men are accustomed to their angry partners, their angry significant others, their angry baby mamas. I am guessing that this is one of the first times they were seeing an angry white mama in action calling out the authorities.

I give John King credit. He is game.

"My daughter is a teenager," he begins. "I don't ever want her to go out—ever."

The men in the room all begin to laugh and nod their heads in agreement with the universal feelings of daddies everywhere who do not want their little girls to grow up.

"My daughter came to my wife and me and told us a complete lie. She said she was going out with friends, but she really wanted to go out with this boy who had asked her out. Boy oh boy—she played that right. What could I say? I gave her a twenty and told her to go have a good time."

The men respond with reinforcement.

"I've had that happen more times than I want to remember—"

"Hell, we've all been there."

"When I found out she was lying, I had to face that she had lied, that she had fooled us. And then I had to think of what her punishment was going to be. I wanted to whip her, but I didn't. But I had to tell her she couldn't go to the prom. And even though she cried and cried, I had to stick to my decision."

Before I can draw breath, Big Mike turns to the cop who has brought the manila folder and asks gently, "What about you, officer? What's the hardest decision you've had to make?"

The officer's voice shakes slightly.

"I used to like going out with my boys—drinking, going to clubs, y'know, partying. Then I had a daughter. And I know, I can't go out anymore. That was a hard decision. I like going out—I wanna be with my boys. But I can't. I gotta be a man for my daughter. And sometimes I miss it."

The room is utterly still. There is no division between the men with handcuffs and the men who had been locked up. Every man in the room knows this feeling. Every man in the room wanted to hang with his boys. Some of them had—instead of raising their children—and knew the price they had paid. The air is filled with regrets unspoken.

The silence is broken by Ronald. He wears a dark purple cap and sunglasses and has dreadlocks. He looks old weathered, tired.

"The hardest decision I ever made was to tell my woman that a new baby boy born at the hospital that day was my son with another woman."

There are gasps, and laughter.

"What did she do?" I ask, just above a whisper.

"That woman came to the hospital with me and saw that baby and saw my girlfriend and told her, we gonna take that baby home and raise it up."

"She must love you very much."

"She do."

Terrance raises his hand.

"We are real here. We are all real here. This doesn't mean we have to spill our guts out, but we gotta take some chances—all of us. With that in mind, what I have to say is this: the hardest decision I ever made as a father was to leave the mother of my children. We have four children together. She is an amazing mother. But we're no good together. We fought all the time. I hit her sometimes—I'm not ashamed to tell the truth, although I'm ashamed of what I've done. But I couldn't stay there. I couldn't let my kids see me do that to their mother. But I also felt like I was doing what my daddy had done to us. And when I had my kids, I had promised myself I wasn't gonna be like my daddy. I wasn't gonna leave. But I had to. And I am working now to make sure we do things together on the weekend, we come together for our children. But that was—and it still is—the hardest decision I have ever made."

The dynamic in the room has shifted, and the Latino cop who had attended the week before volunteers his feelings.

"I have a son. But, y'know, sometimes I wish I had a girl instead of a boy. The hardest decision I have had to make has been to tell him no. He wants so much—too much. He's always pushing me, always asking me for things. I've gotta tell him no. And I've gotta stop being afraid he won't love me if I tell him no."

"He's gonna love you more if you tell him no," Leelee offers and all of the men around the table nod their heads in affirmation.

"Yeah," Debois agrees, "but we gotta know how to tell ourselves no first."

The cops look on.

"Amen," one cop offers.

"Amen," the group answers.

FIFTEEN

Checkmated

We are all gonna have to change—our attitudes, our beliefs, even what we do as our behaviors. But change takes time.
                                                    —Michael "Big Mike" Cummings

I have tried to keep tabs on Matt, but he remains elusive. Big Mike has seen him leaving school and checked in with him, but he rarely sees Matt around Jordan Downs. Matt seems to spend most of the time indoors with his girlfriend. When Matt first joined the group, I had been concerned that he could be at risk for gang involvement. My fears were unfounded. Even now, he is not in the least bit interested in Grape Street or any of its cliques. Matt lives at Jordan Downs at a remove. I catch word that he likes to party, mainly to drink and hang out.

"Listen, he's not interested in dope at all. He's not interested in money. The only thing he's interested in is school," Big Mike tells me. With his soft eyes and gentle manner, Matt is not assigned the role of potential gangster. Everyone is protective of him. Even when I ask some of the local gangbangers why they never went after Matt—neither recruiting nor rejecting him—they all tell me the same thing.

"Nah, we leave Chicago alone," one offered, calling Matt by his nickname. "He's smart."

"He's does good at Jordan, so we let him be."

"He's too soft, and he's good at school," Buddha elaborated. Buddha was one gangster whose name fit, intellectually as well as physically. Large and thoughtful, he offered a new spin on the hood code of ethics. "Someone's good at school, we leave 'em alone. They'll do something good for the community, we support 'em. That's all. We don't wanna jack them up. Y'know, some of these youngsters, they're gonna go to college. I figure we gotta do what we can for them."

As usual, gang culture never ceases to surprise me. Evidently there was some sort of neighborhood waiver that operated when someone was smart and—the key words—*in school.* This somehow differed from someone who was intelligent yet useful to gang life. I had seen too many youngsters with good business sense and street smarts snapped up by one of the neighborhoods—black or brown—because gangsters were good talent scouts. I knew multiple wannabe MBAs at work in gang life right now. But Matt was left alone. The local cliques recognized an intellectual.

Among the fathers, Matt is the example the men hold up to their children. I hear Debois tell his twin sons, "See, you can be like Matt. He is getting ready to go to college." When Matt returns to Project Fatherhood after missing several sessions, the men are happy to see him. They all openly express their collective pride and welcome him with open arms. He listens quietly during the meeting but tells the group he has an announcement to make near the end of the session.

"My girlfriend is pregnant."

The men listen to him in silence. They are stunned.

"You sure, man?"

"Yeah."

"You know we're here for you."

"Yeah."

"You reach out if you need something."

"Yeah."

"How do you feel, man?"

"I can't wait—we had a sonogram and it's a boy." Matt is clearly excited. No one knows quite what to say, although several men pat Matt on the back and offer their support as the group breaks up.

As I review my field notes, I am still trying to figure Matt out. He is an honors student at Jordan High School, earning superior grades in math and science. With this record, he is catnip to the world of higher education: a thoughtful young man from an impoverished community who wants to be a biologist or a doctor. Several universities have expressed interest in him, sending letters to his aunt's unit at Jordan Downs. I have even made some inquiries at UCLA, only to discover that they have already reached out to Matt.

The problem is that Matt is not responding to any of them. He is focused on his beautiful and very pregnant girlfriend. The pregnancy is intentional, not accidental, and Matt is proud and happy. I am mystified by this and meet him after school one day, shortly after he returns to the group. We have set the time up by phone and he is eager to talk. I know his auntie is raising him, and I have fallen into a similar role.

"You are so young," I tell him. "You want to go to school—to college. Why did you decide to have a baby now? I'm not judging, I want to understand."

Matt looks at me very seriously.

"Having a baby doesn't have anything to do with going to college. I want to go to college. I want my girl to go to college. As soon as she has the baby, I want her to finish school. But we gotta get our family started."

"Why do you feel that way? I wasn't a mother until I was much older." I omit that this was not something I ever envisioned in my life. Mark, my husband, was a widower with a very young daughter. Shannon was seven years old when she came into my life, and I adopted her after Mark and I were married. Now, I cannot imagine my life without her—and I feel as if I gave birth to her. My love for her is so deep that I now regret not having had more children. There is a part of me that understands Matt's wish for family, but I am thinking, *Not yet, not yet.*

"I know, but you have a family—you've talked about your dad and your mama and your brothers. I don't really have a family. But I'm gonna make one with my girlfriend. My auntie is sick, and I don't know what's gonna happen with her. She's old—I don't know how much longer she's got."

I refrain from asking Matt how old his auntie is. Several homies have referred to "really old" mothers in their forties and to "elderly" grandparents in their sixties. "Elderly" is a relative term. I don't completely understand Matt's urgency about having a child.

But he is far from my mind the following week before Project Fatherhood. Big Mike and I agree that the fathers should discuss homosexuality. When it comes to attitudes about gay men and lesbians at Jordan Downs, everyone has an opinion. Overall, there's a subtle homophobia at work among the black men and women in this neighborhood. Gay black men exist mostly in the shadows, with very little said about them at any time. Lesbianism is somewhat more acceptable, although in the Baptist tradition such men and women are regarded as sinners who will suffer the fires of Hell when they die. Still, it's on the Project Fatherhood list of approved topics, so the question is raised: "How would I feel and react—as a father—if my son or daughter tells me they are gay?"

"I would kill him," one of the fathers answers very calmly.

My jaw drops.

"*What?*" I say.

"Okay, maybe I wouldn't kill him. But I would never see him again."

"But that's your son."

"Look, with your people, it's okay—"

Sy again. I ignore him.

"Why do you think people are gay?" I ask, trying to steer the discussion into a possibly more positive direction.

"You don't know what you're talkin' about even askin' that question."

"You don't—if a man goes with a man, he goes with the devil. You need to understand that. It says so in the Bible. It says that spreading your seed on the ground is a sin."

"That's not about homosexuality," I insist.

"Then what the fuck is it about?" One of the more volatile fathers, Scorpio stands up and is questioning me.

"It's about masturbation," I calmly answer.

"How do you know that?"

"Because it says you spill the seed on the ground, not in someone's asshole."

The men all burst out laughing.

"Excuse me, Dr. Leap," KSD says, "but you know that any man who goes with another man is sick in the head! They need to be locked up, and put the key away."

"Fuck it—they need to be killed."

"Language, language," Big Mike intones.

This is a departure from how the way the men usually conduct themselves. I am no stranger to profanity, but the number of expletives uttered trumps that of any other conversation thus far.

"They're fucking perverts—"

"You know in the pen—you know what they were—"

"Don't talk to me about it. If my son were a faggot, I would want to kill him and kill myself."

I am not prepared for the onslaught of homophobia, but then I notice that Matt is trying to break into the conversation.

"Be quiet and listen to Matt," I tell the group, and they immediately shush each other.

"No one wants to be gay. No one chooses to be gay," Matt begins but the men immediately drown him out.

"No way—"

"You may be smart in school, but you don' know what you're talkin' about."

"You are way wrong on this—"

"I am one of the leaders here," Pirate begins, "and with all respect, Dr. Leap, you are wrong. You are talkin' about the devil and you are with the devil. You are talkin' about evil. You are talkin' about sickness. How do we know it is sickness? It is being punished with the AIDS and the herpes. It's a sign—God is against homosexuals. He wants to smite them down; he wants to kill them. It is God's will. And God's will be done. You, Dr. Leap—and you, Big Mike—I can't believe you would even have us discussin' such an evil thing."

I suck my breath in. Pirate has offered a direct challenge. Meanwhile, all of the protectiveness surrounding Matt has evaporated. Instead, there is so much blatant homophobia and biblical scripture being discussed that even Mike Huckabee would blush. No one will allow Matt to speak. He looks at me and rolls his eyes.

"Matt is right, and I'm wondering why no one listens to him." I am almost shouting. The men all continue talking at the same time.

"Radio," Big Mike inserts. This is hood shorthand for "listen up."

I speak as quickly as I can. "There is research that shows biological differences between gay men and straight men. I'm sure Matt knows about this. Men and women are born this way—we don't know if someone would choose to be gay or straight. But any child would be afraid of their father acting like you."

"You need to understand what scientists say—the truth," Matt chimes in. "They have looked at the brains of gay men who died and noted actual differences in their brain size and structure."

"And they're dead because God killed them."

"God didn't kill them. No one killed them. You need to understand. People who are gay have no choice. They are born that way. Why are you judging them? The Bible says, 'People who live in glass houses shouldn't throw stones.' Why don't you listen to the Bible, since you love it so much?" Matt is furious, and the men look at him with disbelief. He stands up and carefully looks at each face.

"I can't believe how ignorant you are. You say you wanna help me and you believe in me, and then you say these things that are so stupid. I can't stay here."

The men watch as he leaves the room.

"He'll be back," Leelee reassures everyone.

I am not so sure. Big Mike is quiet and doesn't enter into the fight. I wonder what he is thinking.

The next day, I run around Jordan Downs trying to find either Mike or Matt. While I keep running into dead ends, I am trying to figure out just what is going on—something is not being said. Is Matt gay? The thought has crossed my mind about a thousand times since the session ended. He is certainly sensitive and gentle; in the Jordan Downs community he is not hyper-masculine in the way of so many of the men. Would that explain his need to father a child so deliberately at such a young age? I have all sorts of half-baked psychological theories about what is driving all of this. As usual, it is a lot simpler than I think.

I finally find Mike standing at the front gate of Jordan High School. School isn't dismissed yet. This is a good time to talk.

"Do you know what's going on with Matt?"

Big Mike looks at me carefully.

"Okay—meet me at three thirty at the community center. We'll talk about the men, and we'll talk about Matt." He heads towards Jordan High School, and I know I've been dismissed. Half an hour later, Big Mike turns up with a serious look.

"You and I gotta be honest with each other," he begins, shutting the door to the conference room behind him.

"I'm not gonna tell anyone what you are saying to me, Mike. You know you can trust me."

"I know. But you gotta stop running around worrying about Matt—that boy is fine and he is strong. But," Mike pauses here as if to add emphasis, "are you gonna listen to me?"

At this point, Mike and I have been through the wars. A year before, in a brief article in *Los Angeles* magazine about our work together, Big Mike was incorrectly identified as "a founding father of the Grape Street Crips." Mike's association with Grape Street was nebulous. I couldn't begin to understand the ins and outs of it. But one thing was certain: he had *not* been a founding father of the Grape Street Crips. And even though Big Mike had enjoyed the attention that accompanied the publicity, there was blowback in Watts. Mike and I had a huge fight about the accuracy of the article. Mike insisted I ask the magazine for a retraction. I told him that would never happen. We were equally stubborn and fought to a draw.

Andre later told me that a lot of people were angry.

"For God's sake," I said. "What were they angry about? It was a one-page article—it barely said anything at all."

"You don't understand. Watts is different."

I understood by now that Watts was, indeed, different. Jordan Downs was different and, most significantly, what Big Mike was about to tell me *was different*. It could not be part of the general discussion at Project Fatherhood.

"Look, we can't keep talking about gay men and lesbians. It's hard for the men. They're trying to understand, but they're old school."

I nod.

"Matt is the future—Matt is *not* old school. He really is the future. But it's gonna take time. And the men don't wanna be reminded that the future is coming. So they're gonna give Matt grief about how he feels. And—without upsetting folk—we gotta support Matt in how he feels."

"Well, what do you think, Mike? What would you do if Booboo were a lesbian?"

Big Mike is obviously uncomfortable. I know that from what I am witnessing. A man who weighed over three hundred pounds is literally squirming in his chair.

"Y'know, Drjorjaleap, I believe God made all of us in his image. I would have to believe in that."

I decide not to push this line of argument any further. Instead, I switch gears.

"Okay—but what if we talk about this with the men? Won't they understand that Matt was just expressing his opinion? That they don't have to feel threatened?"

Big Mike has a look on his face that says what he cannot or will not put into words. But I know what he is thinking: *How stupid are you, Doctorjorjaleap?*

"Nah. They'd think he was disrespectful, that he should listen to what his elders have to say. And, y'know, the men want to see Matt do good, but they are also—what's the word?—intimate—"

"Intimidated?"

"Intimidated by how smart he is."

"But they love him!" I try one more time.

"Well, Dr. Leap, we can't change the men."

Here was a problem that I suspect Hershel Swinger had not contemplated. The gender politics of Watts were crazy and inconsistent. And right now, there was little I could do.

SIXTEEN

The Nation

If we cannot get along in peace after giving America four hundred years of our service and sweat and labor, then, of course, separation would be the solution to our race problem.
  —Louis Farrakhan, *Meet the Press*, NBC, April 13, 1997

For several weeks, three men wearing identical dark suits, bright-white shirts, and bow ties sit in on Project Fatherhood, just listening. Once the formal meetings end, they talk outside the community center, but they connect only with the black fathers. They don't talk with the Latino fathers; they don't talk with me. After a month, their behavior shifts. They begin to speak up during meetings, subtly—and then not so subtly—urging the group to change direction. While I have yet to fully understand what they are doing, I feel the threat soaking through my skin. I am not the only one. Big Mike turns to me and asks, "What are we gonna do? It's the Nation. They don't belong here." Of course I know this. The men in bow ties are Black Muslims.

After the meeting, we sit down to talk about what is going on. Our exchange is tense, because two members of the leadership team—Andre and Ele—flirt with Black Muslim affiliation in a big way. I feel particularly uncomfortable about Ele. Andre insists that the men can attend; they just can't stir things up. I am worried about what it will mean for the Latinos in the group.

"I worry about the Nation," I offer. "They preach a lot of hatred."

"No, they don't—" Ele immediately disagrees, but I cut him off. For the past few weeks I have kept my feelings to myself. But now that the presence of the Nation has been more consistent and their blatant disrespect for me has become obvious, it's time for a confrontation.

"Ele, let's all admit one thing. If it were up to the Nation, I'd be out," I announce.

Ele and Andre are both silent.

Big Mike nods while I speak and then says, "We don't gotta worry—they're not taking over." Ele and Andre nod in agreement. My concern about the Nation and the role it might play in Project Fatherhood vanishes in that moment. I know that Ele both admired and loved Mike deeply. He had once spoken to me about how deeply he depended on Mike, and his eyes had filled with tears. Beyond this, I also know I have to give up my own fear and try to think about the deeper meaning of Ele's attachment to the Black Muslim agenda.

I understood that Ele was still struggling with post-prison issues. Andre warned me that he and Ele both suffered from post-traumatic stress disorder. Their everyday existence was fraught with hypervigilance. Ele also was filled with guilt that his incarceration amounted to unintentional abandonment of his wife and family. For solace, he often turned to the Black Muslim faith he initially encountered in prison. When the men in the bow ties began to show up, he welcomed them to the group and reinforced what they had to say. Whenever the opportunity arose, Ele blamed white people for the community's collective troubles. I was afraid I was really going to have problems getting along with Ele.

I was never against Ele becoming part of the group, but I was unnerved when I showed up one Wednesday and was told he'd been brought on as a co-leader. "I think it might be too soon after prison, Mike," I demurred. But I understood. Just being part of the group would not put money in Ele's pocket, beyond the crumbs of the gift card, and Ele needed a job.

Reentry from prison represented a major challenge. Author Michelle Alexander has noted that one out of three young black men is unemployed, while the jobless rate for black high school dropouts who have been incarcerated is 65 percent. I didn't know where Ele fit on that employment continuum, but I knew that Mike was trying to help him get started. Ele was working hard trying to survive and rebuild his relationships with his five sons.

As I learned Ele's story, I began to understand more. He'd had a tumultuous upbringing: his parents separated when he five years old, and the family bounced around different locations, even moving to Cleveland for a year. When he was ten years old, the family settled at the Jordan Downs projects. Ele grew up in Watts, but never graduated high school. Instead, he explains, "I bought into the street system, the street life." He had been to prison and had his first son by the time he was twenty-one years old. He hustled and used drugs, and was soon back in prison after he caught a drug sales charge and was convicted.

He was part of Grape Street and had been trying to prove his worth to the neighborhood when he caught a murder case, but he beat the murder charge and managed to stay out of prison until 2004. By his own account, he wanted his life to be different. Like so many of the men I had known from my research at Homeboy Industries, he reached a turning point. His time out of prison was marked by a long period of reading, learning, and introspection. It was during this period that he began to read more about the Black Muslim belief system that he had first heard about in prison. He formulated his thoughts about, as he describes it, "four hundred years of miseducation. Instead of white people transforming us, really teaching us if they really cared, they put us in projects like this and start dropping bombs that don't say boom in our community. It's the drugs. It's warfare. It's chemical warfare, the schools, the lack of education without the proper facilities." Ele began to think about the chronic violence that was taking the lives of the young men in Watts. He played an active role in the peace treaty negotiated between the Bloods and the Crips in 1992, and he is still proud of this achievement.

"They would call me Ele Mandela. We went to the table with some of the influential brothers from the neighborhood. I am not going to say 'leaders,' because Grape Street don't have leaders. The peace table was so big. It seemed like every hood from everywhere in the projects was there. We got Bounty Hunters, we got PJ's, and we got Grape Streets in the room. It's eighty of us probably all together, twenty people from each neighborhood. How'd this happen? When we got in there with them cats all in the room to talk peace it was like, what took us so long? I can't explain it today, but I couldn't do nothing but cry. Big tears just roll down my face, man. We shoulda done this a long time ago for the sake of a lot of our people."

However, Ele's personal resolve began to crumble. He had been working for Shields for Families for five years but started dabbling in drugs and stopped going to work. He wound up catching another case; he was arrested and charged with murder. "I just let somebody use a pistol, and they killed somebody and told the police I gave them the gun," he explains. "Later on they was saying that I was an accessory or accomplice. They couldn't get me on that, but I was in an all-white town and they was playin' dirty. They made up a charge to hold me and then they filed a murder charge on me. And I ended up taking a four-year deal."

Ele's case was not unusual. Most of the men in the group had described how they would settle for reduced time rather than deal with a system they view as intractably racist. Ele served his four years and was released, returning to Los Angeles. A year later, he caught a probation violation for having pistols in the house. "The police drove me all the way back to Ohio. Took ten days, twelve states—in a little van. Wow, that was an experience. That changed things for me. When I got out, I was done. Since then, I haven't needed to pull no capers or no crimes in order to feed my family."

He became a member of Watts United and helped "birth Project Fatherhood," as Ele explains. "And being a good father is all I care about. I'm a bummer husband. I got three kids outside my family." But he cares for all of them. All of his children, except for the youngest, have graduated high school. Both his twin sons and his daughter have completed college, and his eldest son has returned to school. The twins are successful youth football and basketball coaches. Now there are even grandchildren, who are the center of his life. Ele says his newborn grandson, Malakai, "brought life to the household. You know, it makes me proud because I wanted another son. But my wife can't have no more kids. So boom, God gave me him. Even though he's not my son, he's my grandson, but it's like he's mine. Now I gotta save all my sons—all my people."

Ele's thinking from his time in prison and his feelings about the community meshed with much of Black Muslim ideology. What the Nation had to say fit with what most of the fathers believed about who was to blame for their poverty and for the lack of upward mobility—those problems were the fault of the LAPD, the Department of Children and Family Services, the government, and, of course, white people.

Recently, a new group had been added to the list of who was to blame: Latinos. This posed many problems for Project Fatherhood. South Los Angeles in general, and Watts in particular, had long been identified as synonymous with "the black community." However, in the first decade of the new century, the demographics shifted. An influx of Latino families—Mexican, Salvadoran, and Guatemalan—changed the ethnic profile of South LA, and Jordan Downs—more than any other housing development in Watts—had evolved into a combination of brown and black families. There are racial tensions, which occasionally arise inside of Project Fatherhood, although overall the group is turning out to be a petri dish of blacks and browns cooperating. There are three young black fathers in the group who are raising toddlers with Latina significant others. Both CII and HACLA aggressively pushed for diversity in the group's composition. Early in the project's existence, HACLA hired a Latina resident to recruit more Latino fathers. However, her efforts yielded little. More recently, John King had spent part of a meeting telling the men that if they wanted the group to survive, they had to bring in more fathers from other cultures. Everyone knew this meant Latinos. The men immediately discussed how this might be accomplished. No one remarked on the fact that, in the midst of their discussion, the men in bow ties left the room.

"We need to get to them through their women," Leelee suggests. "In Latino culture, the women run the household." I refrain from pointing out that this is no different from how the fathers have described the gender dynamics in the black community.

"Maybe we need to meet on Saturday?" Andre ventures.

The men all shake their heads in disagreement. They love Project Fatherhood, but aside from the occasional special event, they want their weekends free.

Aaron is one of three Latino fathers who have been with the group from the beginning. He suggests holding a separate session for Latino fathers. "Maybe we should have a separate group just until they feel comfortable."

"I think that's a good idea—maybe Latino fathers will come," John King is quick to agree.

"No, no, no, no. It's wrong." Sy is emphatic. The other fathers agree.

"No way."

"We don't want two separate groups—it doesn't make any sense."

"It's way wrong. It's like we are saying that we want to be separate. Isn't this how all the problems start?" Leelee protests loudly. While the other men limit themselves to simply saying no, Leelee is off and running.

"So many of the problems we've got here in Jordan Downs are because the blacks and the Latinos aren't getting along. So if we go ahead and do that with two separate groups, we're just reinforcing the problem. This is Project Fatherhood. We don't say Black Project Fatherhood. We are all in this together."

"All of us are one group," Sy agrees.

Only the two men both known as "Twin"—Donald and Ronald James—are silent.

"We are Project Fatherhood for Watts United."

"Well . . . but if we get a lot of Latino fathers, the group may become too big," John King begins. He still likes Aaron's idea.

"Then we'll deal with it. We'd rather have one big group and stay together," Leelee says and then looks around for approval. The men all nod. The unity is palpable. I could not have predicted this. The group is completely pulling away from any kind of separatism.

John King pauses and then comes up with a new suggestion.

"We have a translator here for the Latino fathers," he gestures to Dave, who sits off to the side. "What if we tell the Latino fathers we are going to conduct the group in Spanish and then have a translator for the black fathers?"

The men start to agree. Then a young man, who has appeared at the group for the first time tonight, begins to speak. Carlos Espinosa is poised and articulate. He quickly reduces the older fathers in the room to silence as he shares his story. He begins in halting English, then speaks more quickly as he gains confidence.

"Language doesn't matter. And color doesn't matter. I am going to be a father for the first time in another month. I heard about the group, but I didn't want to come. I wanted to do it myself. I said I don't need help. I realized I needed a job and I said, 'I don't need help, I will find the job myself.' But I realized something—I do need help. I need the group.

My baby is coming next week and I am going to be a father. I don't know what I am going to do."

The men in the room verbally surround him and express their support. Color is not the issue; the point is to help this unemployed, unprepared young man adjust to becoming a father.

"You don't have to worry. We will help you. We're all fathers helping each other," Big Mike begins.

"We gotcha—"

"We understand."

The men quickly gather around Carlos and shake his hand.

Leelee announces, "You got a problem, you call me."

"You just gotta come every Wednesday."

"We are here for you."

This is not exactly fertile territory for the Black Muslims. While most of the fathers in the room warm to the message of black pride and black history and the evils of the white race, they are not in a big hurry to unite against the Latino fathers in the projects or elsewhere in South LA. But I intuitively know the men in bow ties aren't going to give up so easily.

Despite all this, I don't spend a lot of time worrying about the Nation. Instead, I wonder if we are going to see Carlos again. When I read his intake form, his birth date jumps out at me—he was born two weeks before my daughter, Shannon. When I think about the trajectories of their respective lives, I find it painful.

Carlos makes me think about Matt, who had not shown up for a long time. I tried calling him, but there was no response. Occasionally, Matt sent messages through Big Mike that he was fine. He repeatedly told Mike he would get in touch with me. Mike said he had gone to Chicago to see family. I knew it would be up to Matt to resurface. Somehow, I had faith he would tell me what was going on—but he had to decide when and where.

SEVENTEEN

Hero of the Neighborhood

It's like iron sharpening iron. We come and share our stories, and it gets contagious, and everybody goes around speaking on their flaws. Some people were scared to speak about those things—abuse, neglect, pain. But we need to close that chapter. And the only way we can close that chapter is we need to speak on it.

—Terrance Russell

"I want to talk about the *Los Angeles Times*."

I open the meeting with my own check-in. Three days earlier, a page-one story about Project Fatherhood appeared in the Sunday edition of the *Times*. The article was written by Kurt Streeter, a reporter I had long known and trusted. He attended meetings and grew close to the men, and he spent time with several of them just hanging out. His account was thoughtful and sensitive. It was accompanied by photographs and the banner headline, "The Father of All Support Groups: The Men of Project Fatherhood Are Trying to Rise Above Their Own Life Experience and Help Their Families Along the Way." I was excited and looked forward to discussing the article in depth on Wednesday.

But when I bring up the topic, the men are less than interested in discussing how the media portrayed their lives.

"It's good."

"I thought it was fine."

"Well, how did you feel about it—the stories about the group and how we came together?" I am ignoring the signs, trying to pull something out of the group that isn't there.

"We're telling you—it was fine."

"Yeah, great."

End of story.

I can't figure out what is going on. Kurt and I met repeatedly while he was writing the story—we both worried about how the men would respond to the article. Would they object to the public airing of their group discussions? The article mentioned some of the men's resistance to changing their child discipline practices, and it noted their defensiveness around any intimations of physical abuse. Would they be angry? Upset? Excited? I couldn't understand their lack of interest.

Big Mike takes over.

"Let's talk about Christopher Dorner."

Five days before Streeter's article hit page one, an African American former LAPD officer named Christopher Dorner shot and killed himself in a mountain cabin following an eight-day killing spree. He had been the target of the largest manhunt in LAPD history. The case drew national media attention, and it had been of great concern in my home.

Among Dorner's victims were the daughter of a retired LAPD captain and her fiancé, who were shot and killed in a parking garage. My husband, Mark, knew the captain, Randy Quan, and had worked beside him. At first there was no motive or suspect for the killings.

Within days the details emerged. The assailant was Dorner, a man with a distinguished record as an officer in the United States Naval Reserve. His reputation was further enhanced when he joined the LAPD in 2005. Dorner's image had been displayed proudly on internal LAPD web posts. A photograph showed him shaking hands with then police chief Bill Bratton, accompanied by the announcement that Dorner would be on leave from the LAPD to serve his country in the Persian Gulf.

After Dorner returned to the LAPD from Iraq, he was accused of lying about an excessive force charge he filed against his training officer. Following a Board of Rights hearing, he was terminated by the LAPD. He appealed the ruling, but a civil court judge upheld the dismissal.

Dorner returned to the navy and eventually earned an honorable discharge from the reserve on February 1, 2013. Two days later, he went on the shooting rampage, killing four people, among them three police officers. A few hours after he killed Monica Quan and her fiancé, Keith Lawrence, Dorner posted an eleven-thousand-word manifesto on his

Facebook page naming all the LAPD personnel he planned to kill in retaliation for what he perceived was his unjustified firing.

The case generated a huge reaction from law enforcement, community activists, and the news media. There were rumors that gang leaders from Nickerson Gardens had offered personally to protect LAPD captain Phil Tingirides, whose name appeared on Dorner's hit list. Civil rights attorney Connie Rice left no doubt about her feelings, entitling her *Los Angeles Times* op-ed "Christopher Dorner's Web of Lies About the LAPD." Rice argued that Dorner's murderous actions discredited the black "pioneers" who had worked to change racial politics from within the LAPD.

I was sure that as soon as Big Mike broached the subject, the men of Project Fatherhood would reinforce Rice's view. I expected to hear outrage that Dorner had tarnished his achievements as an African American professional and contempt at the fact that he had killed someone's child, some father's daughter. I thought the fathers would understand my concerns about Shannon's safety. They knew that both Mark and I loved our daughter beyond measure. I wasn't totally wide-eyed. I expected *some* anti-LAPD sentiment—after all, Watts had a long and painful history with law enforcement. Still, I waited to hear reassuring echoes of my fears and of my sorrow at what had occurred.

"So what do you think of Christopher Dorner?" Big Mike asks.

"Christopher Dorner was a hero," Donald James begins, and I almost gasp.

I have been deep in denial, but now I am in shock. And I can see Donald waiting for my reaction. I remain expressionless, thinking, *The men are gonna disagree; they'll take him on.*

But I am about to be reminded—yet again—that I still have much to learn.

The uniformity of their reactions is shocking to me. It isn't just that the men express anti-LAPD sentiment. I expected that. The problem is that *everyone* is anti-LAPD. Without exception.

"You know, when I heard what he was doin', I wanted to call the brother. I wanted to send him money. He did the right thing."

"Someone finally stood up to the LAPD."

"Someone finally did to those muthafuckas what they've been doin' to us."

I manage to ask a question.

"What about that young girl—the daughter of the LAPD captain—did she deserve to die? She was just an innocent victim—"

"Boohoohoo, Miss Leap. Why doncha go cry somewhere else?"

I don't even need to look where this is coming from. It is Donald James.

"How many innocent victims we got in Watts, killed by the police?"

"Really, Miss Leap." Leelee joins the discussion. "I gotta disagree with you and agree with Twin here. We are losin' children to the police alla the time. No one cares about the innocent victims *here*. Instead, because they are black children or Latino children, no one pays attention. We still don't count as whole people—just like in the early days of the US. I say, 'Good for Christopher Dorner for putting everyone on notice.'"

"Yeah."

"It's just too bad that he had to die. We'll never know the story. They're gonna cover it up."

"Just like they cover everything up."

"And we're never gonna know the truth," Sy concludes.

Big Mike is silent through all of this, as is Andre. They let the men unload about Dorner. I stop talking, but I am growing steadily angrier. The meeting ends, and I tell Mike I want to go home. There is no debrief.

By the time I get home, I am furious, but I *know* that Mark will sympathize with my plight. Instead, when I start to tell him how betrayed I feel, he starts to laugh.

"Sweetheart, forgive me for saying this, but are you for real?"

"*What?*"

"Are you surprised these men feel this way? Of course they feel this way! They go back to the old LAPD—when Daryl Gates believed in anything but community policing. I know. I was a part of that. They've seen police brutality—my guess is most of them have been victims of it. Or, if it didn't happen to them, it happened to someone in their family. Their experiences with the police are all horrible."

"But they were so angry—"

And then it hits me. None of my distress is about the police. It is about me. And Shannon. That could have been our daughter. Mark is retired, but he knew the men named in Dorner's manifesto. He served alongside Randy Quan. *That could have been Shannon, and these men wouldn't have cared.*

The next morning I wake up and my head is banging.

"I don't even know how I am going to go back there," I tell Mark. I start crying.

"You are looking at this the wrong way," he insists.

"Oh, tell me the right way. That they would say, because you used to work for the LAPD, we had it coming?"

"No. That these men feel comfortable enough with you that they will say all of this in front of you. In their own way, they are telling you they trust you."

This time, I'm not buying.

"I don't think so," I tell Mark.

The next week it is as if Christopher Dorner never existed. The men are angry about the jobs that have failed to materialize, and they are directing their ire at Big Mike.

The relationship between Big Mike and the other fathers is complex. The men admire him and are suspicious of him at the same time. *Watts is different,* I think. The community responds with equal parts paranoia and attachment to whomever might be under the microscope at the moment, whether it's Barack Obama or Big Mike.

There is a backlog of negative gossip about Mike. A handful of men express heavily veiled suspicions that he is taking money from the Project Fatherhood group and keeping it for himself. But he is also seen as a hero, a model of accomplishment. In the group, the men listen to him carefully as he speaks with a messianic zeal. But all of this is undermined by the fact that, instead of making his home in Watts or even in South Los Angeles, Mike lives over ninety minutes away. He is seen as someone who leaves his hood. Squeak often tells me, "You can't be a part-time homie. It's good you stick around." If you're not consistently seen in Watts, you're counted among those who use and abandon the community. Big Mike is a presence, but it's confusing: *He doesn't live in the hood.*

Tonight Big Mike has decided to address all of the haters.

"I know that there's rumors about me. People say things about me, so I want to have everything out in the open. I want to talk about my work and how I make money. I am not makin' money through Project Fatherhood. I am not pimping out the hood. I make my living with my tow truck. Does anyone have any questions, before I go further?"

Big Mike pauses for a good thirty seconds, then continues.

"I am gonna pass around my towing license. It's very precious to me."

He hands me a peach-colored card and instructs me to pass it around, making sure everyone sees it. I glance at the card. It is a towing license from the City of Los Angeles.

"I had to go all the way to the police commission to get that. They denied me and denied me. They said I was a former felon and that I shouldn't get a tow license. I took my appeal to the police commission, and finally Chief Bill Bratton was there. He said, just give the man his tow license, and I got my license—because of Chief Bratton."

I look at the license more carefully. It lists his weight as 340 pounds. (I almost faint when I read this.)

"I don't know if anyone's noticed it, but times are tough." Mike laughs and adds, "Times are always tough here in Watts, but now it's worse than ever. It's hard out there. I'm an independent businessman. I gotta compete with Triple A and all these people who have towing contracts. And I gotta be at the right place at the right time, ready to tow when they call me. Let me tell you my day: I get up at four so I am out the door at four-thirty. Then I get to LA so I am ready to take a call. I get home about ten, have something to eat, then go to bed around eleven. I am up at four again the next morning. And that's it—six or seven days a week. Except I did find a church that's closer to my house, so I don't have to drive so much on Sunday."

"Now, I been thinkin' about what happened last week, when we talked about Christopher Dorner. Everyone was negative. And now I am thinking about this week, when we talked about my job and my commitment to Watts. Everyone is negative again. We gotta stop this. We gotta pull together. This is always what happens in Watts—we attack each other instead of bandin' together. It's time to change. We gotta be what our organization says—Project Fatherhood, Watts United."

"Yeah, Mike, you're right."

"I love you. I don't know what we'd do without you."

"Just one problem, Mike. I'm sorry I got me a Triple A card."

Mike is smiling.

EIGHTEEN

Twins

We gotta tell the truth in here—because no one else is gonna be this real.

—Donald "Twin" James

The men in the bow ties have come—and gone—again. When the Black Muslims are around, I am afraid the emphasis on color obscures the real problem in Watts: chronic, cross-generational poverty. This comes up during a discussion of the 2012 presidential election and Barack Obama, who the fathers relentlessly insist is *not really black.* What they mean is that he is not street—and I am inclined to agree. He is college-educated, has money, and—even though he never really knew his father and was raised by a single mother and his grandparents—his upbringing did not take place in traditionally black communities. But I hope the men see that whether or not Obama is "street," the upcoming election is not about race.

"The presidential race is about money," I tell them.

It has been twenty-four hours since a tape appeared in which Republican presidential nominee Mitt Romney says he would not get the votes of the 47 percent of people who do not pay income taxes and who "see themselves as victims."

"You in the room with the 47 percent," Sy tells me. "But we ain't victims."

"You know that's what the Nation says," Ele begins. "Maybe we should talk about that."

"I don't wanna talk about the Nation—they aren't part of Project Fatherhood," Andre says.

"We don't do anything here—let's just go home." It's Ronald James again, stirring the shit.

The Nation is gone, at least temporarily, but Wednesday meetings continue to be tense. They have come to be dominated by the presence of the pair of men each known as Twin: Ronald and Donald James.

While everyone in the group is street, something is different about the James brothers. Despite the sing-songy, innocent sound of their names, Ronald and Donald have emerged as the group's major trouble-makers. And despite their biological assignation, they do not look anything like each other.

Ronald is angry, profane, and often threatening. With his perennial sunglasses, he is central casting for an OG—original gangster. He is also the hood obituary man. About once a month he comes in to announce that someone has died. He collects money for the funeral and repast. Sometimes he shows me photos of the dinners that follow the funerals. On one occasion, the meal featured a salad with the name of the departed spelled out in red grapes, honoring his affiliation with the Grape Street Crips. Ronald is tied to the hood, even though he was never part of Grape Street. Instead, both twins claim a "family" called the Pygmies, a Watts neighborhood that began in the 1970s. Ronald is now far from his former life of street "business" and incarceration. But he is still unruly and undisciplined, always hustling.

Donald is different. He appears as squared away as a member of the LAPD, neatly groomed, head shaved. At the end of each meeting, he produces a plastic bag and collects empty plastic bottles to recycle for money. Whenever someone asks Donald how he is doing, he answers, "I am blessed. I have a cell phone and a car. And I walked out of San Quentin alive."

I know only three other men who have been in San Quentin State Prison. One of them, James Horton, walked away from death row when a witness recanted and the case was thrown out. The two others—Andre Alexander and Eric Robinson—are still there waiting out appeals. San Quentin is the worst—and most authentic—prison, a place most people cannot comprehend unless they visit someone there. It sits perched on a beautiful peninsula surrounded by San Francisco Bay. Inmates can smell the salt and hear the waves—and sometimes catch a glimpse of sun on the water—while locked up. Having the beauty so close by seems to me a particularly odious form of torture. It is the oldest state prison in California, having opened in 1852. While it is located on property worth close to half a billion dollars, the facility itself is overcrowded and filthy. I spent many days there interviewing inmates and moving my chair to avoid rats. Donald James had somehow survived it, and I was ready to issue him a blank check in terms of his sanity, but it didn't mean I felt any safer being around him.

Ronald joined the group first. He is a middle-aged man who wears dreadlocks and a baseball cap and never, ever removes his sunglasses. He occasionally makes comments that are negative at best, provocative at worst, but otherwise keeps to himself. A few months after he entered the group, Donald appeared. The day Donald joined, Big Mike warned me, "He did thirty-two years in San Quentin. We don't know when he's gonna explode." I am already thinking that his potential instability is matched by that of his twin, Ronald, who doesn't so much double the anger in the room as act as a force multiplier.

Although Donald disrupts meetings whenever he can and is a generally negative force, there is something in him I like. He never said he was wrongfully convicted of any crime. He takes responsibility. In fact, disturbingly, he even seems to brag about his bad reputation, and he often talks about crimes he has committed in Watts. I was certain he had killed people—but then again, he wouldn't be the only one in the group who had. He is angry and sad and hopeful and frightened.

While Donald was in San Quentin, he acted in a prison production of *Waiting for Godot*. The prison was an appropriate setting for that particular play, given that San Quentin inmates are locked up for anywhere from twenty-five years to life. The production spawned a documentary that was highly successful in Europe; Donald believes he is owed some of the profits. The performance also inspired in Donald a love for the works of Samuel Beckett. He dreams of going to Germany to visit Beckett's home. I thought about putting together a fund-raiser, until Mark pointed out that the likelihood of someone who had been in San Quentin going to Europe was very slim.

Donald came to me—half proud, half hustling—and told me in detail about the play and his role. After one session of Project Fatherhood, he showed me his scrapbook, which contained newspaper clippings along with information he had gathered about Samuel Beckett, including a photo of his birthplace. Twin had journals, poems, and notes that he had written carefully in pencil while he was incarcerated. While I looked at this compilation, he loudly announced, "That filmmaker made money off me and I want it back. He needs to pay me. Jorjaleap, I need you to get me a lawyer." I was still poring over his journals but stopped and looked up at him. I didn't even want to begin a discussion about how the word *profit* probably never entered the vocabulary of most documentary filmmakers. Instead, I waited to hear what was coming next.

"I need you to get me a lawyer," he repeated.

"I can't promise I'll get you a lawyer, but I *will* talk to someone about you."

"Good. Can they get me my money?"

"I doubt it."

Twin started laughing maniacally.

"That guy owes me money. He made money—from me."

I sighed.

"Let me take your scrapbooks and your materials, and I'll show them to a lawyer I know and see what they say."

"Okay. You gonna ask him?"

"Her."

Twin considered this for a moment.

"Okay. Her. *Who is she?*"

"Her name is Elie Miller. She was a public defender and then she was the lawyer at Homeboy Industries, and I trust her with my life. She will give you some good advice."

"Okay."

"But I gotta show her this stuff."

"Well, that's my whole life you got there. How do I know you're not gonna lose it?"

For once Twin was quiet. I thought about this carefully. Then I reached into my purse for my wallet.

"You gonna give me money for it? No way."

"Don't be an idiot."

Twin started laughing at me. I opened the wallet and took a battered piece of paper out of the billfold. It was a small reproduction of a painting of an angel.

"You know, my daddy died thirty-five years ago," I began.

"Yeah, you told us."

"He always carried this in his wallet. I took this out of his wallet on the day he died and put it in my wallet, and I've carried it with me ever since. I am gonna give this to you so you can have it while I have your scrapbook and journals. You'll give me back that part of my daddy when I give you back all of this. You trust me, and I trust you."

Twin looked up at me and nodded.

"Well, all right."

Eventually Elie and Twin connected on the phone. She told Donald what I intuitively knew, that there was no case. I gave Twin his scrapbook, his manila folder with his prison writings, and he immediately gave me back—perfectly preserved—my father's angel.

A few weeks later, Ronald appears at the group meeting pushing a stroller with a baby in it. At forty, he now suddenly finds himself the father and caretaker of an infant whose mother has just been incarcerated in state prison.

"His mama is a gangbanger. She's crazy. She deserves to be locked up. But this is my son, and they were gonna put the baby in placement," he tells me. "With strangers. I ain't gonna have the County raisin' a child of mine."

I pull the baby out of the stroller and immediately realize he needs changing. Ronald starts nodding.

"Yep, I need money for diapers."

I allow myself a moment of cynicism, thinking, *My God, he is using the baby to hustle*, and then I walk off, still holding the baby, to look for John King. I tell him to speak to Ronald.

Ronald is already at work with the group, however, sharing his thoughts on raising the baby.

"What am I gonna do? I am a good father when they grow up a little, but this is a . . . baby."

"Do you have some kin you can give the child to?"

"Is your mama alive?"

"Do you have a sister? Daughter?"

The men are offering their version of kinship care. But Ronald begins laughing.

"I can ask my brother."

The fathers all start to laugh. I am wondering what is going to happen to the baby. Is foster care an unreasonable alternative?

"What about having the baby just placed—temporarily—for a short period of time?" I venture.

"This is my son," Ronald insists. "I'm not havin' the County raise him."

After the session, Big Mike, Andre, John, and I gather to debrief. We immediately start to talk about Ronald. I bring up his financial problems and his other parenting challenges. John announces that he gave him money for Pampers. Big Mike says he has given him money. I add that I gave him money for Pampers several weeks earlier. Andre starts laughing and weighs in. "I gave him fifteen dollars for medication."

"Looks like he's playing all of us," Big Mike observes ruefully.

He may be hustling, but there *is* an infant involved. I try to call Ronald several times over the next week, but he never picks up the phone. I check with Andre to see if the cell phone number I have for him is correct. He arrives the next week with the baby and tells me things are better. He is limping, and from what Big Mike has told me, I know he is in excruciating pain much of the time. His lower left leg does not move. I want to say something, but there is something about Ronald that warns me not to ask any questions.

A few days later, when I am talking to Ronald he slowly opens up about his life. It is not what I expected. He tells me he is in constant pain after having been shot in the leg in two separate incidents. While Ronald is evasive about his activities, he is very clear about his injuries. In one instance, the bullet shattered his femur. In the second, he was shot in the kneecap and the bullet passed through a main artery. As he bent his knee at a ninety-degree angle, Ronald explained that he had "what you call a step foot—my foot was up like this, so while I was locked up I went to the jail clinic, and the doctor wanted to bring it down, but I didn't want the jailhouse doctors to do nothing to me." I understand his trepidation. Many gang members have told me that county jail doctors are frequently less than competent, and many are rumored to have had their licenses revoked. Most of the men who have been locked up in CJ have told me that no matter how bad the pain or severe the injury, they will wait until they are released to seek medical attention.

"When I got out, I went to Martin Luther King [Hospital], and Dr. Long did the surgery on me, brought my foot down." Ronald's wild days are long past, though, and—despite his rather unruly appearance—he lives a settled life at Jordan Downs with "a beautiful, nice wife who been in my corner from day one."

Ronald has unpredictable visits from his new son. "His name is Saj-jon James," Ronald explains, "but we all call him Baby Boy." The child is the product of an extramarital relationship with the young gangbanger, an active member of the Bloods. I am trying to figure out why Ronald stepped out, when he tells me that "after alla my baby mamas, I have a good wife." But when I ask him why he cheats, he tells me, "It's in my blood, in my character. My wife is dealing with a cheater—it's nothing to brag about—but you learn from your mistakes. And I'm not saying Baby Boy is a mistake. He is a treasure. And I am gonna learn to be a good father. In the past, with my other kids, it ain't been genuine. But this child represents a chance to do things right. Right now, Baby Boy is my everything."

Ronald limps along, literally and figuratively, in the situation for several months. Then his son's mother is released from custody. I never find out exactly why, and Ronald is not talking. All I know is that the baby is living in Hemet—out in San Bernardino County—and the mother won't let Ronald see him. Before one of the Project Fatherhood meetings, Ronald is on the phone with her, and he asks if I will speak to her. I am not prepared for the anger on the other end of the cell line.

"Who is this?" the woman asks suspiciously. When in doubt, I revert to professional credentials.

"This is Dr. Jorja Leap. I am one of the co-leaders at Project Fatherhood. Mr. James is a member here."

"Yeah, well, what do you want from me?"

"Mr. James says that you need some help with the baby?"

"I don't need any help with this baby."

"He said you might need money for diapers and for baby supplies."

She yells: "You tell him to leave me and this baby alone! I don't want any money, and I don't want him around! You hear me?!"

"Yes, ma'am, I do. May I give you my cell number if you need any information or help from me?"

There is a pause.

"I guess so."

After I give her the information, she abruptly hangs up. I turn and look at Ronald.

"She sounds pretty pissed."

"She's crazy."

"Well, she didn't want money and she didn't want you to see the baby." I am more upset than Ronald. He smiles.

"She'll get over it. She always does."

I am ready to drive him out to Hemet, hire a lawyer, and launch into a diatribe about the importance of fatherhood, but Ronald is remarkably calm. I am wondering why. A week later he appears with the baby and I ask him what happened.

"I told her I wanted to spend some time with my son."

He gives me a "sit down, child, and shut up" smile, and I comply.

Ronald never discusses his custody arrangements. But the group turns into a set of godfathers, watching Baby Boy progress into toddlerhood. The child is thriving, and when I see him I subtly examine him for anything that might cause concern, but he is a happy little boy.

Ronald may be silent about his child, but he and Donald do not keep quiet when it comes to expressing their opinions on childrearing in general and on discipline in particular. Every time I start to explain that what they are saying isn't healthy, I fumble around with their names. I finally give up and resort to calling each of them "Twin," just as the men in the group do. The twins are both intractable in terms of their opinions. But one night, during a discussion of child abuse, the glacier that is Ronald slowly begins to move.

"There are all kinds of information about why hitting your child is gonna backfire," I say, in the midst of what feels like my millionth admonition about child abuse, when Ronald interrupts.

"That's true. You don't need to hit these youngsters."

In shock, I stop talking. Twin is probably the last person I expect to back me up. He usually makes a hobby of disputing every single word that comes out of my mouth.

"What do you mean, Twin?" Big Mike steps in.

"Well, my daughter—I remember when she was young, she was mouthing off. She got into some trouble at school and I told her, 'You just need to be punished.' So I made her go sit in the closet for eight hours."

I am trying desperately not to start screaming. I am also trying to figure where this daughter exists on the family tree. In the gap left by my silence and my total ineptitude, Ronald continues.

"That didn't work so good. I'm not sure she turned out so good. She's kinda . . . a mess. So this time I am gonna be different as a daddy. I wanna raise my son. I don't want him going into the system. Not because I'm not there. Not because I hit him. So I'm raisin' him right, and I'm takin' everything day by day. His rash has gone away and he's doin' better. We're doin' better. Day by day."

I am smiling now. The baby has changed Ronald. I can see he loves his son.

"That sounds good, Twin," I announce, momentarily blissful.

"But I got one complaint."

I forgot. This is Twin.

"What is it?"

"You know we had toys at the last meeting? They passed out toys. And my boy didn't get any toys. Some kids—those Mexican kids—*they got double toys*. And my baby didn't get any."

The men are all shaking their heads.

"We'll look into that, Twin," Big Mike says soothingly.

"My boy should get toys."

"You're right, Twin. We'll talk to Mr. King."

"I think my brother has said something good here." Donald is talking now.

I have no idea what is going to happen next. I always end up feeling this way in relation to the twins. Ronald and Donald faithfully attend Project Fatherhood and frequently disrupt the group, but their outbursts are catalyzing and often lead to greater insights among the men.

"What's going on? What happened, Twin?" I ask.

Donald launches into a story about De'Shawn, the sixteen-year-old nephew he is raising. Where the parents are, and how the boy came to Donald, has never been discussed. But Twin is immensely proud of De'Shawn. He is a basketball star at Jordan High, and Donald attends every game.

"He was late for dinner and he started mouthing off, telling me he didn't need to tell me when he was goin' out or coming in—y'know, he just was gonna come and go as he damn well please. He's yellin' at me and talkin' at me, and all the sudden he's up there, standin' next to me—"

The men in the room collectively suck in their breath at once. De'Shawn had invaded Donald's personal space. There are boundaries that men do not cross in relation to other men, part of a set of social behaviors surrounding respect. Signs of disrespect can be as threatening as throwing a gang sign, and just as indecipherable. Slowly, by talking to gang members, ex-convicts, and their families, I have learned part of the codebook of behaviors—what is allowed and not allowed. You cannot cross personal boundaries. Taking your shirt off signals that you are ready for a fight. You do not turn your back to anyone—it is a sign of the greatest disrespect. Donald's nephew had flouted the rules by walking into his personal space.

"I didn't do so good. I felt like I was back in prison," Donald explains. "I wanted to whup his ass, beat him up. Y'know, that's what happens."

The men were all nodding.

"He's seen how I was gettin' ready and he ran out of the house. I didn't run after him right away. I started thinkin' about what happened. Then, after he was gone a while and didn't come back, I went lookin' for him. I couldn't find him. He was gone for a week—he wasn't sleepin' in his bed or anything. But he would sneak in to eat. I knew he had been there. He ate some chicken I left for him in the fridge."

The men are all silent. A few of them hang their head. Many of these fathers struggle with how best to support their sons as the boys navigate the pathway to adulthood. Leelee speaks up.

"It's hard to wait on them. Did you know where he was?"

"I think he was stayin' with his girl. I don't know. I don't know where he went. But I started thinkin' about what I'd done. Maybe what I did was wrong. So I went to see a psych. I want to be a father, but I don't know what I'm doing. I don't just got him—I got other children. I got women claimin' their kids are mine. I don't know if they are really mine. But I want to be a father. I just don't know how."

The room is silent.

"I feel so honored that Twin has shared all of this with us . . . ," I begin.

"Yeah."

"Good job."

"It's important."

The men are supportive and yet hold back slightly.

" . . . And I think it's good that Twin went to see someone—a psychiatrist—to talk about it."

The room goes silent again. Then Jeff begins to speak.

"Twin's not the only one who felt this way. I got two daughters and then my son. He got in my space—just like Twin's boy—and I wanted to just throw him off the roof."

Everyone is yelling at the same time.

"I know how you feel—"

"I've done the same thing—"

"You can't talk like that. It's your boy—"

I am the only one not talking.

Big Mike puts both of his hands up.

"We gotta take turns. I know this is a problem, but we gotta take turns. But before any of us talk, Drjorjaleap is gonna give us some background."

I am reluctant to interrupt the fathering by committee that has taken hold in the meeting, but I bring up puberty.

"Some of this is biological—"

"Yeah. Hormones. They. Are. Horny," Debois offers up. My entire discussion has been summarized in three words. But I soldier on.

"The other part is psychological. It goes back as far as the Bible—the sons rise up and challenge their fathers. It's a part of becoming a man— you show your father you are a man. It's up to the father to understand. The most important thing for everyone to understand is that every boy going through puberty needs a father."

. . .

A week later the meeting picks up where it left off. Leelee speaks for the group.

"A lot of us have been talking about what you said last week."

"What did I say?"

"You said every boy going through puberty needs a father. And we're lookin' at some of our young men here in the community, and they don't have fathers. No one is there for them. They're just runnin' the streets. But it's crazy now—not like we used to know."

The men all nod in agreement.

I've heard this story many times talking with gang members, black and brown. Somewhere the street codes and systems of organization have broken down. Gangs used to be totally dependent on a sort of mentoring system—big homie would look out for little homie and bring him through the ranks. This no longer holds true. I repeatedly hear, "There's no respect for elders," and "These youngsters aren't listening to anyone." It's the street version of "Things weren't like this when I was young." The group is focused on taking action.

"We gotta do something for our youth. They are all our sons," Big Bob proclaims.

Chubb, a young father not that many years older than the youths he wants to reach, jumps into the conversation.

"I have learned things from my past, from my childhood. And now that I'm older I have that wisdom enough to go in and pass that message on to my children and not just to my children, who are girls. I wanna pass this on to the younger cats that's around my neighborhood."

I listen carefully. Big Mike takes the lead.

"Remember when we talked about Trayvon Martin? And I asked what we would do for our young men? Now we gotta ask—what do we, as Project Fatherhood, want to do?"

Almost immediately, Leelee speaks up.

"We were thinkin', maybe we could have some group sessions with the youth. Give them some food, tell them some stories about what we have been through, try to mentor them a little."

"Leelee is right," KSD chimes in. "We need to talk to our youth— really talk to them. No one was there talkin' to us, and look what happened—we all got into trouble. We all went to jail, some of us went to the pen. We need to make sure this doesn't happen again."

"We got too many graveyards, and the graveyards are full, they are too full of our babies." Ele is very emotional.

"I like the idea that we invite them, somewhere they will come—like the gym." Debois has always been an instinctive community organizer, and he demonstrates this again.

The fathers begin to plan excitedly.

"We can introduce ourselves—maybe a few of us can tell our stories," Andre suggests.

"We can also think of some activities to organize for them," Leelee adds.

"Go to the California African American Museum."

"Go to some college campuses."

"Some of them have never seen the ocean."

I am silently witnessing the men organizing for something beyond themselves, beyond their own families. The idea of the youth impact session has begun to take hold.

"Go get Johnking, Jorjaleap. Tell him we gotta talk to him."

I run down the hallway to get John, who is meeting with the women. The men quickly outline their idea and John begins smiling.

"This is a great idea—we can call them youth impact sessions."

"Yeah, but we gotta buy food and stuff like that," Leelee begins.

"I think there's money in the budget for that—" John begins.

The men look at each other warily—they have always suspected there was money they didn't know about.

"Let me find out when we can get the gym, what's the next date it's available. You guys are gonna need to publicize this in the community."

"We gotta make fliers. We can do that—can you print them, King?" Andre asks. I'm not surprised he is placing himself in charge of fliers. If there is an event planned for Watts even six months from now, Andre is out making a flier for it.

"Who's gonna take charge of passing out fliers—letting people know?" Big Mike asks.

"I will," Leelee starts. "With KSD and you—Ele. We'll talk to people about it."

"What do you think, Drjorjaleap?" Big Mike asks. The men all stare. "I think this is great."

But I can't put what I'm feeling into words. I am humbled. I am witnessing a miracle.

One year before Barack Obama announces his "My Brother's Keeper" initiative to address the challenges young men of color face, the men of Project Fatherhood are already on the job. And these men, who have never heard of social policy expert Lisbeth Schorr, are living proof of what she and others have described as "collective efficacy."

Hershel Swinger has been dead for almost two years now, and I am wondering how he would have responded to the fathers' work. They have gone far beyond his original design and yet held true to its premise—that within fatherhood there are solutions and strengths for a community.

NINETEEN

We Are All Family

There's always folk that say it's not gonna work for us to try to help one another. But the ones that's naysaying, they're the ones that's doin' nothin'. All they can do is point fingers, but if you ask them what you are doing, they have a mouth full of peanut butter.

—Elementary "Ele" Freeman

I arrive late because all of the streets are closed off with yellow tape and a fleet of black and whites. It's obvious there is what the radio always calls "police activity." When I get to Project Fatherhood, I ask the men what is happening a few blocks away, and Mike quickly answers, "Someone got killed by the sheriff."

"Some Bloods and Crips cliques are warring and someone got killed," Leelee adds. "Let's start the meeting." It's business as usual in Watts. Leelee is not interested in discussing the particulars of the gang warfare—he has moved beyond that.

"Should we talk about this?" I ask.

"No—we wanna talk about goin' to the UCLA football game." One of my students, Katie Thure, an unofficial and much-loved member of the family at Project Fatherhood, has obtained free tickets for the men and their children to attend one of the upcoming home games. The men are focused on this. I ignore all logic and try one more time.

"I just thought maybe we should talk a minute—"

Ronald turns his head my way and says, "You just don't get it, do you? This is the way life is here. White folk aren't like this."

I erupt.

"Are we doing this again?" I ask, my voice rising and becoming—in a word—shrill. I am getting excited, but Twin is calm.

"You just don't get it, because you're not from here. You're not ghetto," he laughs.

"Again—"

At this moment Ele cuts me off.

"Don't bite," he says to me, very quietly under his breath. I can barely hear him, but I know he is trying to protect me, and somehow the words register.

I stop talking. But I am hurt.

The room is silent for a moment. Then Donald begins singing "Georgia on My Mind," and I start laughing. I know that this is as close to an apology as I am going to get. We spend the rest of the session planning for the football game. What I finally understand is that the men need a break. I can drive away from the violence at the end of the meeting, but they cannot. In a way, they understand our differences at a much deeper level than I do. And they are constantly schooling me, helping me to know what it is like to live this life. Tonight they needed to think about something else, something positive—a day trip to a football game at the Rose Bowl in Pasadena.

Why would I deny them that?

The morning after Project Fatherhood, Luis calls me, crying. In his half English, half Spanish vocabulary, he tells me that a social worker from the Department of Children and Family Services has come and taken his three children away.

"I will do anything—my children—I need them, Miss Jorja."

I promise Luis that I will help, but when I call around to the DCFS worker I know and trust, it soon becomes apparent that there is extensive documentation of physical abuse. I call Luis and tell him what is happening. I will meet with the social worker and with him. I ask if he will come to Project Fatherhood. He is ashamed and asks me to explain what is going on, to tell the men he will return after the case is settled.

The next week I tell the men what is happening with Jorge. I am on shaky ground. The session on child abuse feels like it happened a hundred years ago, when in reality it has been less than two years. Still, I am not sure I want to reopen those wounds. But the men listen closely and several ask for Luis's phone number. "I'm gonna tell him he's gotta come back to group," Big Bob announces.

"We gotta reassure him," Sy says.

"And tell him we're here for him," Leelee adds.

There is no black-brown division. And the men don't change the subject. This is yet another sign of how far the group has come.

"We need to talk about this," Ele insists.

"I got something to say," Debois begins, with great difficulty.

"My family sent me down south one summer—to Tennessee—to stay with my cousins. My one cousin—I don't know—he stole some sweets from a neighbor's house. The neighbor came over and told my auntie. The next thing I know, she's beating my cousin with an electric cord. She kept beating him and beating him—all over the face, all over his head."

The room is silent. Debois drops his head and looks down at the floor.

"I remember someone ran in and told her—'Don't beat the boy that way! Don't do it to his head!' My cousin passed out and they took him to the hospital."

"What happened?" Sy asks.

There is a huge silence. The fathers are almost willing Debois to tell them something other than the ending that they dread.

"He died."

No one talks. I am not sure what to say. I wait.

Then it happens.

One of the fathers begins to speak.

"I used to believe in givin' my kids a whuppin'. But now I'm gonna do things different, I decided. It's a challenge, being partially crippled and having a baby. Because if he goes outside, then I gotta be outside too. I can't be in the house, 'cause he'll be way down the street. But, he's a good kid. He listens. He ain't like, 'No, no, no, no, no.' Sometimes he starts acting up, then he sees I'm serious 'cause I can hurt him with my mouth. I don't have to put my hands on him. I can hurt him by hollering and, you know, shouting. You know what I'm sayin? He'll pretty much know I'm serious."

I cannot believe this is Twin—Ronald James. Before I can stop myself, I check him.

"So you're saying, you don't believe it's really effective to hit Baby Boy as a form of discipline?"

"I'm never gonna hit Baby Boy," Ronald replies. "Watching him come up, that's something I never really got to do with other children. I was doin' other things and I couldn't pay as much attention to them. But to see this one from birth . . . you know what I'm sayin? Carrying him around, walking around with him in a stroller, riding around with him in the car. And seein' him go from an infant to talking, it's a brand new thing. It's old, but it's brand new. There's a whole lot of motivation in that—it gives you the mindset to really do something strong. In the past, instead of seeing your kid come up, you don't see him for months at a time. I had one son. I saw him till he was nine, but [then] I didn't see him till he was nineteen. I was locked up, things happened with his mama. We were apart. But Baby Boy—all I wanna do is watch him grow. I don't wanna hit him, but I wanna talk to him, help him grow."

The men are all nodding. I am trying not to cry.

"Twin," Mike interjects. "It sounds like you're tryin' to be a good father. And you *are* a good father."

"I'm just gonna act as a father should act. Do as a father should do. Be what a father should be. Take that role. Don't let someone else take that role for you. You know what I'm sayin'? Because it's no greater thing than being there for your kid and he's there for you. And I guess I am learnin' that here—from alla you. Even her." Twin points to me. "But, really, from the group. It's what we said—we gotta learn from each other."

Over the weekend, I check my voice mail and find a message from Leelee.

"Hello, Dr. Leap. I got a job. Congratulations to me. At Shields Family Services Compton office. Can you come see me at my work? I wanna talk to you about a project. If you can find some time in that busy schedule of yours, give me a call." As always, Leelee jokes, but I know he is just trying to hide his excitement. Without any assistance from Big

Mike or John King, or any of the work readiness sites, Leelee has found a job.

After tracking him down (an effort that involves multiple calls), I speak to Leelee on the phone. He repeatedly interrupts our conversation to explain to his girlfriend that I am not another woman who is after him. We make a plan to meet on Monday. When I arrive at the Shields office, I almost don't recognize him: he is wearing a polo shirt and Ray-Bans. Only his jeans save him from looking completely preppy.

"Come on in, Miss Leap. I wanna show you my work station."

He motions to a cubicle and sits down to demonstrate his computer skills, sending me an e-mail while I watch. He then marches me over to see his mailbox—with his name on it.

"I like this job. I feel like I could do something here and really help the young men."

"Good. What do you need from me?"

"You need to help me make a plan. Shields wants to start another Fatherhood group—but for younger fathers, outside of Jordan Downs."

"How do you want to do that?"

"Well, that's why I asked you here. You gotta help me with my bosses, so they can understand what Project Fatherhood does. We need to get organized. We need to offer the youth something. We need to show them that staying in school is the most important thing they can do. Come on."

With much fanfare, Leelee introduces me to everyone at the Shields office. The staff is welcoming, and the CEO and director of clinical services sit down to talk with us. But instead of discussing programming, they want to talk about Leelee.

"We think he has a wonderful future with our organization," the CEO tells me.

"We want him to go to community college," the director of clinical services adds. "He can be a credit to Watts and a role model for other young men."

Leelee is beaming throughout the discussion.

"I want to do all of this—and Dr. Leap—I believe you can help me."

He looks at the clock. "We gotta get going," he tells me. "We'll go to Jordan Downs together."

Leelee and I drive to the community center. He is bubbling with ideas for his new group. We arrive late and the meeting is in progress. Big Mike is on his cell phone—someone needs a tow. At the same time, Debois is reporting that one of his sons was in a fight and ran away. He wants to teach him to fight back.

"What?" I can't stop myself. "It's never a good idea for kids to fight— it's really violence. It might even be bullying."

"Oh, Jorja, you don't understand. You never had to go through this in your neighborhood." Sy again.

"I am so tired of hearing about my neighborhood—why do you think I am different?" I ask.

"You are so different," Ronald James tells me. "Your eyebrows always go together when we tell you something, like you're shocked." He imitates my facial expression as he says this. It's not a bad impression, which further angers me.

Even Debois tries to explain. "It's different in the projects." This is the mantra. It's different in the projects. It's different in Watts.

"You don't understand—you're never gonna understand. White people are different. If your daughter was in a fight, you'd probably take her to a counselor. But we don't do that." KSD is matter-of-fact. And he is right. I called a therapist when Shannon was failing calculus, even though I knew, at some level, that I was playing a part in a middle-class cartoon.

"Why aren't you saying anything?" Sy asks.

"I'm thinking," I say, struggling to be honest.

"Y'know, you're still shocked." Twin continues. "White people are all alike."

"First of all—why do you think we're all alike? Black people all get mad when white people say you're all alike, but now you're doing the same thing. I bet a rich black person is exactly like a rich white person."

"No, Miss Leap." Leelee smiles. "If a mother in your neighborhood had a sixteen-year-old daughter dating a twenty-year-old, you'd just call the police. Not here."

At this point we are all screaming at each other, but I am amused, not threatened the way I was during the discussion of Christopher Dorner. Somehow this feels different.

The conversation takes a turn when Luis asks to speak. I know he has been attending parenting classes. His social worker has called me and praised him for being cooperative.

He begins slowly.

"You know I was reported to DCFS. And now I am going to counseling. I am being very careful about how I treat my children. But today, my son has a bruise on his arm because a Shields worker grabbed him and squeezed his arm. I can't take it. I am not going to come back to Project Fatherhood. Today is my last day."

The room erupts.

"Your place is . . . *aquí*," Bob tells him. No one wants him to leave.

A few weeks ago, Aaron had pulled me aside to tell me he believes there is apartheid in Jordan Downs. But there is no evidence of it here.

The men focus on Luis.

"We want you here."

"Your place is with us!"

"Will you come back? Just next week—try next week."

Luis looks as if he is going to cry.

"I am afraid. Not you, but there are black men in Jordan Downs who have threatened me. I have to protect my children."

"We've got a problem in getting along—blacks and browns—" Big Mike has returned.

Sy quickly interrupts him. "But it used to be so much worse."

"We have to remember we are together—black and brown—we all want what's best for our children," Big Mike intones.

Leelee points to me.

"We are forgetting someone here—Miss Leap. We are all colors—black, brown, white—all together. And we got some of our black boys laying down with our brown girls. You wanna talk about how there's gonna be peace and an end to violence. This is how. Look at what we're doin' in Project Fatherhood. We're all comin' together."

"We are brothers," Big Mike agrees.

"I will stay," Luis says quietly. "I don't want to leave."

Without missing a beat, Donald shrieks, "We are your family!"

"You are part of our family," Big Mike adds.

The men stand up and begin coming over to Luis one by one. Each shakes his hand, or gives him a fist bump, or hugs him. Once all the men have comforted Luis, they return to their seats.

"We need to have more money on our gift cards," Tiny starts. Mercifully, Ben interrupts him.

"I wanna talk."

"Go ahead, Ben Henry," Big Mike encourages.

"I told my wife about my child—my son, who it turns out is autistic."

It has been months since Ben divulged that he had kept the child's existence from his wife. The group had urged him to come clean but had never followed up to see if he took their advice. There was an unspoken agreement that Ben would report back when he was ready. Evidently the moment had arrived.

"My wife—she kicked me out of the house, and I went over to my brother's place—"

At this point Sy nods in acknowledgment.

"But my wife called me the next day, and she said, 'We gotta take care of this boy.'"

"You got a good one, Ben Henry," Pirate decrees.

"Yeah, but now my baby mama, my son's mother—she doesn't want me to see him."

"Well, you got to get you some legal representation. You have rights as a father." Leelee is very clear.

"Yeah, you send him to that lawyer, Elie Miller. Even if she didn't help me, she was a nice lady," Donald offers. I make a mental note to tell Elie that Twin has just offered up a rave review.

"Your baby is the most precious thing in the world. You gotta take care of your son," Debois reinforces.

The men all offer their suggestions to Ben, vowing they will support him. At the end of the session, Luis walks over to Ben and shakes his hand. "I am sorry for your troubles," he adds.

One week later, Big Mike and I are standing outside of the Jordan Downs community center watching two LAPD officers patrolling the area in their car talking to a pair of homies on bikes. The scene is filling me with dread. I am trying to talk, but Mike is half listening and half watching what is going on in the street. He is also looking beyond the police and the homies, trying to gauge what is going on in the cut between the housing units. As he watches the landscape, I tell him we need to make a plan.

Two days before, a black, teenaged gang member on a bicycle killed a fourteen-month-old Latino baby on the front porch of a house on Grape Street. The bullet was meant for the baby's father, who was wearing a purple shirt that read "I own a Honda, be nice to me" while he held the child in his arms. A man was wearing the wrong color, someone was a bad shot, and a baby was dead. The cops are on red alert, the community is filled with tension, and there is talk of retaliation. Andre joins us and we walk out to the picnic tables, trying to figure out what to do.

"This isn't good," I begin.

Big Mike waves me off.

"Don't you trust the group?" he asks.

"I don't know." I am not looking for reassurance. This is my honest assessment. I can never tell which direction things will go.

"You gotta trust the group, young lady," Andre reassures me. It doesn't work. If Watts erupts, it won't be pretty. It's been such a tranquil spring. But this shooting and the death of the baby threaten to blow apart the fragile peace that has emerged.

Two hours later, the group takes up the issue of the baby and the shooting.

"We gotta do something."

"We can't just let this go."

"That was a Latino baby, killed by a black man—this is going to make things worse. We got to do something to stop the hatred between our two cultures, between our two groups."

All of the men in the group are talking at once. But what is clear is *they want to do something.*

"We need to have a peace march," Debois suggests. The men immediately respond.

"We can walk from Jordan Downs to the parents' house."

"We can buy them flowers."

"We can buy them some toys for their other children."

"And some stuffed animals with the flowers—to remember the little boy."

"We need to march together—get more browns and blacks."

"Why do we gotta march together?"

"Shut up, Twin."

"Okay. All right."

"When do you want to do this?"

The men agree they will march together in two days. KSD and Andre are already planning to recruit members of the community. Big Mike says he will call ahead of time, to let the family know and ask them if they are comfortable with having the community hold a brief vigil in front of their house. John King asks if the men want to let the media know what they are planning.

His suggestion is met with a resounding *no*. The entire group is adamant that they do not want any attention. The peace march is meant to comfort the family, not provide a photo opportunity.

Two days later, a huge swell of people is waiting in front of the community center. It is as if all of Jordan Downs has come together on this quiet afternoon to pay their respects. Big Mike and Andre organize the line of people, and they move across the grass field, past the picnic benches, out to Grape Street. This file of sadness moves and turns left on Hickory Street, where the family lives. They halt in front of the house that already has a group of neighbors, black and brown, standing on the front porch. Big Mike approaches the group, holding a small bunch of white flowers.

"We just wanted to come here, on behalf of the Jordan Downs community and Project Fatherhood, to express our sadness and love for your family," he says solemnly.

"And we would like to pray for you," Andre adds.

Each of the fathers steps forward to the porch and leaves a bunch of flowers or a small stuffed animal. Several community members tie balloons to the chain-link fence in front of the house. The father momentarily steps out on the front porch and says, "Thank you, thank you, thank you"—over and over again in heavily accented English.

What he sees in front of him is the community of Watts, black and brown, together, feeling the depth of this loss.

TWENTY

Letter from Scotland

*We all gotta talk about death. But then we gotta
end up talkin' about something uplifting.*
                                        —Andre Christian

Near the end of the last session of Project Fatherhood, before we take
two weeks off, the men are talking about buying life insurance in their
children's names.

"I don't understand," I say, confused. "You buy the insurance in the
name of your son or daughter so if they die, you are the beneficiary?"

Sy starts, "You don't understand 'cause you're not from the ghetto."

"I know, I know," I tell him. "I'm having my T-shirt printed. You'll
just point to where it says 'I AM NOT FROM THE GHETTO,' and it
will save you a lot of time."

Sy starts laughing.

"Well, you do understand what it's like not to have money," he admits. "You're not ghetto, but you're not rich either."

"Yeah, you are right." I am more than ready to accept progress in
Sy's attitude towards me.

The men then launch into a discussion about how they want to care
for their children *even after they die.* I learn that it is a common practice
for families to buy term life insurance on their children. I want to hear
more about this, but the conversation stops when a man looks through
the window into the conference room.

Andre immediately orders, "Everyone stop talking," and the men
comply.

I ask Mike what is going on, and he whispers, "That's Big Dave. He
lost two kids."

Mike waves him in, but Big Dave shakes his head. I go outside to talk with him briefly and invite him to join the group. He thanks me but apologizes, explaining, "I'm not ready. I heard about these meetings, but I'm not ready yet. I'll come back another time."

When I return to the room, the men are trying to talk about death. Most of the fathers are uncomfortable with the subject, and some of them openly admit it.

"I don't want to talk about it. I've seen too much death," Debois offers.

"We all know about it, we live with it," KSD adds.

"But we gotta use that knowledge to do something." Leelee is like the Energizer Bunny. "We gotta focus on the youth impact sessions."

"We gotta focus on life."

"We gotta make sure no more babies die. I don't wanna be involved in another peace march," Ele reinforces.

The men clasp their hands together and pray. This ritual has evolved at the end of each session. Mike volunteers different men each week. Tonight he picks Dwight, one of the fathers who rarely speaks up but faithfully attends the weekly meetings.

"Father God," begins Dwight, "let us pray for all the children in Jordan Downs. We want to make certain that no one dies too young, that we all live to an old age, to enjoy our lives, to love our children and our grandchildren. We ask this in your name, Father God. Amen."

As the group breaks up, Ronald motions that he wants to talk with me. I am worried that something is wrong with his son, but he quickly hands me a flier.

"I'm having a party," he explains, "and I want you to come."

"Okay." I stare at the piece of the paper in shock.

"I expect you to be there." I laugh, and he says, "I mean it."

I hug him, although he seems slightly reluctant to have contact with me. After he leaves, Andre and Ele tell me I cannot go to the party.

"Boundaries," Ele says.

"Young lady, you cannot go that party. Just take my word for it," Andre adds.

"Calm down," I tell Andre. "I really want to go to the party, but I have to pack."

"Why?"

"I leave tomorrow night for Scotland."

"That's right, ya told me. I am just going to miss you."

"Me too. I'll bring you a kilt."

"No way," Andre laughs.

The trip is not a vacation but a cross between a speaking tour and fact-finding mission. Mark and I are traveling with Father Greg Boyle and James Horton, the man who walked out of death row when his case was overturned. Our hectic schedule includes speeches in Glasgow, Edinburgh, and Kilmarnock, interspersed with visits to government programs and, finally, to a Scottish prison.

During the trip, the sea of pale faces at the prison astonished me: devoid of black and brown visages, the sterile building felt more like a community college in some rural suburb than a penal institution. At most, it could have been a halfway house for men gone astray, men without homes. But this was in reality a maximum-security facility, with a population that included murderers, rapists, and high-level drug dealers—and not one black or brown man.

The fathers always insisted that the composition of the prison population was deliberate. It was all part of the white conspiracy to keep the black man down. Most of the time I had to agree.

The day after we land in Glasgow, a key provision of the landmark US Voting Rights Act is struck down, and I find myself wondering what the fathers in the group back in California would say. The decision was racist and disturbing, but I wondered if the men would even know—or care. They weren't particularly interested in politics or mainstream activism. Two months earlier, I had brought up the fiftieth anniversary of Martin Luther King's "Letter from Birmingham Jail." I had worshipped the document from the moment I read it. King's letter was a manifesto for nonviolence and a brilliant piece of writing; it is still regarded as a seminal text of the civil rights movement in America. King offered a stirring rationale for nonviolent resistance to racism, upholding people's moral responsibility to rebel against and break unjust laws. I need to talk about the letter, and I am certain the group will also want to discuss it at length.

I get as far as "Birmingham" when they started in.

"Why do you wanna talk about that?"

"It's bullshit."

"Forget him, he's not really black. He's white, always siding with the white man."

"All you white people wanna talk about that letter when some of our people still can't read."

"We don't wanna talk about King—let's talk about our real problems."

There is one holdout amid the fusillade of anger—Andre Christian is the one father who actually wants to talk about Martin Luther King. A month earlier, he had been on an airplane for the first time in his life. He took a jet to Montgomery, Alabama, for a gang conference, where he led a training session about street intervention. He texted me photos of himself standing on the balcony in Memphis, Tennessee, where MLK had fallen.

"You can't imagine that place," he told me. "There's something about it, something you can feel. It's a holy place. You wonder what King would have done had he lived. Someone was afraid of him living."

I knew what was coming. Even Andre, the king of psychological insight, is prey to conspiracy theory. This belief is all too common among many of the men of color I have known. No matter how far from the street they travel some harken back to the idea that they are not in control. So many insist that there is something organized and sinister "out there"—powerful outside forces that control their destinies.

Although I don't believe there is any sort of "secret council," as some of the men insist, the notion is not far from reality. I have plenty of conspiracy theories of my own, related to the Koch brothers and the Republican Party. Certainly, when one considers the obstacles the fathers face in terms of education, jobs—even housing—it feels like a conspiracy, as if white America wants to ensure they will never get ahead. The fathers struggle with this on a daily basis. They feel out of control but are working valiantly to exercise some sort of power over their own lives. And beyond this they are determined to help their children, protect Jordan Downs, and rebuild the community. Over and over they tell me: "We tried to destroy this community once. Now we gotta heal it."

Healing is very much on my mind when I return from Scotland. The George Zimmerman trial has started. Instead of focusing on community concerns, the group's discussion has a thread of anti-white sentiment that is strong—and unpredictable.

"Y'know, it's all a plot," Donald told me. "It's a big conspiracy. Your white boys want us all locked up. I don't need that stupid book about Jim Crow. I *lived* it."

The men in the group all hold white society responsible for the time they spent in prison. They constantly described how prison was "*all* black and brown" or "niggas and more niggas—black niggas and brown niggas."

"Dr. Leap, how come there are no white folk in prison?"

"Because the system is racist."

The men all stop mid-sentence. I am not using a tactic; I believe this with all my heart. I knew the statistics about racial disparities in sentencing. In addition, I had been working on two death penalty cases and was taken aback at the latest death penalty statistics from Amnesty International: In the United States, from 1977 onward, in 77 percent of all executions the murder victim was white—even though African Americans comprise half of all homicide victims. In the same time period, 35 percent of the individuals executed were African American.

Death Penalty Focus put it baldly: "The race of the victim and the race of the defendant in capital cases are major factors in determining who is sentenced to die in this country."

"This is why we gotta save our young men," Leelee affirms.

"We can't let the white man keep putting us down."

"No we can't."

"Besides, we have the oldest history and the greatest leaders." Andre Christian is on a roll here. "We need to understand that we had scholars and leaders in ancient times, even before ancient Greece. No offense, Dr. Leap."

"No offense, Andre. We all know that Africa is the site where the oldest skeleton on the earth has been discovered. All of the human race probably began in Africa."

The men regard me curiously.

"If we all began there, how come some of us are whiter and different shades?" Debois asks.

I am floundering at this point, and Big Mike steps in.

"We all know that the Garden of Eden was in Africa. And that fits exactly with what Jorjaleap is saying. We are all God's children, and we started in Africa."

I flash him a grateful smile. Big Mike has just returned from vacation with Sauna and Booboo, and I have felt his absence. Ele and I tried to run the group without him, but the men were disorderly and wouldn't stick to the topic. When the session was over, I was dripping wet with sweat. At home I told Mark it had been a disaster.

"I don't know why," I whined.

Mark started laughing.

"Big Mike has gravitas. He keeps the men in line," Mark observed. "They admire him and want to be like him—he is sort of a father figure or a big brother. You're talented, honey, but you can't do that."

I knew Mark was telling the truth. And it was good to be reminded of my limitations in the group. I loved the men, they drove me crazy—but I was not their leader. I would leave that to Big Mike. He was living proof of everything Project Fatherhood was teaching me: that the real solution to the problems of Watts—the violence, the family dysfunction, the inadequate education—was going to come from the community. Leadership and strength could not be imported. Here was where lessons of the past and pride in black history could ultimately have the most meaningful impact: helping these men and others grow from the fathers of the community into the leaders of the community.

TWENTY-ONE

Photo Finish

Most of the time, you come in here and they put you on
that grill. But instead of you burning up, you gonna come
to yourself. 'Cause a lot of times, I used to come in here
and have attitude about something that went on and
don't wanna talk about it, but at the end of the day I talk
about it and get it off my chest, so I feel better. Come in
with attitude, leave out with gratitude, gratification that
some of the brothers will reach out to you and tell you
and talk to you, you know. That's basically it.

—Ronald "Twin" James

Two weeks later, an hour before the meeting, Matt comes by to tell me he has enrolled in community college and that his girlfriend has graduated high school. I begin to breathe more easily.

"I feel like I am really on my way, and I have some great news."

"I am so happy! What's going on?" I am imagining that he has a job, a scholarship, or an internship for the summer. While I travel around fantasyland, Matt hands me a small piece of gray paper folded in half. I don't need to unfold it. I know it is a sonogram.

"I want you to have this. The baby is coming, and it will be born in about five months. Jasmine is okay—she's not gonna have a miscarriage." Matt's eyes are shining. I hug him.

"I'm so happy for you," I add. This is not the time to talk about missed opportunities and financial support and where the new parents are going to live and how the fuck is a high school graduate going to support his family and go to college. None of that matters. Matt desperately wants this baby, and he is overjoyed.

"And the doctor says if you look at the sonogram you can see there's a—" He hesitates here.

"A penis," I finish for him. "It's a boy. That's so great—I know you want a son. And now you really do have to come to Project Fatherhood—it's important for you."

"Ah, Jorja." Matt laughs. "Always recruiting."

"You know the men want you there. You know they love you. And now you're gonna have a son." I look at Matt carefully. "Your father would have been proud."

"I think so." He smiles and I pass the sonogram back to him.

"No, keep it," he says. "I want you to have it. You're the auntie."

He starts to walk out of the community center but then turns around.

"Y'know, I've got my problems with the group—well, you know why—but that doesn't mean it shouldn't be here. I really think it should. It does a lotta good for Jordan Downs and for the folks around here. You gotta keep it going."

"Thanks, Matt. I will."

Easier said than done.

I am worried about Matt, but this is not something I want to share with the group as they gather around the table. They are all concerned about bigger problems.

There is tension in the air tonight. No one is talking about it, but everyone can feel it. Many of the younger fathers are missing. There has been a spike in violence in Watts, and Jordan Downs is particularly unsettled. There have been four murders in Watts over the past week and it's clear that something has got to be done.

The men are restless. Big Mike tries to introduce the topic of good nutrition and health habits, but several fathers are disruptive. I have arrived late and the group discussion was already under way. My not being on time tilts things further.

"You're late."

"Yeah, you're always late. You got important things at UCLA?"

"You been on one of your trips? When you gonna take me on one of your trips?"

"I wanna lecture to your class."

"You gonna get us some money?"

There. Finally, something I can sink my teeth into.

"I met with Guillermo this morning—" I begin, and Donald jumps down my throat.

"So you've been in City Hall. *That's* why you're late—"

"I said, this *morning—*"

Both of the twins can turn into such bullies that I've learned I can't do anything but shut up or bully them back. Both responses have to be used strategically. Right now I just want Twin to stop.

"I was with Guillermo this morning. We are all working on getting some money for Project Fatherhood and for Watts."

"Well, we need it."

"There's gonna be trouble here if they don't start helpin' out."

"How come they help out in other places but they never help out in Watts?"

I am listening to the latest version of the culture of martyrdom that exists in Watts. *Watts is different.* This is rapidly becoming my favorite catch phrase, because it includes everything—the severe poverty, the lack of opportunity, the rumors, the anger, the checking, the paranoia—all the side effects of chronic poverty and deprivation.

Project Fatherhood is a microcosm of Watts. Even after being together for three years, the men remain suspicious, particularly about funding matters and police issues. Some were less vitriolic and more thoughtful, including Debois, who—when he wasn't working or tending to his large family—served as a de facto community organizer.

Debois focuses his normally relaxed visage on me with laser-like intensity.

"Jorjaleap, I want to know why no one is telling us if all the cameras they got around here watching us got any pictures of who got shot this weekend and who did the shooting? Do you know someone who could tell us?"

These were tricky questions, on many levels.

A year earlier, the LAPD, with the assistance of the Advancement Project—a civil rights organization—had installed cameras throughout the Jordan Downs development to track crime. Despite the high rate of violence in the projects, the move was controversial. Americans have a particular aversion to security cameras. The idea has not been embraced as it has been in Britain. Still, the cameras were installed, the denizens of Watts complained, and life went on.

Now Debois is asking legitimate questions.

Over the weekend, one of the four fatal shootings occurred right in the middle of Grape Street. Aside from providing the name for one of the most notorious gangs in Los Angeles, Grape Street was infamous for other reasons. Its designation as an outer perimeter of gang territory had warranted the positioning of cameras up and down the street. Now Debois rightfully wanted to know what the cameras had picked up during the shooting. There was general concern throughout the community regarding who had done what and who knew about it. But there was also more specific uneasiness that anyone could use such knowledge to snitch to the LAPD *or* to inform active gang members about what was going on. And I was concerned about my own credibility. I knew plenty of people who could answer the questions Debois was asking, but I was not anxious to remind the men of my official ties. In the end, the need for information won out over my need for approval, so I texted Mark. I also texted Reggie Zachery, the director of the Watts Regional Strategy at the mayor's office.

I worked with Reggie, argued with Reggie, and loved Reggie as we continuously tried to structure and supervise the mayor's plan for Watts. I didn't know if he would have any information about the cameras, but he had a good communications system all his own, and there were folks at the LAPD he could call. I wasn't sure who would respond first— Reggie or my husband.

Mark texted me right away.

"If there are cameras and they're activated, the LAPD and HACLA will know about them."

This was progress of a sort. I was still waiting on Reggie, but I started yelling over the din of the group, "Where's John King? We gotta ask him."

"I know, I know. He texted and said he's coming," Big Mike answered.

"Mark says if the cameras are activated, the LAPD and HACLA have the films and they will know what happened."

No sooner are the words out of my mouth than Reggie texts me. "Come outside. I am in front."

All of the men are screaming.

"If the LAPD has the information from the camera, why aren't they doing anything?"

"Does King know?"

"Does Captain T know?"

"They know and they don't care—just crazy niggas killing each other."

I stand up and move for the door, but no one is paying attention.

Except Leelee.

"Miss Leap, now where are you runnin'?"

Leelee has always possessed a wickedly accurate sixth sense about what I am doing. I would be an idiot to avoid the issue. I quickly decide that if a stampede of fathers wants to join me, Reggie will have to deal with it.

"Reggie is out in front, and I am gonna ask him about the cameras."

"And can you ask him if I can get a job with Summer Night Lights?" It's Donald, always trying to make the most of an opportunity.

The men start laughing. I know a break when I see one and walk out the door.

Reggie is standing right next to his city-issued Prius, shaking his head.

"The cameras weren't pointed in the right direction," he begins.

"I don't wanna tell them that."

"I don't think you should."

"I think this is a job for Mr. John King."

I duck back into the room and tell a half lie.

"Reggie says to ask John King."

On cue John King enters the room. I whisper to Big Mike that he needs to present the concerns before the meeting deteriorates into a scream fest.

"Mr. King—"

"Yes."

"All of us have been talking, especially about the violence that has been happening here and the shooting on Grape Street."

"I know. This is serious." John matches Mike in severity of tone.

"Well, what all of us at Project Fatherhood wanted to know is what happened with the cameras? We have them posted everywhere. What did they show?"

There is a moment of silence.

"The cameras were not working."

"*What*?!"

"What are you talkin' about?"

"Stupid cameras. They be working if you need to catch someone jaywalking but not if someone is shooting."

"Why do they even have them?"

I've got to hand it to John King: he absorbs all the flack until the men run out of energy. Then he continues:

"We are calling the company that runs the cameras to see what happened—to see why there is nothing recorded from the weekend. This is not the way things should be. We want to make sure nothing happens in Watts. And that's the other thing I wanted to talk with the group about."

The men are listening.

"All of us at the Housing Authority are working very hard with the mayor's office to try and get some funding so we can go on—so Project Fatherhood can continue, so Safe Passages can continue, so we can have services in the community."

In an instant, the men have forgotten about the cameras. They are hanging on Mrjohnking's words.

"Mr. King," Big Mike begins, "when will you have word on this?"

"I will let you know as soon as I know."

"Can I get a job with Summer Night Lights?"

Donald again. He is nothing if not persistent.

"We'll see, Twin, we'll see."

In a matter of days a deal is struck. In a special arrangement between the mayor's office and the ever-embattled HACLA, for the second time in two years housing funds will be "loaned" to the city to set up a gang intervention program in Watts.

A week later I am sitting in Guillermo's office while he outlines a three-pronged strategy—the Summer Night Lights program, Project Fatherhood, and ongoing gang intervention—that will serve as part of

Mayor Antonio Villaraigosa's crime prevention and anti-gang effort in Watts. The mayor wants to keep the crime figures low—he is eyeing his next office, and there are rumors he will run for governor of California.

Here we go again, I think, but the men are all happy. Project Fatherhood will be funded for another year. I keep my mouth shut and nod. Whatever is going on in City Hall politics— keeping this group going is what truly matters.

TWENTY-TWO

We Are Your Daddies

We've got to watch out for our youngsters. I think about that.
You're not doing this just for the baby. You're doin' it for yourself
too. We've got these young kids that think it's what you do by the age
of twenty-five, not living past that. To want to live past that and be
able to raise your kids past that—it's a challenge for a lot of them.

—Debois Sims

The following week, concerns about the cameras and the violence are temporarily suspended. Something much more important is on the agenda: the men have decided to devote tonight's session to planning for the youth impact session.

But there is an outburst during check-in. The men are up in arms about developments at the alma mater of most of the group, David Starr Jordan High School. Founded in 1923, it is one of the few public high schools in the United States to have produced three Olympic gold medalists, including one woman, Florence Joyner Griffith. Flo-Jo retains the world record in the 100-meter and 200-meter races. In addition to the Olympic athletes, the school's alumni include African American luminaries such as jazz musician Charles Mingus and NFL star James Washington. To this day, alumni pride in Jordan High School flourishes. Most of the fathers retain a kind of advisory role in relation to the coaches, and they attend games as an unofficial booster group, harking back to their glory days as student athletes.

However, tonight everyone is agitated about one of the assistant football coaches. The men insist he needs to be fired.

"I like Coach. He's great. But it's this other guy—Evans—he's the defensive line coach. He uses the *n*-word alla the time. He expresses *his* anger, but he won't let the boys cuss or even express their anger." Craig McGruder is talking. His son, Victor, is a star athlete at Jordan. I am trying to figure out how the son has integrated his own fatherhood into his plans to be a college athlete and maybe go on to be a professional. But then I remember Jim Foley—my high school classmate who got his girlfriend, Lupe, pregnant in eleventh grade. His devout Catholic family took her into the household and helped her with the infant. Jim went on to become a high school sports hero. Victor's family supports him. His mother helps care for the baby while both he and his girlfriend continue to attend school.

Craig McGruder is Victor's greatest fan, and he is particularly upset, recounting how Evans had wanted to suspend a player for using profanity. "The kid said he felt fucked-up when Jordan lost the game to Centennial. When the administrators told Evans he better have a better reason for the suspension than using the *f*-word, Evans accused the kid of breaking into his car."

I am incredulous.

"But Evans had no proof," I begin.

The men are all nodding.

"Yeah, that's what happened," McGruder says.

"He can't go accusing a kid of that with no proof. This is America—you are innocent until proven guilty."

The words are hanging out of my mouth like a cartoon caption, and I already cannot believe what I have said. The men all burst into laughter.

"Missjorjaleap—" Leelee is yelping, he is laughing so hard. "Haven't we taught you anything?"

"Where do you think you are?"

"Really, gentlemen, I think we are failures if Dr. Leap can ask that question." Andre is laughing the hardest.

The men are all teasing me, but I am horrified. White privilege rears its head and I feel it in a way I have never felt it in my life. The men's talk of white conspiracy and of how the Man is against them has always made me angry, defensive. But right now I am not threatened, I am not defensive, and the men are not angry. They are teasing in an affectionate way. But they are telling the truth, and I start to shake.

What I take as my everyday reality, these men will never trust. I am near tears but cannot cry. I am struck by my ignorance and feel ashamed. I am grateful for their laughter. I cannot talk.

Thankfully, Craig McGruder continues.

"You know, the vice principal wants to come to our impact sessions as soon as we get them started with the young men. We should tell them our first session is coming up."

"I don't know if we should invite him," I say.

"Of course we should invite him—if we get him on board, he can send us the youngsters who need the most help."

"Yeah, but he's at high school. We need youngsters from middle school."

"We can have the vice principal come. Maybe he can reinforce what we want to do."

"We need to plan *what* we are going to do at the impact session."

The men organize quickly, drawing up an agenda for the impact session. They assign tasks swiftly, and there is little argument and no back talk. Everyone is united in their desire for the session to flow smoothly and effectively. John King reassures the group that food will be provided to all of the youth. KSD, Debois, and Andre take charge of recruiting the youth, intent on insuring a good turnout. The men are excited and animated in their efforts. They agree that next week they will fine-tune their plans for the session.

A week later, the fathers do not bother with check-ins. They want to focus on continuing to prepare for the first youth impact session, scheduled for the following week. For many of them, this effort was linked to their own redemption.

"I used to be wild," Andre once confessed when we were sitting alone outside of the community center. "I think about what I did on these streets and I am ashamed. So are most of the men in our group. We all want to give something back. And we want to help the youth." Andre eventually shared these thoughts during the group session, as did many of the other fathers.

Sy was one of the most vocal. In his role as one of the Fatherhood elders, Sy repeatedly spoke about all of the men's responsibility towards

youths "coming up." His words resonated throughout the group, form-
ing a theme I began to hear repeatedly. It wasn't enough that the men
wanted to help their own children—they wanted to help the children of
the community. They gave their help in the form of advice. They also
gave whatever money they might have in their pockets. Although most
of the men of Project Fatherhood were poor, jobless, and living off of
entitlements or disability, they would reach out to small children in the
neighborhood, talk to them, and give them dollar bills "for ice cream" or
"for pencils." Sy tried to explain this to me as we walked around Jordan
Downs.

"I recognize other children that's not my children—I try to help
them out. When I see a little cat doing something he shouldn't be doing,
I pull him to the side and have some words with him, see where he really
coming from, and little cats get help with a few dollars. I help him out,
and let him know the world that I been living in is not the world they
wanna live in, because things are much tougher now."

"What do you mean?"

"It was easier then. I know it sounds crazy, but it was. If you did the
same things I did—if you do it now, I might not see you again. So you really need to think about it, weigh it out, use your brain. I try to let them
know, 'Don't be afraid to talk about the situation you are in and how you
feel about certain things and issues.' I am trying to communicate with
all youth. I am learning to communicate better with the Latino people,
people of other races, period."

After this exchange, I ask Sy to share some of his thoughts with the
men as the group prepares for the youth impact session. He is much
more succinct in front of them.

"We gotta make sure these youngsters don't make the same stupid
mistakes we did."

Ben picks up from there.

"It passes from one generation to the next. We had our time. I had
my time. The cats younger than me—now they're doing their thing. I
don't knock them. But I try to tell them, there's always consequences,
repercussions. You know if you robbing a bank, do the math. See how
much prison time it carries. You selling crack, talk to one of your homies
and see how long you'll be locked up."

"All right," Big Mike rubs his hands together. "What are we going to offer these youngsters?"

Ele takes control of the discussion. He poses a critical question.

"We gotta think of how we can get our kids to buy into the educational system, because coming up in this environment, you don't see kids doing that. All they understand is instant gratification. They want it now—right now. Maybe if we lived in a community where a doctor lived next door, or the lawyer lived across the street, and the judge lives up the street, maybe one of our sons, maybe he could see and feel that's what you need to do—go get an education. But when next door's the homie, Big Killa, and you know, Big John and Mad Dog, and Hustlin' Willie, and dope fiend Denny. So it plays on your psyche and it blurs your vision, weakens your senses. That's why the graveyard is overcrowded with our people. Prison is overcrowded with our people. Now, we gotta use these impact sessions to stop this happening into the next generation. We don't have those role models up the street. So in a way, we gotta be the role models."

"Well, first we gotta make sure the kids will get here," Leelee offers. "So me and KSD will organize a group of you to walk around Jordan Downs with fliers, put 'em up where people will see them, announce what is going on. Then we'll go down to Markham Middle School and invite the cats there. We want the youngsters before they get into anything too deep. Then we gotta talk to their mamas and let them know what is going on, ask if it is okay for their boys to come to this."

The men discuss how they plan to tell young men that if they attend the impact session they will have a good dinner and earn credit for gift cards, and that they will talk with the men of Project Fatherhood. Everyone is full of ideas and anticipation. And of course, they fight about what the impact sessions will accomplish.

"What about inviting the LAPD?" Andre begins.

"No, not here, not with our youngsters. It's stupid," Ronald objects. The men all nod their heads.

"I like Captain T. I do," Big Mike offers. "But I think we gotta settle in with the youth first, build our relationships."

"I think he is okay, but you don't have the police there the first day. These boys—they're afraid of being called snitches," Leelee adds.

But Andre urges them to reconsider.

"Y'know," he begins, "this Community Safety Partnership—they're doing lots of things. They're coaching Pop Warner, they're bringin' in tutors, they're helping start a Girl Scout troop. They've got funding. We could partner with them."

An assistant coach and teacher from Jordan High School, Billy Wilson, is attending the meeting, and he is adamant in his opposition to having police at the youth session. I have always enjoyed the teachers and coaches who attended Project Fatherhood sessions, but I have reservations about this particular coach. He feels like a walking, talking illustration of the saying "A little knowledge is a dangerous thing." His response to Andre does nothing to alter my opinion.

"I don't know how you can talk about working with them. It's not a good idea—not now, not ever. The LAPD is an occupying army. We've got to understand the truth, and that's all they are. And you know when they talk to our youth, our young people, they're gonna use those words *urban terrorist.*"

"What are you talkin' about, coach?" Andre asks. "They don't talk that way. No one talks that way."

"Yes they do. They *all* talk that way."

"Let the coach talk, Andre," Donald insists. The coach is emboldened, and continues.

"They see our young men as terrorists, and they see this as war. The order has come from the top."

I am astonished. Usually it's the Black Muslims spewing this kind of nonsense, and most of the men dismiss them, but the coach has more credibility. On top of that, he is offering up something new: a jaundiced view of LAPD Chief of Police Charlie Beck, who is beloved in the South Los Angeles community. The men stay silent, except Andre, who bravely disputes the coach's claim.

"I don't believe Charlie Beck would give that order." Andre is on familiar terms with the chief and tells the men that Beck cares about South Los Angeles.

I am inclined to agree. While Charlie Beck is second-generation LAPD, over time he has shown himself to be a flexible and innovative thinker. He was a captain in Southeast Division and deputy chief in charge of South Bureau, building a positive and enduring relationship with the South Los Angeles community.

None of this matters. The fathers decide to join in on an anti-LAPD rant.

"I think Captain T is a cracker," Ele says solemnly. "What is he anyway?"

"What do you mean, what is he?" Andre challenges.

"Is he Italian, y'know? What is he?"

"He's Greek," I offer.

"He's just a cracker. They're all crackers—Greeks, Italians, I don't care." Ele is strictly hood right now.

"Well, I don't care what he is—we don't need the cops in the mix with our young men," the coach continues. But Big Mike is upset.

"Ele, don't use that word *cracker*."

"Oh come on—"

"It's disrespectful. It's all that Nation stuff. They're the ones who encourage black folk to call white people crackers."

I feel like I am still picking up pieces of the secret code. We're back to the Nation of Islam, and I am feeling as conflicted as ever. As much as members of the Nation talk about the strengths of black men and the power of the black community, their arguments are invariably undergirded with hatred of white people, often tipping over into the dream of developing a separate black state. It's understandable, but it's ineffective—mainly because it preaches division rather than real-world solutions. But I'm not sure what to say. I am at a loss.

"Let it go," I tell Mike, but he scowls at me, and I know he is deaf to my entreaties.

There is a complicated strategy with the Nation. Members *still* make sporadic appearances at Project Fatherhood, where they try to turn the discussion to the white devils and to black separatism. They still stir the men up emotionally and talk with the black fathers afterwards. After they are gone, the meeting becomes much calmer and the men refocus on what they want to do in the community. But then the brothers reappear and all hell breaks loose. The Nation is represented by the assistant football coach here today, but I am not going to confront the issue. I want to see what will happen with the youth impact sessions.

"Come on, Jorja, you know I love you," Ele tells me, and I smile.

"All right, let's move on and talk about what we are going to do." Leelee is on top of things. "Elementary, come on with our organization."

"These youngsters look up to us," Ele intones. "But they look up to us for the wrong reasons. Because we've maybe had something to do with killing people, serving time, gangbanging, some of these youngsters think we're special. We gotta talk about our pasts. Lay it out there. But explain to them this is not what it's about, that we want things to be different for them, that we want them to go to school. So I think we oughta start with a positive message. Maybe have Coach here talk about how important their education is. Then we can go from there, and a few of us can talk about our experiences."

"I wanna talk about my experience," Donald volunteers. I am leery of this but keep quiet. It's important that the men are organizing. The youth impact sessions are completely their idea. They are not part of the Project Fatherhood curriculum and not anywhere on the list of suggested activities. This doesn't matter to John King, Mike, Andre, or me. What matters is that these fathers are deeply engaged in relating to the youths at Jordan Downs. The fathers' concerns have extended beyond their own children to the community. What could be more meaningful or important than that? The fathers are particularly intent on reaching out to the boys whose own fathers are locked up or are otherwise not around. Debois defines this, saying, "We've got to be their fathers too."

"Debois just said it perfectly," Big Mike reinforces. "So Ele, what is our structure?"

"We'll have Coach talk first about the importance of education. Then when he's done I think three of us should share our experiences— Donald, Leelee, and me. Unless anyone has objections."

"Nah."

"No."

"It sounds good."

One week later, the Jordan Downs gym is filled with young men seated at a series of long tables. The recruitment has gone well. Leelee and KSD have managed to bring in around twenty youths, ranging in age from eleven to fifteen. After they have devoured the fried chicken John King has provided, the coach stands up and begins his address.

"You know me as a coach, but I am also a member of the Nation of Islam, that proud brotherhood led by Elijah Mohammed and Malcolm X."

I want to scream but instead I try to remember where I left a book—stolen from an old boyfriend—that was devoted to a dialogue between Malcolm X and Erik Erikson. I can't mentally locate the book, but I start thinking about rumors that Malcolm was inching toward a more inclusive dialogue when he was killed because the forces backing Elijah Muhammad wanted to continue to preach black separatism. While I am trying to remember the events leading up to the assassination, the coach keeps talking. It is impossible to tell what sort of impact he is having on these young men. I can't pick up any feeling. Their expressions are flat. It is almost as if the words are bouncing off of their blank faces.

"I want to ask you, what do you see as the strengths of the Black Nation? Of black men all over this earth? We have a rich and important history, a history you need to know. What do you know about the history of the Nation?"

No reaction. The coach is just warming up when Big Mike cuts him off and says, "We've got to move on."

The coach looks flabbergasted as Ele introduces Donald, who launches into a vivid description of his life as a gangster.

"I was one of the Watts Original Pygmies," he tells the group, and the boys' faces suddenly animate with interest.

Donald is lively, engaging—a natural entertainer. The problem is that he is not offering a cautionary tale. I begin to worry as he starts his trip down memory lane, detailing the adventure of gangster life. There is very little remorse in the account. Mainly, he announces that he spent thirty-two years in San Quentin. The subtext is that he survived.

Did he?

He tells the youth, "I was the meanest, baddest dude in Watts. People hated me. And they should have. I did bad things."

Donald describes how a rival gang caught him at a party "across the tracks" that he should not have been attending. Their response was to knife him through his back until the blade emerged from his stomach, then hogtie him to the railroad tracks, twenty minutes before the next train, ensuring pain and a brutal death. He was rescued by three of his homies but continued to engage in violent activity until he was caught—and locked up—for murder.

Donald is boastful, not regretful. I am wondering just what kind of game he is running, and then I remind myself to look through a different lens. He was already violent, already an outlaw, and then he was locked up in a prison for over three decades.

What kind of outcome do we expect?

And what do we do with a man like Twin when we finally release him into society?

I am wondering if Watts is one of the few places where he could survive and be understood—or at least find other men whose experiences are similar, if not identical, to his.

Community interventionist Kathy Wooten comes up to me as Donald finishes and whispers, "I'm not sure if this is the right message for these young men."

"I know. I gotta talk with Big Mike and Andre."

"Be careful. These boys, they're right on the edge." She looks at me, and we both have tears in our eyes.

Kathy works around the clock as a gang interventionist in Watts. Her house is a few blocks from Jordan Downs, and the doors are always open. If there is an event or a community meeting, she shows up. I suspect it is how she copes with the deaths of two of her sons from gang violence. The boys died within six months of each other in 2008. Kathy is now trying to find a good lawyer to defend her youngest son, who was arrested for burglary when he was home from college for Christmas break. Maybe she is thinking about him when she tells me, "We gotta watch out for them, because they're not watchin' out for themselves."

Mercifully, Donald's story winds to a close. He is followed by Ele, who begins by describing his experiences while incarcerated. He stays away from discussions of crackers and black supremacy, focusing on the true impact of the prison experience. The young men are all spellbound.

"Yeah, I got locked up—caught a murder charge—but I got out from under that and I got out of prison. I stayed out of prison till 2004. I tried to change my ways about gangbanging because I lost a little homie, name

Ricardo. I was starting to do what you call an introspective. Thinking about my place on this earth and what is my calling, why I'm here. I should have done it sooner, but I had never really narrowed it to the teeth. Next day after Ricardo got killed, I read in the newspaper that it was average for a black man to die before he was twenty-five years old. *I couldn't believe it.* At that time I had five sons and what I was reading was telling me if I lived to be a certain age, I was okay. I was like twenty-eight. So then I'm reading this, and they tell me if I reach a certain age I'd witness my son's death—" Ele's eyes begin to fill with tears here. He reaches one of his core beliefs, something that has been part of his struggle.

He talks carefully as he explains.

"God knows I love my babies. I love my boys. I got some beautiful kids. I thank God for that. And I start thinkin', 'So what I'm supposed to do to save my sons?' Then I come to the realization that I got more than my sons. All of you kids are my sons. All you little dudes is mine."

The boys are hanging on every word.

"I need you to know we are here for you. Project Fatherhood is here for you. Maybe your daddy done messed up, maybe he's locked up, or he's on drugs, or he's gone away. We are here for you. And we are gonna be here for you. We are your daddies."

The men—young and old—nod their heads in agreement.

"Let's all end this meeting with a prayer."

Afterward the youngsters linger, talking to some of the homies. Ele apologizes to Leelee for taking so long. Leelee laughs.

"It was the coach, Ele."

"Yeah, I know—he didn't do so good."

"No, we gotta watch out on this."

"Yeah, and next time we gotta get the youngsters to talk."

TWENTY-THREE

Hood Day

We need to come together to remember our fallen warriors.
—Little Buddha

No more mothers crying, no more babies dying.
—Blinky Rodriguez

Andre and I are eating lunch at Louisiana Fried Chicken. It looks like half of Grape Street is here trying to figure out what we are talking about. It is two weeks before "Hood Day" in Watts. Hood Day began when various neighborhoods decided to designate an occasion to honor gang members who died in "the wars," a sort of Veterans Day for the neighborhood. But there are no graveside remembrances. The memorial celebrations are notorious for drinking, dope smoking, and partying. On Hood Day, the threat of death hangs in the air alongside balloons representing gang colors. There is a history of violence at these events.

Andre is determined to make things different this year. I am helping write the text for fliers declaring it a community day, open to everyone, from babies to senior citizens. Once he reviews my writing, he adds language indicating the LAPD will co-sponsor events. Project Fatherhood is going to be front and center, trying to "flip the story"—instead of being known as a day honoring gangbanging, the event will be redefined as an occasion to remember innocent victims of gang-related violence. Andre tells me that many community members are excited that this may be a day to change the tone of activity in Jordan Downs. The effort is at the heart of what Project Fatherhood is trying to do—heal the community, change the narrative. Andre is almost giddy as he talks about his plans for the future.

A little over a week later—the weekend before the community day—

two young men are gunned down in Watts. The shootings occur within the same hour, and before the sun comes up, both men are dead.

The news is everywhere. The community day is canceled. Then HACLA cancels Project Fatherhood's weekly meeting. I am frustrated. This is when the men really need to talk about how to deal with the violence. But HACLA is worried about its own liability—the agency fears someone might shoot Big Mike, Andre, or even me and hold it responsible. I try in vain to convince John that the last thing any gang member wants to do is shoot at a small white woman who is married to a retired LAPD deputy chief. Gang members did *not* want that kind of trouble. They wanted law enforcement to stay far away from what they were doing. John is kind but immovable. There will be no Project Fatherhood this week.

I travel down to Watts anyway. I have a meeting scheduled with Leelee at his job. But I really want to see what is going on, to talk to homies and find out if there is anything I can do. I drive to Jordan Downs and park my car at the community center. The development resembles an armed camp. Police cars are blocking every entrance, police are checking IDs, and there is a helicopter hovering overhead. There will be no Hood Day, no community day, nothing. Of course, there is the danger that instead of calming things down, this will further inflame the community. I start walking around looking for Andre, whom I find standing on the curb outside the "parole parking lot," a Watts gathering place. The area is hot. "You better leave here, young lady," Andre tells me. "It's not gonna be safe after dark. Everything has changed."

I don't listen to him. I drive over to the Compton Avenue Shields for Families site to meet with Leelee and the Shields leadership team. Leelee has been anxious for a meeting to discuss organizing a second chapter of Project Fatherhood. After I had postponed the date several times, I sit down and listen to Leelee's supervisors talk. Nothing they say is registering. I am worrying about what is going on in the streets outside. The night before, Mark and I discussed what was happening at Jordan Downs. We talked about how one of the biggest problems was that the interventionists and the rest of the community felt let down by the beloved Phil Tingirides—Captain T, as they called him. Instead of talking about resolving the conflict, Tingirides had issued a battle cry—

"No more Grape Street." Worse, at the Monday meeting of the Watts Gang Task Force, Captain T spoke as if he was freshly arrived from traveling in a time machine from 1965.

"The full force of the LAPD is going to be brought down on Jordan Downs," he announced.

The crowd was silent, collectively wondering who this guy was and what had happened to Captain T. I asked Mark—who went way back with Tingirides in the LAPD—what on earth was going on. I was confident that he could link this shift up with Captain T's history. When Mark was in charge of Uniformed Services Group, Tingirides had been a metro cop and a member of the mounted unit under his command. Although Mark had little contact with the LAPD after he retired, he had stayed in touch with Tingirides, and he applauded his approach.

"He's a great cop, but here's the deal," Mark began. "Phil has been out at Southeast and in Watts over six years. Whatever else is going on with him, he really has a sort of professional PTSD. He deserves to be a commander by now. But he's devoted to that community and doesn't want the folks there to feel he abandoned them."

I wasn't really interested in the LAPD promotional process. I already had deep-seated doubts about the objectivity of the people making decisions, but I knew this was a realistic assessment. Anyone who lived or worked in Watts over time just naturally developed post-traumatic stress disorder. This included most of the fathers.

As if to prove the point, in the meeting at Shields, Leelee seemed preoccupied and nervous. It could have been anything—his job, his family, his own PTSD triggered by the shootings and police presence. But when the meeting was over and he walked me out to my car, he told me what was on his mind.

"Dr. Leap, I got a case coming up, and I might be looking at some time in the pen."

There it was. All the pain, all the shame, all the research evidence I needed that the new Jim Crow was alive and well in Watts.

"What happened?"

"Well, it was before I got this job," Leelee offered. I decided to make it easy for him.

"You were dealing?"

"Not much. Just some bud, just some oxy. I had to make some money. The thing is, I got my three sons living with me now, and I got another baby on the way. I got this job. I got everything going right. I don't want to go back to the pen for two or three years. I don't care—I just want house arrest. I'm not gonna do anything. Put an ankle bracelet on me, let me come to work—but don't lock me up. I can't do this again."

I knew Leelee presented absolutely no threat to society. I knew he had dealt drugs because there was no job for him when he first emerged from prison. But his life had changed—he had been hired as a case-worker, he had found his calling. Even today, the executive director at Shields for Families talked about putting him through school. I wasn't exactly wide-eyed about Leelee—I knew there were things he wasn't being completely honest about yet. I didn't push. But I yelled at him for not telling me sooner. Then I hugged him and told him to have his lawyer, Earl Caldwell, call me. Whatever was going on—including what Leelee was not revealing to me—I had to see what I could do.

Caldwell called after I had left five messages, which included an offer to write a letter or testify for Leelee—whatever might be needed. I was not prepared for a "truth about Leelee" barrage from Caldwell.

"Look, I've tried everything I could for this guy," he began. As soon as I heard that, I knew Leelee had not hired the right advocate. "Any way that I cut it, he's gonna do four years, 80 percent time. He'll be out in a little over three years." The percentages were all part of a complicated political and fiscal reality. The California prison system was woefully overcrowded, so sentences were adjusted based on a "good behavior" factor. Unless someone completely sabotaged himself or herself, a sentence could be served in less than the appointed time. The percentage of time one had to serve was based on the seriousness of a person's crime and the degree to which that person posed a threat to society, as well as how likely it was the person would return to a life of crime. "Strikes" figured in the calculus of time served, too. A "three strikes" sentencing law was implemented in California in 1994 to address the problem of re-peat offenders. Under the law, a defendant who had one previous felony conviction (strike one) would be sentenced to state prison for twice the term of the previous felony. If a defendant with two or more strikes was convicted of a new felony, the law mandated a state prison term of twenty-five years to life.

Leelee had two strikes. He was first convicted of armed robbery. The second conviction was for manslaughter. He served eleven years in prison when he had two sons—a baby and a toddler at the time he entered prison. The boys had never known their father.

I knew that Leelee wanted to repair his life and help heal the community. I also knew that before he got the job at Shields for Families, he was doing some slanging. I just wasn't sure at what level. Now I had the lawyer yelling in my ear that Leelee had been arrested for receiving or mailing three thousand Oxycontin pills—I wasn't sure what Caldwell was talking about, but the official charge involved the high-profile narcotic and the US Postal Service. I pretty much stopped listening when I heard the number *three thousand*. There was not going to be an ankle bracelet or a brief stay in county jail. Leelee was going to state prison.

I asked if there was anything I could do and the lawyer resumed his harangue.

"I've been a lawyer twenty years, and before that I was a cop. You don't know what this means—but I can walk down Grape Street any time of the day or night."

Just as he was warming up to recite his street resume, I cut him off.

"I understand. The thing is, I have been working in Watts for thirty-five years. I grew up there. Let's not have a competition. We both know the neighborhood."

This was a real conversation stopper, and that was fine with me. I had just one more question.

"When did you start working on this case?"

The lawyer told me he had started over a year ago, and I hit the roof. I called Leelee back.

"You've been sitting on this for a year and *now* you've told me?!"

"I'm sorry, Miss Leap," Leelee began.

"Don't apologize. You screwed yourself. If you had told me when this happened, I could have done something. Now I can't do anything. Your hearing is Monday."

It was Friday. I had no answers for Leelee. I truly didn't know where this would go, but whatever the outcome, it would not be good.

On Monday morning I called Leelee to tell him that everyone I had spoken to over the weekend, including Elie Miller, said the same thing: there would be no alternative to getting locked up. He could fight his case or take the deal—the outcome would probably be the same.

He answered the phone and his voice was muted.

"Where are you?" I asked.

"I'm here," he said, sounding tense. "I'm already in the court."

"What do you want to do? I can't find anyone to help—everyone I spoke to said you should take the four years."

His reply was heartbreaking.

"I'm gonna take the deal, Miss Leap, but you gotta promise me something."

I waited for him to go on.

"You gotta promise me that you'll help me while I'm in there. I want to get educated. And you gotta help me line something up when I get out. I don't want to go back to my old ways."

After all his progress, the news was devastating, and yet I didn't doubt that he had made the right choice. I just didn't know what to think. How would he deal with it? And he would have another child born while he was locked up.

"I'm not gonna leave you, I promise."

"Thanks, Miss Leap. I'll call you later. I got a month left before they lock me up. I want to talk to you about my plans."

Excitement about the cancellation of Hood Day died down, and a week later Project Fatherhood was back on. I was interviewing two former gang members who lived in an apartment near Athens Park, part of my ongoing work on reentry. This work was proving to be particularly important in Los Angeles because of Assembly Bill (AB) 109, California legislation enacted in 2011 that shifted responsibility for certain offenders from the state to counties in an effort to relieve state prison crowding. The violence many people prophesied would erupt when felons were released into the community had not come to pass, but the atmosphere in South Los Angeles remained uneasy. As I drive from the apartment to Watts, I see a cluster of police cars parked in front of Nickerson Gardens.

When I get to Jordan Downs I ask Sy what happened.

"There was a murder out on Imperial. Right near to the Nickersons."

"Who's involved?"

Sy starts laughing.

"You really gotta ask?"

"Yeah, because I never want to make the mistake that it's always the hood."

Sy looks at me carefully.

"That's fair. I know you're bein' fair. It was the Bounty Hunter Bloods. They're implicated, as you folks might say."

The murder on Imperial is an unfortunate prelude to the discussion tonight.

The men are preparing to confront Captain Tingirides. For weeks, stories about Captain T have been flying around the neighborhood, and because of what they've heard, the men in the group have been very agitated. After being on the receiving end of a series of irate phone calls, I reached out to Andre, who also had been getting an earful. He arranged for Captain Tingirides and his wife, Sergeant Emada Tingirides, to appear at the next meeting of Project Fatherhood. The couple has long been a favorite around LAPD Southeast Division—community members continue to insist they would have protected Captain T and Emada from Christopher Dorner if it had come to that.

Sy and I are sitting at the table, still talking about what might happen next at Nickerson Gardens, when Captain T arrives. After telling us that Emada is on her way, he joins the conversation.

"They killed some kid," he says.

"Things there just don't calm down," I add, and we all know we're talking about Nickerson Gardens and the Bounty Hunter Bloods.

Sy then speaks quietly.

"Y'know, that's always been the most violent place of all. More violent than Jordan or Imperial."

Even now, with the new gang-reduction strategy, the emphasis on community—and the resulting low crime rates—Nickerson Gardens is slowest to change. Violent crime is down over 50 percent at Imperial Courts and Jordan Downs, but at Nickerson it is down "only" 38 percent. The Bloods have always been considered the most dangerous gang in Watts. Tonight, however, they are not the topic of conversation.

By the time the fathers gather around the table, Emada Tingirides has arrived and Captain T starts to talk again. He begins by offering a history of the past year, reminding the men that Halloween 2012 marked the beginning of renewed conflict between Nickerson Gardens and Jordan Downs. He carefully recites from a list of death and destruction.

"Between 2002 and 2011 there were sixty-nine homicides in the projects. This is an unbelievable figure. And then, starting in 2011, there were zero homicides in almost two years. This is not just because of the LAPD. This is because everyone worked together as partners. And this is because we all know what the violence has done here in Jordan Downs and in the projects. It's created a prison—*violence creates a prison*. Now it looks like that prison is starting to be built again. Last weekend— you know what happened. You all remember Flip—he was assassinated. Then some group got together and decided they were going to retaliate. They went to Imperial Courts and assassinated someone else. But they weren't so smart. Within an hour we had suspects in custody . . . they were from here. This wasn't good. That was the third incident with people from Grape Street."

The men are all listening intently. Often so furious at the LAPD, the group has gone silent.

"Let me tell you why I said what I said at the Watts Gang Task Force," Tingirides continues. "I said, 'This is the third time Grape Street has gone out and killed like that, and I'm coming after Grape Street.' And, you know, if we don't do this, it won't stop. The violence will keep going on, and people will die—innocent people will die. And everyone will be living in a prison."

Andre Christian, sitting directly opposite Captain T, has been instrumental in organizing this exchange, acting as the go-between for Project Fatherhood and the LAPD. I sometimes worry if people suspect Andre of being a snitch—or, at the least, a police loyalist. But his hood loyalties and his need for objectivity rear up.

"You're talking about a clique—one group, Captain T, and it's *not* all of Grape Street. It's like you've got some bad cops, but you're not all bad. Perception is everything."

"Look, I know it's not *just* Grape Street. Someone from Nickerson came over here and went after three girls who weren't doing anything. But now I'm going over there too. The whole community has to be a part of this. Not just the Jordan Downs community—I mean the whole Watts community. But all of you have to listen to this message: until we pull together and stop this, your kids are going to die."

Leelee starts to speak.

"If we can keep the kids with some sense—keep them out of trouble—then all the twenty- and thirty-year-olds can stop."

Emada Tingirides is nodding vigorously as Leelee says this. She adds, "We're not looking after Grape Street. We're not out to get Grape Street. You gotta understand, we're looking after Jordan Downs."

Emada may be an African American woman, but she is cut out of the traditional LAPD blue cloth. She subtly moves the conversation to all of the great things the Community Safety Partnership is accomplishing. Right now, I'm agnostic. I know that the CSP is engaging with the Watts community in an almost miraculous partnership that includes the LAPD and the Watts Gang Task Force. Certainly police-community relations have never been as positive. But I can't shake the feeling that we are still seeing the police *coming from the outside* to save the day. Somehow, Jordan Downs needs to build leadership from within the community.

I still fear how heavy-handed the LAPD can be. As if to illustrate this tendency—and despite Emada's talk of partnership—Phil Tingirides expresses his determination to impose order in Jordan Downs. He throws down the gauntlet, announcing, "In the future, there is not going to be any purple celebration Hood Day here."

"But I thought we were talking about Jordan Downs," Andre asserts. He wants to differentiate: "Grape Street is part of Jordan Downs, but it's *not* Jordan Downs." While he is talking, I am feeling uncomfortable with all the labeling. Captain T keeps singling out Grape Street—calling out the gang by name. I don't know if this is the best approach. At the same time, I am struck by the fact that the men in the room—

who have been screaming to me over the phone for the past week—are mute. They almost appear to agree with Captain T.

Bob finally speaks up and complains that the officers lack people skills. "You're not here when they're here, Captain T. They're not always respectful. They are still rough with the youngsters."

"There's another problem," Tiny starts yelling. "The cameras are out there and they're not working. We know. Someone got shot out on Grape Street and none of the cameras were working! What's going on with that?" Leelee winks at me while Tiny is talking. It's not lost on either of us that a blind man is asking the camera question. Captain T tries to explain: "If I had known the camera wasn't working, I would have had it fixed!"

But Tiny interrupts him.

"So—are they working now?"

"No," Captain T answers.

Everyone in the room—including Phil and Emada Tingirides—erupts into laughter. Ele is laughing the hardest. But when the laughter dies down, Leelee starts poking.

"You put all this money in these damned cameras—how come you can't put some money into this community?"

Emada tries to answer, saying that money is being put into the community, but Leelee won't back down.

"It's not just programs. You need incentives in place to get people to change—including these youngsters that we don't want to go bad. What about the youth activities? We could get these young gangsters-in-the-making to play together as teammates. We want them playing together, not getting locked up together." Leelee does not sound like someone one month away from prison. We have agreed he will tell the men when he is ready. It definitely will not be tonight.

"Look, we want to make things better." Captain T now seems much more relaxed. "We want to ask you to help us making things better. We have had three thousand fewer arrests in the past couple of years. Three thousand. That's a huge number. We want to keep on this way. We don't want to arrest the people doing drugs. We want to arrest the drug dealers. I mean it. I care about this community. I want to see it transformed."

I don't know about community transformation, but I am witnessing a personal transformation in Ele. He is listening raptly to every word Captain T utters, nodding and laughing along with him. While Ele gazes at Tingirides, Debois starts talking.

"Look—I know you care, but the cops here have abused community members. You may not know all of it, Captain T, but this has happened in all of our families. The LAPD—they've done a lotta dirt in this community. What about that?"

Before Captain T can answer, Ele starts talking.

"Let me speak to that," he begins. "Captain T—we know you care. That's not you—that was before you." I am finding this quite amusing. He has changed drastically. I wonder if Ele will still be referring to Phil Tingirides as a cracker.

"Thank you for saying that." Captain T suddenly looks tired. The fathers appear satisfied. But the captain has a few parting words of advice.

"You guys need to put some pressure on the youngsters in here. The only tool I have is to be draconian. You're the ones these kids listen to. *Do something.*"

TWENTY-FOUR

Sugarbear

We need to learn to love ourselves.
—Andre Christian

Right after Thanksgiving, Theo Pete died. It was sudden, unexpected. He had been in uncertain health from middle age—a heart attack at fifty, open-heart surgery at seventy, and a diagnosis of Alzheimer's disease at seventy-nine. Because he had always been the family intellectual— a man devoted to George Bernard Shaw, the horse races, and *Playboy* magazine—the diagnosis of Alzheimer's seemed particularly cruel. His life had been dedicated to joy and knowledge. Just when the family braced for a slow and inevitable descent, he developed a horrible cough. He could not swallow and could not breathe. In a matter of days, he was dead of cancer. The tumor, long undetected, had wrapped itself around his heart and his throat and literally choked the life out of him.

Two days after his funeral, I return to Project Fatherhood and share what has happened. I start crying as I tell the men my uncle had died. The fathers are comforting and loving. Many of them get up to hug me and ask how they can help.

I had not seen my uncle as often as I should have in recent years, but I had never forgotten my debt to him. He had stepped into the void created by my adolescent conflicts with my mother and father. After his death, I was worried about my other surrogate father, Papa. Celebrating his ninetieth year on earth, Papa no longer walked ten miles a day as he once did, but he was still full of life, feistily reassuring me whenever I began to worry about his imminent death: "I didn't sign any contract to live a certain amount of time, so calm down."

I am trying not to think too much about this, but I don't want to lose Papa. I begin to explain this to the group when Donald interrupts me.

"Don't even tell me how sad you are—look at how many fathers you got. Most of us in this room don't have one." Donald spits the words out.

"Yeah," Sy laughs. "You oughta share some of those fathers with us."

They had me, and there was no reply. I started laughing.

"You see," said Sy. "Now don't you feel better?"

I was on the receiving end of the hood version of tough love, and I wasn't sure how much I liked it. I wanted more of the Greek histrionics. I felt like I was in the midst of a multiple-choice test on grieving. Which emotional response do you prefer? Was it (a) Greek hysteria, (b) WASP stoicism, (c) hood tough love, or (d) all of the above?

I had no choice. I opted for D, held my breath, and hoped for the best.

A week later, the room is restless. No sooner does the meeting begin than Tiny starts to complain, loudly insisting that Project Fatherhood is not really providing for him. When I ask what he means, he insists, "You're not doing anything for the handicapped." The other men do not take him seriously and are laughing as he yells. Their joking continues, and they start ribbing each other. Mike tries—unsuccessfully—to get the men to focus. They are playful, not focusing, having multiple side conversations.

The disorder magically stops as Andre inserts a DVD into a small television set. The picture is grainy, and the men sitting at the far side of the room can barely see, but it doesn't matter. It is immediately clear what the program is about: a series of still photographs depicts everyone who was killed in Watts in the past ten years, through 2013.

There are infants and small children, elderly men, middle-aged women, and, finally, adolescents, cut down in the prime of life. The birth dates roll by and I calculate rapidly—fifteen years, seventeen years, sixteen years, four years. The roll call is almost unbearable. There is a moment of silence after the portraits fade, then the men all start talking simultaneously.

"That's deep."

"I can't believe how many there are."

"That's all happened in Watts."

"What are we gonna do?"

"We gotta do something."

Andre stands up in front of the group.

"We gotta ask ourselves, '*What are we gonna do?* Why are we ignoring our own lives and our families?' I know that this is because I didn't have a man to help me. I never had a daddy. Every man needs his daddy. I did and I still do. And I know I have to heal myself. You know I talk a lot in here about how important it is for a man to have a daddy, but I was so angry at my daddy for so long. I was so mad that he left me. I was so mad he wasn't there to help me. I didn't believe I could ever forgive him. Over the holidays I finally went to see him. I finally sat down and talked to him. I gotta practice what I preach and make peace with my own father. And now we gotta be good fathers to the community and stop these babies from dyin'. We've got to be peaceful and keep the peace. If we're gonna be good fathers, we've got to be peacemakers."

The room is silent. This is not a good sign. No one wants to talk peace.

The men are focused on the faces that have just flashed on the screen. KSD turns to the issue of the dead babies.

"We can't go on like this. We gotta do something when kids get killed. Maybe we should have a green light on baby killers."

This is a throwback. I have only heard about the "green light" from Mexican gangs; it's the equivalent of taking a contract out to kill someone. When I was in Tortilla Flats conducting interviews with help from Kenny Green, I heard a lot about green lights from the members of 18th Street. But this was the first time I was hearing it in the black community.

"We gotta teach a lesson to anyone who kills a baby. It's wrong."

I am stifling my impulse to ask if it is bad to kill babies, but open season on older people. Big Mike beats me to it.

"So it's okay to kill someone if they're not a baby?"

"Look," Ele starts in, "sometimes violence is the only way to bring about peace."

The men quickly agree.

"You know, it's a way to drive the lesson home."

"Malcolm X said it: the way to change people is through violence."

"This is what the United States government does—why can't we do it?"

My disbelief turns to anger as the men interrupt each other trying to preach the gospel of violence. I cannot control myself.

"This is the most ridiculous discussion I have ever heard in this group."

The men all stare at me. I have officially lost my shit.

"Who died in December? Who died? I don't mean babies—I mean someone who was probably one of the most important people in the world."

"Nelson Mandela, yeah, yeah, we know. It's time for another history lesson from Dr. Leap. He did it all because of a soccer game."

It's Donald, wiseass as ever. The men shout him down.

"Listen to her."

"Do you know what Nelson Mandela did to his jailers—to the men who kept him in a tiny little cell, who imprisoned him, who ruined his wife, his children, his life?"

"Yeah," Spider blurts out. "He forgave them. Then they made him president. But they had a motive. They knew that the blacks in South Africa were going to rise up and be violent and destroy everything and kill everyone who was white. They made him president because that was the only thing to keep things in one piece. And it's because Mandela knew *how* to use violence to make peace."

I am speechless. Spider has just effectively synopsized a political movement including the strategic use of violence.

"How'd you learn that, man? That's deep."

Spider looks proud.

"I can get the DVD of *Long Walk to Freedom.*"

I am trying to keep a straight face. The film has just opened in wide release in theaters. Spider has to have a pirated DVD.

"I'll get copies if anyone wants to buy one."

"You can't say that here," Big Mike warns. "It's a crime. And there's only one thing we've got to think about, and it's keeping the peace."

The fathers are struggling. They want to do something but there is the simple issue—they don't know how.

"We need to create a safe haven—for our babies." Elementary is clear. "We have started the youth impact sessions, but we gotta keep 'em going. You heard Captain T. He told us to put pressure on the youth. We gotta do more than put pressure, we gotta have an impact. And not just our sessions. We gotta reach out to them in between, talk to them in between. We said we are gonna be their daddies—we need to make good on that promise."

Andre looks at Ele and then speaks.

"Yeah, Elementary, you are right. But we gotta slow down. Before we have an impact on anything else, we need to learn to love ourselves."

The room goes dead. It's a different kind of silence than when the men come to attention. This is a silence I rarely hear. Andre has brought everything to a standstill.

"We are sitting here talking about what we can do for others. So much of our trouble is that we hate ourselves. We have never learned to love ourselves. Everything we talk about is about this—we don't have daddies, we don't have peace, we've done dirt in the community. It's all because we don't love ourselves. I think we've got to focus on this first."

No one knows where to go from here.

Mike is the leader and he does what any good leader should—he delegates.

"Andre, you gotta do a session on that. Let's plan for that next week."

This is a good place to end, and the men clasp hands and pray. But I am far away. I am thinking about Leelee. I know his court date is nearing, and it is the first night in a long time he is not at Project Fatherhood. Tiny interrupts my reverie, screaming, "Where's my hug from Jorja Leap?"

I go over to embrace him and promise him that I will sit down and spend some time with him soon. After he leaves, I turn to Andre and ask how Tiny is doing. We're both concerned about his health, which is ruinous, and his eyesight, which continues to deteriorate. But he is not alone in his needs. Many of the fathers are severely lacking in basic health care. Our talk morphs into a discussion of what has been going on at Project Fatherhood. It's been over three years. The current funding will run out in October. Is anything working? Andre tells me that I have to evaluate things realistically.

"You can't think about this like regular research," he tells me. "Look at what's happened here. The men come every week. They talk. They plan things. They go back out into the community and do things."

I am thinking about Sugarbear.

Sugarbear began as the most reluctant member of the group. He would leave midway through most meetings. Then he began to stay until the end—partly to collect his gift card, partly to make some sort of comment. But something strange had started happening recently. Sugarbear arrived early. He helped set up chairs; he made sure everything was in place. Tonight he had gone a step further and passed out water bottles to every man in the room. It didn't sound like much, but Sugarbear represented the change.

As if reading my mind, Andre looks carefully at me, then speaks.

"Sugarbear passed out water."

TWENTY-FIVE

Twelve More Days

What kind of help really worked for me? Being honest, being truthful. Standing up to the truth. If I'm wrong, I'll stand up to it, own up to it. And that's a whole lot more relief instead of trying not to own up to your wrongdoings.

—Elementary "Ele" Freeman

A week later, the men gather to discuss the next youth impact session. Andre motions for me to come in. But Leelee is waiting for me outside the entrance to the meeting room.

I try joking. "I call you and text you and e-mail you and you never answer. I'm beginning to think you don't love me anymore."

Leelee looks at me and then quietly says, "I've got twelve more days, Miss Leap. Twelve more days."

"Okay—so when are we getting together?"

I have decided to be matter-of-fact. Leelee doesn't want anyone to hear what we are talking about. We're just having a meeting, I think, another meeting.

"Next Tuesday or Thursday—I can take you to breakfast. And don't think you're gonna do what you always do and not eat, Miss Leap," Leelee's voice begins to rise. I am not going to out him to the group, and we proceed with our charade. He even announces where we are going. The men ignore us.

When I sit down, Ele is next to me and he looks like he is going to jump out of his skin. I can't figure out what's going on. Things between Ele and me have never been easy. I think he is torn between affection for me and his affinity for the Black Muslim doctrine. I know that I represent the "white devils" to him and he is trying to integrate two opposing ideas. This conflict is particularly acute right now because I have offered to help him with his son, Jamel, as their relationship continues to fall apart.

At the beginning of the school year, Ele had assumed custody of Jamel.

"His mama told me she couldn't handle him anymore, so she sent him to me. He's a good boy. And smart, really smart." Ele had looked anxious about having full responsibility for Jamel, and I tried to be reassuring.

"I think you're gonna be a great father to him, Ele. I really do."

The next week Ele brought Jamel, who sat sullenly at the end of the table, listening to the conversation. He didn't want to be there. I couldn't blame him. There was no one near his age and on top of that, what the group was discussing had nothing to do with him. I spent a few minutes with him after the meeting, and it was clear that he was furious at both his mother and father.

"I wanna finish school and get my GED and start a business. Then I'm outta here. I wanna go to New York City."

"What kind of business?"

"Something with the music business. I gotta friend who raps, and I think we could get a label. Do something good, make a lotta money."

This had an all-too-familiar ring to it. Music and entertainment—the way out, the way up. The icons were less Kevin Durant and LeBron James, more Tupac and Jay Z. In fact, rap and hip-hop have replaced sports in the methodology of upward mobility, mainly because most kids in the hood felt they stood a better chance of being a rap star than a point guard. With sports there was a need for size, muscle, and talent. But music involved so many levels—you didn't need to be a hip-hop star, you could be the person who promoted the hip-hop star, you could be the agent. Many young men saw career opportunities in the entourage. Jamel was no different.

But Jamel also told me that, although he didn't care about school, he was interested in books. At the next meeting of Project Fatherhood, I offered Jamel a supply—a book of Tupac's poetry, DaShaun Morris's *War of the Bloods in My Veins*, Cupcake Brown's *A Piece of Cake*, and my own book, *Jumped In*. I told him that as soon as he finished one I would pay him twenty dollars and we could talk about it. Even with the financial incentive, I didn't hold out much hope. Jamel never told me he finished a book. He would drift in and out of Project Fatherhood. I began to catch bits and pieces of his story from Ele, who got called up to school because Jamel kept getting in trouble for fighting. After the first incident, he had to serve detention after school. Then things spiraled downward. Jamel was suspended for two days, then a week. Most recently, he had been arrested. I felt like I was watching a slow-motion car accident.

Today Ele has news. Jamel has been caught fighting again. This time he has been expelled from school.

One thing that was lacking in Watts was some sort of a program—a curriculum, a plan, a defined way of reaching the young men who were consistently getting into trouble. I couldn't send Jamel to Homeboy—it was too far and too alien. This kid had been relocated enough. I thought of Brotherhood Crusade, an after-school program outside of Watts but still in South Los Angeles. It was having remarkable success tutoring and mentoring young black men, keeping them in school and out of the county probation system.

I am sorting through my mental Rolodex as the Project Fatherhood meeting begins with a pleasant man, Jon Jefferson, who has been sent by the office of US Representative Janice Hahn (D-CA) to present a proposal for a job-training program. He wants to offer the program "right here at Jordan Downs, in the gym." He truly doesn't know what he is dealing with. The men start screaming.

"Another training program?"

"We've been through every training program."

"Can you get us a job?"

"Can you guarantee a job?"

The man looks completely crestfallen. He had probably come here thinking that the men would fall upon him in gratitude—eager and excited to receive job training.

Leelee looked at me and rolled his eyes.

"I got a scrapbook full of certificates. And you know what it got me? Squat. None of that helped me. I tried and tried and tried, and finally I had to find myself my own job." Leelee gives up on addressing the man.

He is disgusted. He has also temporarily abandoned the use of any internal sensor. "Twelve more days, Miss Leap," he leans in and whispers to me. "You gotta set me up."

I am wondering where Leelee will be sent. Despite all the information his lawyer has divulged, I still don't know the complete contents of his prison CV. I am certain there are many negatives in his record. I don't fear him losing control in prison—he is not someone who will get in a fight or in trouble. I am just wondering how far away the prison will be.

"Remember breakfast," he tells me. "The Serving Spoon."

The men are oblivious to our conversation. They are too busy running the job services man out of the room. Once that is accomplished, their discussion turns to what they are truly interested in—the younger men in the community. They are continuing to focus on the impact sessions.

"We need to make a plan for what to do with them next," Donald begins.

"And it can't be us just mouthin' off about ourselves," Ele adds, looking pointedly at Donald.

"It's Black History Month," Donald says. "Doncha think we should take them to the African American Museum?"

Leelee weighs in, as if it is just another Wednesday at Project Fatherhood.

"We can't just take them to the museum. I did that with a group of kids at my agency. They were bored. They didn't care about anything; they didn't care about their ancestors. They wanted to go outside. But I noticed this other group there that was playing a game like a treasure hunt. They had these little cards that had a list of things they had to find. The kids were all excited and they were running from one display to another—looking at things and then writing the answer to a question on their card. We should do that."

The men are all nodding their heads in agreement, while I am preoccupied.

Twelve more days. The phrase keeps repeating in my brain.

Leelee continues talking as if nothing is the matter. When is he going to tell the men what is happening to him? While my mind is wandering, the men have turned to a different discussion that I could never have predicted.

"I think we should set up youth impact sessions in the other projects. I think we should take this show on the road," Big Mike begins.

"What do you mean?" It's Debois.

"I mean we should bring together the youngsters from all three of the developments. Have them all together in an impact session. That's the only way to end what has been going on in these projects."

The fathers are stunned.

The room splits straight down the middle; I can see the fault line opening up. Some of the men look at Mike as if he is half crazy. The expressions on their faces say: *What the fuck? He wants us to go into enemy territory.* Forget that they are approaching middle age and almost all have served time. It doesn't matter. The old lines are drawn. This is as tightly formed a battle as that between the Union and the Confederacy. In a certain sense, this is all these men have left—identification with their neighborhood. They don't have money or jobs. What each has is his street CV, and he wants that honored. Still, there are those who tentatively nod their heads in agreement. One is Donald James.

"I am all for this," Twin begins. "I went to the Watts Gang Task Force and there was a guy there, a businessman and a financial manager for the entertainment industry. He says he will help us set up a small recording studio. I think it's a good idea. If there's one thing that will attract young people, it's a studio—they can come and try out their songs, rap, maybe make CDs. They'll come for that. And it doesn't matter what neighborhood they belong to."

The men look confused. More than one of them still wears the WTF expression. No one could have ever imagined Donald as a peacemaker.

"What is going on here?" Ben asks.

"Well, I agree with Donald," I quietly offer, and everyone starts to laugh.

"Well, hell just froze over," Sy observes. I push through.

"But we need to focus. How does everyone feel about what Mike is suggesting? A studio is more of a long-term plan. I think what Mike is talking about is a short-term plan. What does everyone think about having meetings at each of the projects and drawing youngsters from other, er, sites into our youth impact sessions?"

Silence again.

"Just what are we talking about here? Going across the tracks?"

"Yes, we are." Andre has come alive. "We are talking about peace. We are talking about becoming men. When I joined a gang, I made a childhood decision. Now I ask myself, how can I call myself a man and act on childhood decisions?"

The room is silent and then KSD starts to talk.

"I think it's a good idea, Mike," KSD begins. "We say we want peace and we want to be all together—one Watts. That's what we're trying to do—unite Watts. And if that's what we want, well, we gotta get some real muthafuckas to do this."

Everyone except Big Bob erupts in laughter.

"What are you *talking about*?!" Bob is yelling. "We can't do that! We are gonna be riskin' our lives!"

"We can't just show up," Debois adds. "We gotta have some kind of agreement in place."

"Do you know we'd be risking our lives?" Bob says. "The youngsters in those projects don't understand Project Fatherhood. They don't understand group meetings. They just want an excuse to shoot off their guns."

Andre puts his head in his hands.

"We can go. We can get protection. Nothing is gonna happen to us," Big Mike proclaims.

"Who's gonna support us? Who's gonna protect us?" Debois isn't angry, he is genuinely interested in the logistics of the situation.

"We have support from the principal over at Markham Middle School," Big Mike insists, but Debois responds immediately.

"Oh yeah, the school, of course we're safe on the school grounds. But what about getting back and forth from here to the schools?"

Sy views all of this cynically. "You are not gonna be able to do this without the agreement of the neighborhoods."

Ben looks at his brother long and hard. "We can get the agreement. No one wants to see the babies dying."

"Would anyone oppose this?" Ele asks.

"I oppose it on the grounds we might get shot!"

"You want us to get killed?"

"All right, then," Andre offers. "So we are going to teach our youth to fight one another for the next generation?"

"You men remember when Trayvon was shot and we all recognized we was killing each other? We gotta bring our youth together to stop it." Big Mike is imploring the group. "You say we want to heal the community? We gotta heal all of Watts, *not just Jordan Downs*. Anyone who doesn't want to plan this can leave. Otherwise, you stay and we will talk about organizing a youth impact session for *all* our children."

He waits thirty seconds. It feels like fifteen minutes. No one moves.

"So what's our plan?"

The fathers are practical, agreeing they can't just walk through Imperial Courts or Nickerson Gardens recruiting youth to come. Instead, they decide to meet with the principal at Markham Middle School first and ask his help on outreach to classes. Mike has known the principal for two years and is confident he will not only help the group but will allow it to meet with the young men on campus, where everyone will be safe.

I am driving home from Project Fatherhood that night when Andre calls me.

"For the first time, I really have hope about the future," he tells me. But I am still wondering when Leelee is going to tell the group.

TWENTY-SIX

Walking Through the Door

You know, when I go through that door my face is gonna change.
—Leelee Sprewell

I meet Leelee at the Serving Spoon for a goodbye breakfast. He is the mayor here. Everyone knows him, waves to him, or comes over to our table to greet him. He is upbeat, acting like a man a few days away from a vacation. He tells me what to order—a cinnamon waffle—and warns me that I need to gain weight. I can't take too much of this. I am beginning to feel like I am seeing the black spin on WASP denial. I am starting to really believe that Leelee and Mark may have more in common than I could ever imagine. They both remain positive and upbeat, even in the most extreme of situations.

"Okay—quit it. I can't take this anymore." I am crying, and everyone in the restaurant is looking at me. They probably think I'm in love with Leelee and that he is letting me down gently over a waffle.

"Come on, Miss Leap, don't worry. Everything's good. It's all good." Leelee then leans in, confidentially. "But I do need to talk with you about my current situation." He launches into a long explanation of his rather byzantine connections with multiple women. He shows me a baby picture of his newest daughter—Rae Lynn—the product of a one-night stand. Meanwhile, he has a long-term woman "friend" who gets crazy when she drinks and keeps begging Leelee to make her pregnant. I don't comment on his grand total of five children—three sons and two daughters by different women (I am not sure how many). But Leelee laughs as he explains, "You know my daddy had kids all over the place— and I am my daddy's son."

He continues. "But I do love my girl now—Akisha—KK. I think I might have something serious with her when I get out. She says she's gonna wait for me. But I'm not worried about that. I wanna talk to you about something else."

Thank God, I think. I can't take this.

Leelee's personal life makes me long for the days when I was studying the warring factions of the Balkans. The four-hundred-year-old conflict in the former Yugoslavia is easier to understand than this.

"Let me tell you what I am worried about," Leelee continues. "I wrote Shields for Families my letter of resignation, but I told them I want to go back to work when I come home. And I keep wondering—are they gonna start the redevelopment before I get out? I don't know. I know the bureaucracy is slow, but I think it may not be *that* slow."

"I don't know," I say. "HACLA is a wreck. They haven't even gotten the project started. They don't even have the first piece of funding they need." Every word I was telling Leelee was true. I wasn't trying to sugarcoat things. No one knew when—or if—the redevelopment was going to get started.

"I want to know what's going on. I want you to stay in touch with me." Leelee is practically beseeching me.

"You know you can call me anytime. I'll accept the collect charges. Just call me."

Leelee and I both know he stands a good chance of being able to obtain an illegal cell phone in prison. I have been called by way too many people who are locked up and still manage to get ahold of me. One particularly technically savvy homie sent me an animated cartoon card on my birthday.

"Don't do anything illegal to get ahold of me," I warn Leelee.

"Don't worry Miss Leap. I don't wanna go back."

That night at Project Fatherhood Leelee tells the men he is going away "for a while." The men all take the news in and no one asks why or what happened. Instead, they seem to accept this as part of the natural course of events. When Big Mike prays at the end of the meeting he asks for God to help Leelee in the new chapter of his life. It feels way too much like Lee is leaving the group to attend college instead of heading to an overcrowded and violent state prison.

Two days later Leelee calls and asks if I will show up at court when he is remanded into custody. I am sick with the flu and throwing up, but I refrain from telling him this and drive down to the Airport Courthouse. I wait for nearly an hour. Leelee is late. He finally texts me saying he is on his way. I don't know whether to throw up or kill him, so I go into the court bathroom to rest until he texts me that he has arrived.

By the time I get out of the bathroom after receiving his text, Leelee is ensconced in the courtroom cafeteria, eating eggs while his mother and his girlfriend, Akisha, look on. I hug everyone and then ask him when we are supposed to be in the courtroom.

"Oh, we'll go as soon as I am done."

I don't blame Leelee for being in no particular hurry, but I am also worried about him getting penalized for being late. I keep my mouth shut until we go upstairs and look for Leelee's attorney, who is already in the courtroom. We are all sitting together waiting for the judge. Leelee leans in to me and points to a door next to the judge's podium.

"You see that door there, Miss Leap?"

I nod.

"You know, when I go through that door my face is gonna change."

Leelee looks at me seriously. I understand. He is not going to be his charming self inside the hell that is the state prison system.

"I am gonna take care of myself and get outta there as fast as I can," he promises. "And you gotta take care of yourself and get me a job when I get outta there. I don't ever want to do any time again."

"I promise. But I am gonna come see you. And I am gonna bring your mama with me."

Leelee reaches over to hug me. He then reaches over me to his mother.

"You hear that, Mama? Miss Leap is gonna bring you to see me."

"Well, God bless you."

The judge enters and the handoff is over in a matter of minutes. Leelee waves to all of us as he walks through the door.

My face is gonna change.

I sit outside with his mother and KK. For several minutes no one speaks, then I begin.

"You need to tell me if you want anything from me. I have written down all of my numbers for both of you."

"Well, bless you, child. You are so kind. But you are so small. How do you stay so small?"

I am in love with his mother in about thirty seconds. She is dignified and determined to avoid drama.

"I forget to eat." This is the simple truth.

KK starts laughing. "I never forgot to eat in my life."

"Amen," Mama adds.

"You two need to call me. You know how much I love Leelee."

"And he loves you."

"And we'll go see him."

"Yes, we will."

I stand up and say that I am going to go home. Mama and KK tell me they want to sit until the bus leaves.

"You go on, girl," KK advises. "That bus isn't gonna leave for a few hours. We'll call you."

I leave, reluctantly. I understand. They are standing guard until Leelee goes.

I am still thinking about Leelee the next week as I drive to Project Fatherhood. When I get there I am confused. I'm wondering if there is going to be a meeting when I see Ben sitting in the middle of the room with his two daughters—Angela and Ariel. The men are all talking simultaneously until Big Mike hushes them and then summarizes what is going on.

"Girls, this is Drjorjaleap. She is a professor from UCLA and she will help us sort this out. Dr. Leap, Ben has brought his two girls, who have been suspended from school"—Big Mike pauses dramatically here— "for fighting *with each other.*"

I am wary of the big buildup Mike has given me, so I tentatively ask, "What happened?"

I can barely hear the girls' answer when Ben steps in impatiently.

"I'm tellin' you, I don't know what to do. I got called by the school that they were suspended and I just picked them up and drove straight over here. I can't handle this. I wanna hit them, but I know that's wrong. So I'm hoping the group can help me with this."

"What happened?"

Ariel, the older of the two girls, starts to speak haltingly.

"Well, she disrespected me. She started makin' fun of me. So I started hitting her and then she hit me back, and then it just kept goin'."

I sit quietly. Angela then offers her account.

"I started hitting her because she *just made me so mad. My own sister, disrespectin' me.*"

There is a moment of silence and then the fathers start responding. For once, they make their comments one at a time.

"You need to communicate," KSD asserts. "The problem is that you started hittin' each other instead of communicatin'. That's no good, that's never good. You need to express how you're feelin' to each other."

"But most of all," Sy adds, "you need to love each other. Really love each other."

Sugarbear, who literally never has spoken in the group even though he has attended for two years, stands up.

"You need to remember one thing: Blood is thicker than water." He sits down quickly, and the men start clapping.

Dwight then raises his hand.

"I lost my sister when I was a little boy, and I lost another sister two years ago. There isn't a day that goes by that I don't miss them or wish they were around. I wish I could talk to my sister—the older one. We used to talk every day. You gotta cherish each other, because someday one of you might pass—I hope when you are old—and then you're gonna miss your sister so much—" Dwight's voice begins to shake and he lowers his head.

Terrance quickly fills the silence.

"My brother died. A car hit him right out there in the street—right in front of Jordan High School. I'll never forget it. I still miss him. You don't want this feeling, believe me. I'll never get over losin' my brother."

Ariel begins to speak.

"But that's what hurt me about what she said—because I love her. Why did she say that? Why did she disrespect me?"

Both girls are crying.

"Silence is wisdom," Ele offers. "Sometimes you gotta not talk—even if you're hurt, you gotta wait. Being silent—it allows you the time to think about what you're gonna say, what you're gonna do. Then you can talk. Then you can communicate."

"And you gotta forgive yourselves—and each other," Debois adds. "You're both young. You'll grow up, you'll learn. You gotta learn from what happened today."

I think about my brothers and how we have fought, but always kept our differences between us. The girls have been crying through the entire session and show no signs of stopping. KSD brings them paper towels, and they continuously blot their eyes while tears slide down their cheeks.

"You gotta be careful not to give your power away," I tell the girls. "You don't want anyone to know what is going on between the two of you."

"I know, I know. Everyone at school was laughin' at us," Ariel reports, and Angela sobs.

"I feel so bad—I never want to hit my sister again. Ever."

"Me either."

Ben starts to cry and has to leave the room.

"I know you girls, I know your mother." Sy—their uncle—enters into the exchange. "I know you are good girls."

Ben comes in and sits next to both girls while I ask them how they feel.

"Embarrassed."

"Ashamed."

"I am ashamed I disappointed Dad."

They both stand up and hug Ben.

Terrance then warns the girls, while the other men nod in agreement.

"Don't act out on your anger. This is why we are where we are—this is why we wound up in jail, or in the pen. Don't do what we did."

"There is no one like your sister, no one like your blood."

I am crying along with the girls.

Aaron suddenly stands up.

"I haven't seen my sisters and brothers in so long and I miss them. I go to Facebook and I see they're having events and I miss them. I wish

I could still see them. We've been fighting and we can't seem to get over it."

"All you need to do is look at the Scripture," Big Mike offers. "All over the Bible it says how important family is."

But the men do not stop here. They are also thinking about the future.

"When the suspension is over," Sy begins, "when you go back to school, you should stay together for the whole day. Don't be apart. Let everyone see you together."

"Go to the administration and apologize for what you did and promise it will never happen again."

"Don't say you're sorry, just apologize. In the pen we never said we're sorry."

I am not sure what the difference is, but it doesn't matter.

Andre stands up and the men lean forward.

"We are all giving these young women good advice. But I want to applaud Ben and praise him for bringing his girls in. He trusted us, and we trust him. We want to honor his trust, and I want to say, Ben, you've done a great thing bringing these girls in."

"I told you when I got here—I just put the girls in the car. I didn't even tell them where we were going or what we were going to do."

Donald has been silent through the entire session, but he now tells the girls, "I want to sing to you." He breaks into the melody of "You Are Everything," which he sings beautifully. The group listens attentively until he reaches the end of the song. Everyone applauds.

"Remember, you can't trust anyone but your family. I can't see you, but I know you are beautiful. I know it." Ben reaches over and clasps Tiny's shoulder after he says this.

"I will never forget this night," Angela tells the group.

"We love you."

"We all love you."

"And we are proud of you."

"Me too," Ariel adds. "I will never forget this night."

I will never forget this night.

TWENTY-SEVEN

Jamel

The things that I know as a father I learned as time went on.
So it was like, as I was teaching my kids, they were teaching me.
—Delvon "Chubb" Cromwell

Leelee's first letter has arrived. I am glad I have something to talk about during this week's session. Last week was a pivotal moment for Project Fatherhood and I am preparing myself for the letdown. It is inevitable with groups when there is a highly emotional session.

Of course, I am completely wrong.

Big Mike is waiting for me in front of the community center.

"Okay, Miss Drjorjaleap. You need to get ready for this week, because we have a new problem. Ele has brought Jamel in, and we've got big trouble."

I wasn't about to tell Mike what I already knew about Jamel. Two weeks before, after Jamel had been enrolled in a different high school, I had called George Weaver, the executive director of Brotherhood Crusade. I called in a chip and asked if Jamel could enroll in their well-structured and highly effective youth development program as soon as possible. Even though the program was mid-session, George graciously said Jamel would be welcome. While Ele and I were assembling the necessary paperwork, Jamel had been spotted in Long Beach during school hours riding around on a bicycle. When the police stopped him to issue a truancy ticket, they searched his backpack and found a video camera and projector marked "Property of the Los Angeles Unified School District." Jamel already had a court date and a bad attitude by the time Ele hauled him into Project Fatherhood.

"I don't know what to do with this boy." Ele is explaining when I walk in with Big Mike. I stay silent about Jamel's backstory.

"I got the call from the cops in Long Beach to pick him up, and when I got him I was so mad. I wanted to hit him; I wanted to choke him out, but I couldn't do it. I couldn't. I wasn't always there when he was young—this is on me. I wasn't around. I was locked up. I wasn't there, I was in the pen. How could I hit him, how could I blame him? *I wasn't around.*"

The men in the room nodded solemnly. This was the all the data anyone needed about the impact of the new Jim Crow.

"I need all of your help. Jamel needs your help. I don't know what to do."

Following the pattern they had established the week before with Angela and Ariel, the fathers immediately take charge.

But this is different.

The sixteen-year-old boy in the chair, crying, embarrassed, sullen— even looking stoned at one moment as Big Mike called him out—*is* them.

They remember the past and talk about what happened to them. The men all speak, but they aren't exchanging war stories. There is urgency in their voices. *They are trying to save Jamel, and they are trying to redeem themselves.*

KSD, who often takes what feels like hours to get to the point, speaks more briefly than I have ever heard him.

"You are paying for the mistakes we made."

Sy quickly jumps in.

"All the things we did on these corners, that's what created these laws, the gang enhancements, the gang injunctions. You are paying for our sins. You are paying the price for what we did. The cops see you, and they want to make an example of you."

"Sy is right," Dwight says. "My son stood guard over a robbery that turned into a hostage situation and then a kidnapping. My son got five years for standin' in the doorway, just like this." Dwight stands up to demonstrate his son's actions. "I knew what was comin'. I saw what was happening—he was gangbanging. He got shot and still he did dirt. And now he's still locked up, and it's my fault. My mama raised seven kids [without my] daddy. I guess I didn't know how to be a father to my son, but I tried."

The men are silent for a moment.

"Listen, son, you think it's so cool," Sy implores, "but you don't wanna get locked up. You don't know how bad it is. Hell, we had it easy, and it was bad then. Now prison is worse than when we were there. It's a bad place, and you'll be lucky to get outta there alive."

"You don't want prison to teach you to appreciate life," KSD says, looking directly at Jamel. "I was in county jail so many times. I never saw the sun. I never heard the birds sing. One day when I was out, I woke up in the morning and heard the birds sing and I thought, 'I don't wanna get locked up again.'"

In the midst of this outpouring, Tiny moves his hand back and forth, gesturing that he needs water. The men motion to each other to find him a water bottle, while the conversation continues without a break.

"Jamel, I know you think you know better than we do—that we're old, that we're out of the life," Andre says quietly. "But we have wisdom. We've seen a lot. Some of the men in this room have killed people; some of the men have almost been killed. We don't want you to go through what we've gone through. So I'm askin' you—we're askin' you—what do you want?"

Jamel answers swiftly.

"To take care of myself. I want to make money. I want to take care of myself."

"And you're willin' to take all these risks to make money?"

"I am willing to take the risks to get the money."

The men recognize what Jamel is thinking.

"We made that mistake, and we gave up our lives," Sy quietly tells him.

"I don't wanna wait."

"Don't be stupid," Chubb says. "You need your education. You'll be thirty and it will be easy for you, while all of your friends are in the pen. You gotta go through this stage of your life, my nigger, but stay in school. We want you to get an education—none of us got an education. We wanna see you get an education. That's the only way to get ahead."

Jamel hangs his head.

"You got a better plan to make money?" Andre asks, then says, "I will pay you twenty dollars a week every week you go to school. We'll get the dailies—the sheets the teachers sign saying you are in class. Maybe some of the other fathers will pledge money."

Everyone's hands shoot up—Mike pledges ten dollars. Ben, Sy, Debois, and Dwight all chime in with five dollars each. I pledge five dollars. Big Mike keeps track, and we reach fifty dollars.

"That's $200 a month, my nigger," Chubb tallies, "just to stay in school."

Big Mike asks Jamel what he wants to do.

"I want to be an auto mechanic."

"I can take you to Rufus—he'll show you what to do. And if you like it, I'll buy you equipment." Big Mike always has a connection.

I am amazed. This is a therapy group, a case management system—an entire healing community. There is no priest, no guru, no one leading the way. *These men are doing it.*

"We don't want you winding up in the pen."

Big Mike turns to me.

"Speaking of the pen, Dr. Leap has a letter from Leelee."

I start to read Leelee's letter but midway through I begin to cry. The men are incredulous.

"You went to court with Leelee?"

"You saw Leelee into prison—I thought you were sick."

They can't believe it.

I begin again and read Leelee's latest update about where I can bring his mother to see him. The men look confused, so I quickly explain that I have promised to bring his mama up to him. The men begin clapping.

"You're gonna go to prison to see Leelee—" Even Ele is incredulous.

"I know, I'm a cracker," I start, laughing and crying, "but I'm your cracker."

"You're one of us."

I have never quite felt it until this moment.

My life is forever changed.

These are my people. I belong to them.

. . .

Three weeks later the fathers are conducting group therapy again. Jamel has done well for the first two weeks of the Project Fatherhood allowance program. He goes to class and his teachers all fill out his attendance sheet, adding positive, encouraging comments. I suspect that the teachers' surprise matches the fathers' devotion.

However, on the third week, Ele and Jamel both arrive at the community center looking furious. I know exactly what this means—something is wrong, and they are embarrassed and hurt. But instead of expressing this, they mad dog each other, staring with fierce anger. Ele tells the group that Jamel has been kicked out of school for three days for fighting.

The fathers immediately go into response mode.

"You're on thin ice already, and now this?"

For once, Donald almost sounds Zen.

"Why are you doing this? Why do you start fighting? In San Quentin, the man who held back—the silent man—is the one who had the most power. Everyone wondered what he was thinkin'. Everyone wondered what he was gonna do. He had all the power. The people that were poppin' off and fightin' had none."

Ele then comes forward.

"I have read a Chinese philosopher somewhere who says, 'You must stand still like a tall reed and not move in the wind.'"

He looks like an angry but thoughtful Buddha. I am starting to see that he has so much caring that it scares him. He buries this love inside a mountain of anger. But while I am feeling admiration for Ele, most of the fathers are not interested in philosophy. Sy, for one, wants the details of the fight.

Jamel explains that one of his friends was being disrespected, so he stepped in to defend his friend's reputation. Sy is incredulous.

"I wanna understand—how come you defended someone who wouldn't defend himself?"

"'Cause he's my boy."

Sometimes I wonder if all the gang activity and all the hood activity is really a cover for the men's need for love. But I look at Sy and I think, damn—he has killed people. It is equal parts love and rage. I have spent the last two days at UCLA lecturing about social disorganization theory and strain theory and differential association theory—all the general explanations for why juveniles commit crimes and how they wind up in the system, and I am looking at these men now and understanding—it is about their manhood.

Jamel doesn't want to listen to any of this, but the men continue undeterred. They appeal to him with their understanding and their experience.

"I know how you feel—I do," Sy says. "But unless someone comes after you, you gotta walk away."

"Walk away," Bob echoes. "There's nothing in it for you."

The men are all adamant about this point. No one is urging Jamel to fight. They desperately want him not to get involved. But Jamel looks unconvinced.

"If you were in the situation with your friend being disrespected, what would you do now?" I ask.

"The same thing," Jamel answers.

The men actually stay calm. They understand too well. But they support Jamel and tell him they will still pay him an allowance.

"But you gotta try again," Big Mike reminds him.

"We're not giving up on you."

"We are never gonna give up on you."

"You are gonna give up on yourself before we give up on you."

Jamel starts to cry.

"I'm sorry," he sobs.

"Don't be sorry, son," Ele says. "I love you."

The men echo his words.

"We love you, we all love you."

"We've got nothing but love for you."

"Ele—he's your daddy—but we're all your fathers."

Jamel lifts up his head.

"I love all of you. I won't let you down."

EPILOGUE

Project Fatherhood has come a long way from the night after Trayvon Martin was shot. The men still focus on their own children, yet
their concerns have extended far beyond their families. What began as
a group formed for men to explore their individual struggles has grown
into a launching pad for social activism. The men of Project Fatherhood
want to ensure that Watts is a place that is safe for all children and all
families. As they work to transcend drugs, gang life, violence, and severe
poverty, their devotion to their sons and daughters—and to all the children of their community—provides the greatest of all protective factors.

Over time, the focus of the group has shifted and expanded. Many of
the fathers feel increasingly in control of their own lives. In early 2014,
Project Fatherhood Jordan Downs received a major grant to fund its
work, as well as activities for members and their children, for another
year. At the same time, many of the group members' original struggles
are moving towards resolution. Andre Christian is a lead gang interventionist and community organizer for the Los Angeles mayor's office. Big
Mike—Elder Mike Cummings—has been awarded the California Peace
Prize and is seeking a major grant from the California Wellness Foundation to support his efforts with school-aged youth. Leelee Sprewell
continues to serve his sentence, now out of state at a prison in Arizona.
He remains in contact with the men of Project Fatherhood through

the US Postal Service and by phone. In 2014, the Children's Institute named Ben Henry one of three "Fathers of the Year." Matt Givhan and his girlfriend, Jasmine, are expecting their second child. He works full time and attends community college at night, dedicated to completing his college education.

The youth impact sessions have continued on a monthly basis and remain limited to young men in the Jordan Downs development. But a weekend camp has been established at the nearby Angelus National Forest that will accommodate youth from all three housing developments. The fathers believe this will ultimately lead to cross-site youth impact sessions.

Plans for the redevelopment of Jordan Downs continue. HACLA has still not broken ground, but has promised the fathers there will be jobs for them when construction begins. In the meantime, Mike, Andre, and John King have managed to obtain full-time employment at other construction sites for eight of the fathers.

Struggles remain, but there is a truth that cannot be denied: these men—most of whom never knew their own fathers—have learned to father one another. As new fathers join the group, the more experienced, original group members tell each of them, "We'll help you. We've got one another. We take care of each other."

And every Wednesday night, in a small room in the heart of Jordan Downs, the fathers of the community continue to meet.

THE MEN OF PROJECT FATHERHOOD JORDAN DOWNS

John "Reddy" Bailey

Thomas Bailey

Andre "Low Down" Christian

Delvon "Chubb" Cromwell

Elvozo "Redman" Cromwell

Elder Michael "Big Mike" Cummings

Carlos Espinosa

Alphonso Foster

Jamel Freeman

Willie "Elementary" Freeman

Sean Fudge

Matt Givhan

David Guizar

Ben Henry

Sy Henry

Donald "Twin" James

Ronald Bebit James

Sajjon "Baby Boy" James

Wendell "Gangster" Jenkins

John King

Herbert De'Shawn Kirkwood

Charles "Pirate" Lewis

Craig McGruder

Victor McGruder

Vincent McGruder

Dwight Palmer

Ronald Perkins

Aaron Pineda

Juan Romero

Terrance Russell

Julius E. Sanders

Orenthal J. Sanders

Jerome Sanford

Juan Scoggins

Aqeela Sherrills

Debois "Debo" Sims

David Smith

Terrence Smith

Lee "Leelee" Sprewell

Ronald Stringfellow

Jorge Villegas

Tiny Walker

Sylvester "Sugarbear" Willingham

King Spider D Willis

Robert "Bobby" Windom

ACKNOWLEDGMENTS

I will forever be grateful to "Big Mike" Cummings for calling me on that long-ago summer night and asking if I was a "master social worker." Working alongside him—with Andre Christian and Willie "Ele" Freeman—has enabled me to learn about change and hope in ways I could never have imagined. However, my deepest debt is to the men of Project Fatherhood Jordan Downs. Without them, this book would not exist. As we talked, fought, laughed, and cried together, they taught me the meaning of love. This book exists because of them, and all of the proceeds from its publication will go to their organization. But I will never be able to repay them for what they have given to me.

For their ongoing support during every meeting and every funding renewal, my thanks go to John King, Jennifer Thomas Arthurs, and Jessica Lopez of the Housing Authority of the City of Los Angeles and Kids Progress Inc. We all owe a debt of gratitude to the late Dr. Hershel Swinger for this remarkable program. I am thankful that Alan-Michael Graves and Anthony Young, along with Children's Institute, Inc., have kept his vision alive.

This is the second book I have worked on with Beacon Press senior editor Alexis Rizzuto. "Work" is a misnomer—collaborating with Alexis has been a pure joy, and she has helped to fulfill my vision for this story, even at a point when I began to lose my way. I greatly appreciate her intelligence and honesty but most importantly her warmth in what has been an emotional, often challenging, process. Along with Alexis, the entire staff of Beacon Press, including Helene Atwan, Tom Hallock, and Pam MacColl, embodies a writer's dream of professionalism and support. The copyediting provided by Susan Lumenello and Peggy Field was—in a word—incredible.

This book has grown out of some of the countless lessons I have learned from Father Greg Boyle, the founder and executive director of Homeboy Industries. I am eternally thankful for the love and friendship we have shared for almost thirty years. He was the first to help me appreciate the "father wound" and its meaning for the gang members—all in search of redemption—whom we continue to care about and love.

Karrah Lompa has overseen and organized research efforts, community commitments, and policy work with intelligence and care. Her insights abound while her hard work never stops. I am constantly in danger that both she and Laura Rivas will succumb to the never-ending job offers they receive. For as long as they are part of my life, I am fortunate they help make up a team that cares about children, youth, and families. Additionally, I thank Katie Thure, as well as Susana Bonis, Charles Lea, Gina Rosen, Louisa Lau, and Marjan Goudarzi for their intelligence and effort. I am grateful to Dr. Cheryl Charles for taking care of my family and ensuring I stay in good health and humor. The amazing journalist Celeste Fremon and the devoted homie attorney Elie Miller are my two sisters of the heart, whose compassion knows no limit. Beatriz Solis, of The California Endowment, is an ongoing inspiration and a thoughtful advisor, who gives generously of her time and spirit. I also wish to thank my colleagues for their wisdom and support: first and foremost, Julio Marcial, Aquil Basheer, Aqeela Sherrills, and wonderful Angela Wolf.

There are no words for the bond I share with Carol Biondi. She is my friend, my partner-in-crime, and a cherished confidante. I am blessed to have her in my life.

Since September 10, 1972, I have known Dr. Joseph Rosner. Over the past forty-three years, he has been my therapist, my mentor, and my papa. I would not be where I am without him and I am grateful every day of my life for knowing him.

I am fortunate to have been given the gift of time with my Thea Ernie—Virginia Pappas—who talked with me at length about my father and their experiences growing up. The bond between us is something I will forever cherish.

Throughout my life, I have been lucky to share the love of my two brothers and their families: Tony and Margie, Chris and Kim, Stacey and Danni. Along with them, so much of my heart belongs to the members of my chosen family, who enlarge my life, providing love and support: Tina Christie and Michelle Parra, Todd Franke—AB, Joe and Malinda Kibre, Shelly Brooks and Ben Goff, Nina Bende, Penny Fuller, Larry Pressman, my GT Marcia Berris, Ann Herold, Anne Taylor Fleming, Kenny Green, Karina Lehrner, and Jack Rosner.

I am deeply indebted to my UCLA colleagues at the Luskin School of Public Affairs and the Department of Social Welfare. Their thoughtful support is a testimony to the value and importance of the finest public university system in the world.

Finally, my husband, Mark, and our daughter, Shannon, have lived Project Fatherhood and this book every step of the way. Their love is the miracle that has made everything possible.